Routledge Revivals

The French Debt Problem

Originally published in 1925, this volume was written at a time when the cost of living was rising in France and the currency of the Franc was declining. Uneasiness over possible national bankruptcy or financial disintegration was increasing. The book reveals the true financial situation in France and outlines a plan for the restoration of sound financial and economic conditions. As well as discussing the economy of post-World War I France the book also touches on the social and political problems of the time.

I0096132

The French Debt Problem

Harold G. Moulton and Cleona Lewis

Routledge
Taylor & Francis Group

REVIVALS

First published in 1925 by George Allen & Unwin Ltd

This edition first published in 2024 by Routledge
4 Park Square, Milton Park, Abingdon, Oxon, OX14 4RN

and by Routledge
605 Third Avenue, New York, NY 10158.

Routledge is an imprint of the Taylor & Francis Group, an informa business

© 1925 Harold G. Moulton and Cleona Lewis

The right of Harold G. Moulton and Cleona Lewis to be identified as the authors of this work has been asserted by them in accordance with sections 77 and 78 of the Copyright, Designs and Patents Act 1988.

ISBN 13: 978-1-032-94876-8 (hbk)
ISBN 13: 978-1-003-58216-8 (ebk)
ISBN 13: 978-1-032-94884-3 (pbk)
Book DOI 10.4324/9781003582168

THE
FRENCH DEBT PROBLEM

BY

HAROLD G. MOULTON

AND

CLEONA LEWIS

WITH THE AID OF THE COUNCIL AND STAFF
OF THE INSTITUTE OF ECONOMICS

LONDON: GEORGE ALLEN & UNWIN, LTD.
RUSKIN HOUSE, 40 MUSEUM STREET, W.C. 1
1925

PRINTED IN THE UNITED STATES OF AMERICA

DIRECTOR'S PREFACE

THE INSTITUTE OF ECONOMICS presents in this volume the fourth of its series of investigations of European reconstruction problems. The French debt question has passed beyond the stage of academic discussion, and practical solutions are now being earnestly sought. This volume seeks to accomplish two main purposes: First, to reveal the true financial situation of France; and, second, to outline a plan for the restoration of sound financial and economic conditions. An incidental purpose is to indicate the capacity of France to meet her external debts.

While the book as a whole is concerned only with economic factors, an effort is made in Chapter X to reveal in broad outlines the social and political problems interwoven with the economic situation. That chapter has been contributed by Dr. Louis Levine of the Institute Staff, who has long been a student of French economics and politics.

H. G. MOULTON,
Director.

Washington, D. C.
July, 1925

CONTENTS

ix

CHAPTER V

CHAPTER VI

CHAPTER VII

CHAPTER VIII

CHAPTER IX

CHAPTER X

CHAPTER XI

CHAPTER XII

APPENDICES

APPENDIX A

APPENDIX B

APPENDIX C

APPENDIX D

APPENDIX E

APPENDIX F

APPENDIX G

THE FRENCH DEBT PROBLEM

THE FRENCH DEBT PROBLEM

CHAPTER I.

INTRODUCTION

To THE eye of the casual observer, the most striking thing about post-war France is the fact that, despite her sorry financial plight, France is as ever *La belle France*. Now that the worst scars of the devastation have been removed, things are everywhere apparently much the same as in pre-war days. The population remains virtually unchanged both in number and in character, though there is perhaps an undertone of quiet sadness in place of the natural joyousness which cast a glamour over the life of former times. The basic natural resources of land and water, timber and minerals have been increased rather than diminished, and the whole country wears an air of prosperity. Indeed, there is a new spirit of enterprise, of push and hustle, born of war and post-war industrial achievements. In natural resources, in labor supply, in capital equipment, in managerial capacity, and in all outward appearance France is the France of old, and more.

1

Yet the franc declines, the cost of living rises, harassed ministry succeeds harassed ministry, and uneasiness over possible national bankruptcy or financial disintegration, steadily increases. Little wonder that in the face of these strange contrasts, these economic contradictions, we should find a bewildering confusion of ideas about the true economic condition of France and about her ability to meet the problem presented by the public debt. Frenchman and foreign observer alike are faced with what seems an unreality.

What is the key to this paradox? If all the fundamental factors of wealth creation—natural resources, labor, industrial establishments, and industrial managers—exist in undiminished quantity and capacity, if the people are all employed, and if the production of wealth is abundant, why all this pother about the condition of France? The key to the difficulty is to be found in the truth that the so-called fundamental factors enumerated above are not the only, nor even the most important, elements in the economic life of a country. They are to the body economic merely what trunk and legs and arms are to the human body. Without an efficiently functioning economic organism, these parts of the economic system are quite as impotent as are the various parts of the human body when the vitalizing organs cease to function. The most important part of the economic organism is the financial system by means of which all economic activities—whether conducted by public or private agencies—are carried on. The present plight of France is due to the over-straining of the financial capacity of the nation. As a result of war and post-war economic effort, the financial mechanism which sustains and animates the whole economic organization has become diseased and has been steadily, if slowly, disintegrating.

Now the strange feature of this financial disintegration is the fact that in its earlier stages it makes for great industrial activity, for large wealth production, and for actual, if temporary, prosperity. But, as we shall see, if the process of disintegration is not arrested, the ultimate result is general economic disorganization, accompanied by acute economic and social distress. The great confusion about the economic condition of France is attributable to the fact that she is at the moment at the parting of the ways. Continuing business activity; but a growing shortage of working capital and narrowing margins of profit; rising interest rates and mounting prices; a dwindling market for government securities and a renewal of inflation at the Bank of France; an ever-increasing burden of taxation, and the threat of a levy on capital; a continuing depression of the franc and a persistent flight of capital from the country. Those who look only to the present tangible evidence afforded by farm and factory and marketplace are reasonably complacent about France; those who study the intangible evidences of the financial markets are inclined to be deeply apprehensive about the future.

The primary purpose of this book is to show how

France came to be in her present state, and to indicate what must be done to restore sound financial and economic conditions. To do so it is necessary to give some attention to the economic position of France before the Great War. The general financial and economic problems of France present four main features, which though closely interrelated, must first be studied separately. They are: (1) international trade and financial operation; (2) the government budget; (3) banking, currency, and the exchanges; and (4) production. With each separate problem we first present a brief statement about the pre-war situation; then show the effects of the war; then indicate what progress, if any, has been made toward recovery since 1918. Not until after these several phases of the problem have been reviewed in perspective is it possible to appraise the situation as a whole and to point the way to a restoration of sound conditions in the future.

As a background for the more particular and detailed discussions to follow, the reader should bear in mind a few general facts about the extent of French economic resources and the character of the French economic system as it stood in pre-war days. The area of France, including Alsace-Lorraine, is only 212,659 square miles—less than four times that of the state of Illinois—while the population, practically stationary for fifty years, is about 39 millions, or approximately six times that of Illinois. France is comparatively rich in agricultural resources. Though Paris is as far north as the boun-

dary line between North Dakota and Alberta, and
Marseilles about on a line with Milwaukee, the cli-
mate is mild and equable. The rolling plains of
the north and west are among the most productive
agricultural regions of the continent of Europe,
while the sunny valleys and mountains slopes of the
south have given to France a preeminent position
in the production of wine.

In mineral resources France is not so bounte-
ously endowed. While she has abundant deposits
of iron ore, and since the return of Lorraine, much
the richest deposits in Europe, France must import coal and particularly coke. France possesses
considerable quantities of some of the minor minerals such as bauxite, antimony, pyrites, and—in Alsace, since the war—an abundance of potash; but
she is without gold, silver, copper, and petroleum.
On the other hand, she has considerable possibilities
for water power development, and her timber resources are relatively abundant.

The French colonial empire is of vast territorial
extent, and possesses a population of nearly 60 millions. The colonial area—93 per cent of which is in
Africa—is 5.6 million square miles, nearly twice that
of the continent of Europe. Potentially the French
colonies may be an economic asset to the mother
country. For example, it is hoped that they may
ultimately free the French textile industry from the
need of importing American cotton and Australian
wool; and in general the incorporation of these areas
under French rule may widen the territory within

which trade can flow relatively free from commercial restrictions. But except for such cannon fodder as may be furnished in time of war, the colonies are not likely to supply the mother country with commodities free of charge; the mother country will have to send goods to the colonies in exchange. Thus far, at least, the colonies have been only an economic liability to France, though, as has been not infrequently suggested, such a liability might perhaps be converted into an asset for the purposes of international debt settlement. In any event, we are here concerned only with the economic resources and the economic condition of France proper.

As already intimated, the basic natural resources of a country cannot be effectively utilized unless the people of that nation succeed in developing an efficient economic organization. Without entering into any detailed discussion of its origin and development, the general character of the French economic system, particularly the financial system, may be briefly touched upon. The development of the highly complex economic organization of the modern world has occurred during a period of about one hundred and fifty years, beginning with the so-called industrial revolution of the latter part of the eighteenth century. Although France has suffered severely from a series of foreign wars and has been faced with more acute domestic revolutions than have other important countries during the modern era, yet she had emerged at the opening of the twentieth century with a relatively strong economic organization, buttressed by a monetary and banking system of extraordinary strength and efficiency.

Although France was not a gold or silver producing country, she had acquired through foreign trading operations so large a supply of specie that her banking and currency position was deemed virtually impregnable. The Bank of France, established by Napoleon, had throughout the greater part of its history been a bulwark of strength. Through conservative and skillful management it has at all times met the requirements of business for a sound and elastic currency; and it is noteworthy that France has not only escaped financial panics but that the fluctuations of business activity incident to the business cycle have been less pronounced than in most other countries. The Bank of France has also been of the greatest aid to the government during its many vicissitudes—exercising at once a helpful and a restraining influence.

In the administration of public finance, however, there has been much room for improvement. France has always tolerated defective budget practices, and the methods employed have perennially obscured the true financial condition of the government, resulting in an embarrassing growth of expenditures and public debt. This situation has been in part due to the fact that the many domestic political crises and foreign wars with which the French government has had to cope have exerted such heavy financial pressure that the institution of a budget system which he who ran might read, was for reasons of practical politics deemed inadvisable; but it has also apparently been in some degree attributable to a lack of clear vision on fiscal matters on the part of French statesmen as a whole.[1] In the course of our analysis we shall see how the defective budgetary system has helped to bring on the financial crisis with which France is now confronted, and how also the financial dilemma of the government has affected both the condition and the management of the Bank of France.

The statement has often been made that France is in a peculiarly fortunate situation in that she is economically independent of the rest of the world. It is undoubtedly true that France has maintained a more even balance between rural and urban pursuits than has been the case in most other highly developed nations. Over 50 per cent of the total population of France still live on farms and in small villages, despite the industrial development of recent times; and it is true that France is more nearly self-sufficient in the matter of food supply than such industrial nations as Great Britain and Germany. But nothing is further from the truth than to say that France can stand alone economically. In the course of its development the French economic system has become closely interwoven, both commercially and financially, with that of other countries.

The French people are dependent upon such food

[1] A detailed discussion of the French budgetary system will be found in Appendix B.

imports as cereals, sugar, coffee, rice, and meats. French industry depends upon large imports of coal and coke, and upon such raw materials as common woods and building materials, mineral oils, cotton, wool, hides, skins, copper, lead tin and zinc. France also imports a great variety of finished manufactures. In the years just preceding the Great War, the countries. from which France purchased the largest amounts were, in order of importance: Great Britain, Germany, the United States, Belgium, Russia, the British Indies, Argentina, Spain, China, Italy, Brazil, and Switzerland.

In order to pay for these imports, France finds it necessary to export her own products, particularly manufactured wares, to the world at large. Cotton, woolen, and silk manufactures, and wearing apparel; chemicals, perfumery, soap, and medicinal compounds; metal products, iron and steel, machinery and tools, leave French ports for all the markets of the world. In the years just prior to the war, the countries to which France exported the largest quantities of goods were, in order: Great Britain, Belgium, Germany, the United States, Switzerland, Italy, Argentina, and Spain. Accordingly, changes in social customs, legal prohibitions, and commercial restrictions in other countries are of scarcely less importance to France than to other large commercial nations. The commercial prosperity, even the economic existence of France, is vitally dependent upon the maintenance of trade with other countries.

The economic interdependence of France with the rest of the world is perhaps nowhere better revealed than in her financial relations. While it is something of an exaggeration to refer to France as the banker of Europe, it is nevertheless true that for the greater part of the nineteenth century, the French people annually invested a portion of their savings in the securities of foreign governments and foreign enterprises. At the outbreak of the Great War, they possessed nearly 40 billion francs of foreign investments located in regions near and far: in Italy, Spain, and Portugal; in Norway and Sweden; in Russia, the Balkans, and Turkey; in the African colonies and the Orient; in the United States, Mexico, Brazil, and Argentina. Famine in the Orient, war and rumors of wars in the Balkans, a bad "clip" in Argentina, a poor harvest in Russia, or a drop in the world price of wheat were factors governing the ability of foreign debtors to meet the interest upon bonds sold in France, and were thus of the utmost interest to the individual French money lender. The economic dislocation wrought by the Great War in many of the countries where French money was invested, has, moreover, brought home to the average Frenchman as perhaps nothing else could have done, how closely his own economic welfare is involved with that of other countries.

CHAPTER II

INTERNATIONAL INCOME

THOUGH designated "International Income," this chapter is in reality the explanation of the growth of French foreign investments between 1870 and the Great War, and the growth of French foreign indebtedness since 1914. The growth of French foreign investments in the pre-war period was made possible by the net income derived from international trade and service operations. Conversely, the growth of the foreign debt during the war and the post-war periods resulted from the annual net deficits in international income in the decade in question. The economic effects of the war and the present international economic condition of France can be adequately revealed only by an analysis of France's international income accounts over a period of years.

I. THE INTERNATIONAL INCOME ACCOUNT

In the highly developed economic world of to-day the business relations between the peoples of different countries are of many kinds, involving, in addition to ordinary trade transactions, a wide variety of so-called "invisible" or service operations.

11

The most important sources of income (or outgo) from services are as follows: Interest on foreign investments; shipping; banking and insurance operations; expenditures of tourists and other travelers, including diplomatic and consular representatives and special commissions; remittances of migratory laborers; gifts, including philanthropic, religious, and charitable contributions.

The expression "balance of trade" has therefore become a misnomer, and has been replaced in the literature of international finance by such phrases as "balance of accounts," "balance of payments," or "economic balance,"—terms which include along with the trade accounts the results of these various service operations. When all of the items for a given year are brought together, they show the nation's total transactions with other nations during that period.

In this study we employ a still different term, borrowed from corporation finance, namely the *income account*. What we wish primarily to know is whether France obtains from her operations, exclusive of credit transactions, a net surplus of income from abroad at any given period or whether she has a deficit. If she has a surplus, she is able to expand her foreign investments or pay off foreign debts, as the case may be. If she has a deficit, she is under the necessity of increasing her foreign debt. For this purpose credit transactions must be segregated from the trade and service operations in the international income accounts.

Credit operations take a variety of forms, particularly during periods of financial travail such as that of the last ten years in European countries. A nation may meet a trade and service deficit abroad by means of government borrowing; by private corporation borrowing; by the transfer to foreigners of the title to domestic property, including both real estate and securities; by the sale of paper currency; and by the sacrifice of previously accumulated foreign investments. All of these types of credit operation have been employed since 1914 by the majority of European countries.

The following sections of this chapter analyze the international income of France for the pre-war, war, and post-war periods, and present a statement of the foreign debt and investment position at the end of each period. The detailed discussion of sources of data and of the methods used in making estimates where no data were available is relegated to Appendix A.

II. PRE-WAR NET INCOME

During the period between the Franco-Prussian and the World wars, France possessed almost continually a surplus of international income over expenditure. While imports usually exceeded exports, the trade deficiency was commonly more than offset by the income from foreign investments and from services, leaving a net balance available for new investments abroad. The table on the accompanying page gives the commodity, and the bullion and specie figures for the years 1871-1913, inclusive. In these figures the colonies and protectorates are considered as foreign countries.

TRADE AND SPECIE BALANCE OF FRANCE—1871-1913 *
(In millions of francs)

Year	Commodities			Bullion and Specie			Net Balance
	Imports	Exports	Net	Imports	Exports	Net	
1871	3,600	2,926	—674	301	502	+201	—473
1872	3,648	3,896	+248	383	334	—49	+199
1873	3,656	3,931	+275	565	492	—73	+202
1874	3,574	3,806	+232	952	159	—793	—561
1875	3,586	3,969	+383	875	219	—656	—273
1876	4,046	3,689	—357	804	159	—645	—1,002
1877	3,747	3,551	—196	683	142	—541	—737
1878	4,246	3,297	—949	544	189	—355	—1,304
1879	4,676	3,361	—1,315	332	424	+92	—1,223
1880	5,111	3,600	—1,511	296	470	+174	—1,337
1881	4,934	3,686	—1,248	364	302	—62	—1,310
1882	4,900	3,710	—1,190	411	350	—61	—1,251
1883	4,876	3,585	—1,291	146	231	+85	—1,206
1884	4,406	3,354	—1,052	229	128	—101	—1,153
1885	4,132	3,182	—950	479	339	—140	—1,090
1886	4,254	3,344	—910	445	333	—112	—1,022
1887	4,076	3,351	—725	271	397	+126	—599
1888	4,174	3,362	—812	266	301	+35	—777
1889	4,387	3,821	—566	448	232	—216	—782
1890	4,520	3,891	—629	256	359	+103	—526
1891	4,852	3,722	—1,130	539	381	—158	—1,288
1892	4,254	3,573	—681	508	214	—294	—975
1893	3,915	3,347	—568	464	243	—221	—789
1894	3,927	3,217	—710	552	217	—335	—1,045
1895	3,820	3,535	—285	395	325	—70	—355
1896	3,932	3,576	—356	479	513	+34	—322
1897	4,114	3,789	—325	462	327	—135	—460
1898	4,572	3,659	—913	391	502	+111	—802
1899	4,655	4,349	—306	506	382	—124	—430
1900	4,839	4,309	—530	605	333	—272	—802
1901	4,504	4,192	—312	526	286	—240	—552
1902	4,534	4,438	—96	538	246	—292	—388
1903	4,933	4,436	—497	441	238	—203	—700
1904	4,644	4,640	—4	756	235	—521	—525
1905	4,951	5,088	+137	885	232	—653	—516
1906	5,797	5,515	—282	601	337	—264	—546
1907	6,395	5,839	—556	805	371	—434	—990
1908	5,808	5,269	—539	1,173	184	—989	—1,528
1909	6,438	5,966	—472	540	361	—179	—651
1910	7,352	6,488	—864	406	390	—16	—880
1911	8,242	6,322	—1,920	462	285	—177	—2,097
1912	8,414	6,972	—1,442	531	325	—206	—1,648
1913	8,626	7,166	—1,460	975	431	—544	—2,004

* The data are for the *special* trade, with *temporary admissions* and *re-exports* added. For a discussion of these terms and French trade statistics in general, see Appendix A, pp. 311-12.

Before the war France had almost continuously an unfavorable balance of trade. It will be seen from the table on page 14 that except for a few years in the seventies, when the indemnity was being paid, France continuously had an unfavorable balance in both commodity and specie accounts. After 1875 there was only one year in which the commodity exports exceeded the imports, and only eight years in which the bullion and specie outflow exceeded the inflow. France is not a gold-producing country, and a continuous inflow of specie of greater or less proportions was to be expected. The fact that these importations were very large enabled France not only to maintain gold as the actual circulating medium, but also to build up in the Bank of France an exceptionally large gold reserve. As the table on page 125 indicates, the gold reserve of the Bank of France for many years had averaged around 80 per cent.

The adverse trade and specie balances were met with the income from services. While it is impossible to give precise year-to-year statistics of the income from sources other than trade, sufficient data are available to warrant the following rough estimate of the income derived at different periods from interest on foreign investments and from the service accounts. As the detailed figures in Appendix A show, France also had some payments to make for services. These have been taken account of, so that the figures which follow represent net, not gross, income.

FRENCH INCOME FROM SERVICES, 1871-1913
(Average yearly income in millions of francs)

Period	Interest	Shipping	Tourist	Commissions, etc.	Total
1871-1875....	485 to 585	185	200	70	940 to 1,040
1876-1880....	500 to 600	175	320	75	1,070 to 1,170
1881-1885....	480 to 580	170	370	80	1,100 to 1,200
1886-1890....	515 to 615	155	430	75	1,175 to 1,275
1891-1896....	640 to 740	125	475	75	1,315 to 1,415
1897-1902....	915 to 1,015	138	525	85	1,663 to 1,763
1903-1908....	1,315 to 1,415	160	585	100	2,160 to 2,260
1909-1913....	1,705 to 1,805	215	625	150	2,695 to 2,795

By setting off the adverse balance in the commodity and specie accounts against the net income from the invisible sources, we may obtain the net balance of payments—that is, the net income derived by France from all of her international trading and financial operations. This is shown in the table below.

NET INTERNATIONAL INCOME OF FRANCE, 1871-1913
(Average yearly income and outgo, in millions of francs)

Period	Income from Services	Net outgo for Commodities and Specie [a]	Net Income [b] (available for new foreign investment)
1871-1875......	940 to 1,040	181	759 [c] to 859
1876-1880......	1,070 to 1,170	1120	—50 to 50
1881-1885......	1,100 to 1,200	1202	—102 to —2
1886-1890......	1,175 to 1,275	742	433 to 533
1891-1896......	1,315 to 1,415	796	519 to 619
1897-1902......	1,663 to 1,763	506	1,157 to 1,257
1903-1908......	2,160 to 2,260	801	1,359 to 1,459
1909-1913......	2,695 to 2,795	1456	1,239 to 1,339

[a] Including *temporary admissions* and *re-exports*.
[b] The minus sign indicates an unfavorable balance.
[c] The greater part of this was diverted from new investments to the payment of the war indemnity.

The net international income determines the volume of foreign investments. A nation can not in the long run get something for nothing: The creation of foreign investments always requires the shipment of goods or the rendering of services to foreigners. The rate of growth of a nation's foreign investments is therefore measured by the extent to which its income from exports of commodities and from services rendered to foreigners exceeds its outlays for imports and for services from foreigners. The figures given in the last column of the table above therefore indicate the net income available for French investments abroad at different periods. It is necessary to point out, however, that from June 1, 1871, to September 5, 1873, France paid to Germany an indemnity amounting to about 5.3 billion francs, which prevented any growth of investments during this period, and in fact considerably reduced France's foreign holdings.[1]

In brief, just before the Franco-Prussian War, French investments were expanding at the rate of 500 to 600 million francs a year.[2] During the late seventies and in the early eighties there was little, if any, increase. In the late eighties the expansion was at the rate of about 500 millions a year;[3] in

[1] See discussion in Appendix A, pp. 327-8.

[2] The year 1870 shows a net income of 780, but the adverse trade balance that year was considerably below normal.

[3] French loans to the Russian government began in 1888 with a loan of 500 million francs, followed by still larger loans in 1889 and 1891. As a French historian remarks: "good accounts as usual made good friends," and these Russian loans opened the way for

the nineties at approximately 900 million a year, and in the decade preceding the World War, at about 1.3 billions a year.

At the outbreak of the World War, the total of French foreign investments was approximately 45 billion francs. This figure represents gross, not net, investments. As an offset, foreigners held investments in France to the extent of about 7 billion francs, leaving the net amount of French foreign investments at approximately 38 billion francs.[4] The chart on the opposite page indicates the net growth of French investments abroad from 1870 to 1914.

The geographic distribution and character of French foreign investments were largely influenced by the French government. The official market for securities is the Paris Bourse (stock exchange) where the government exercises control over the official quotation list.[5] For example, in 1909, under the influence of the French metallurgists, the French government refused admission of United States Steel Corporation stock to the French market, and in 1914 it compelled the admission of a new Turkish loan. It is evident that the government is sometimes guided in its control over the market by political as well as by economic considerations. The

the alliance with Russia. Bourgeois, Emile, *Modern France;* Vol. II, p. 306.

[4] For a detailed discussion of foreign investments, see Appendix A, pp. 321-40.

[5] Guyot, Yves, *Annals* of the American Academy of Political and Social Science; November, 1916, pp. 38-40.

French government is, however, by no means unique
in this regard.

GROWTH OF FOREIGN INVESTMENTS, 1870-1914.

Billions of Francs

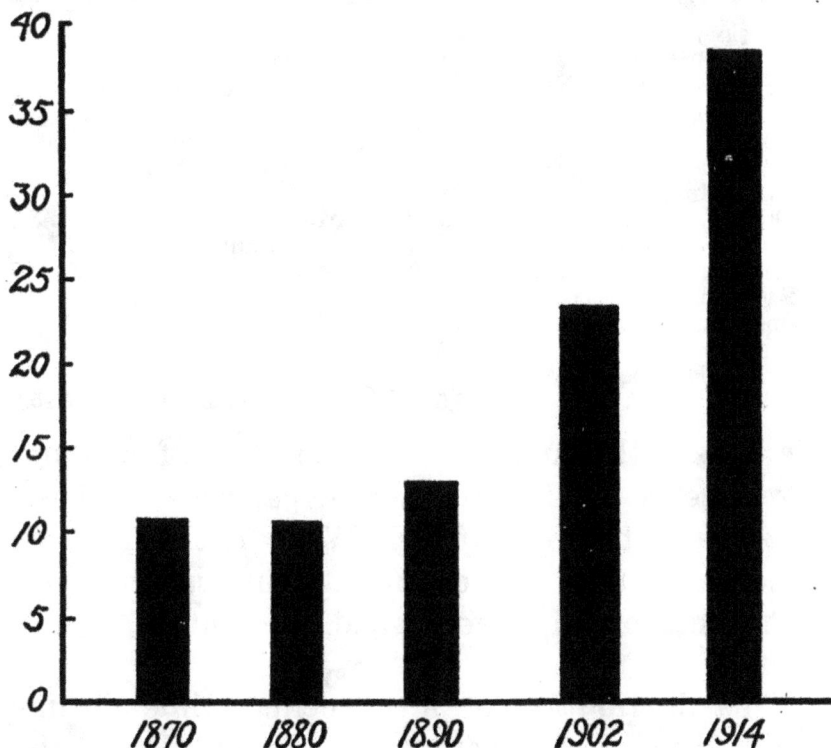

The geographic distribution of French foreign
investments at the outbreak of the Great War is
roughly indicated on page 20.[6]

It will be seen from this table that French finance
was a handmaiden of French diplomacy. French

[6] For references and method used in compiling this table, see
Appendix A, pp. 332-40.

foreign investments were chiefly made in those countries which France was interested in developing and
with which she had contracted alliances. Thus, Rus-

GEOGRAPHIC DISTRIBUTION OF FRENCH INVESTMENTS ABROAD, 1914
(Figures in billions of gold francs)

EUROPE	30.4	ASIA, AFRICA AND AMERICA	14.6
Russia	11.3	Egypt, Suez and South	
Great Britain	.5	Africa	4.5
Belgium and the Neth-		Tunis and other French	
erlands	.5	colonies	4.0
Turkey	3.5	United States and Can-	
Bulgaria and Serbia	.6	ada	1.0
Roumania	3.0	Argentina, Brazil and	
Greece	.7	Mexico	3.0
Austria-Hungary	3.5	Other South America	
Italy	1.3	countries	.6
Switzerland	.5	Asia	1.5
Spain and Portugal	4.0		
Scandinavia	.5		
Other European coun-			
tries	.5	TOTAL, ALL COUNTRIES	45.0

sia constantly ranked as the borrower of first importance in the French market, particularly in the
latter years before the World War. It is interesting
to observe that French investments in the New
World comprised a very small percentage of the
total.

This distribution of investments, while of un-
doubted political advantage before and during the
war, proved in the end of enormous economic dis-
advantage. France's largest foreign investments
happened to be in those portions of Europe which
suffered most from the economic disorganization resulting from the war; and a considerable portion
of them, as we shall see, have been rendered practically valueless.

The character of French foreign loans was disclosed by an investigation under the auspices of the French government in 1902. It was found that over 55 per cent were invested in state and municipal loans; 15.2 per cent in railroads; 12.2 per cent in mining and other industries; and 7 1/3 per cent in government securities; while commercial houses, banking and insurance, shipping, etc., accounted for the remaining 10 per cent.[7]

Briefly recapitulating French economic history as revealed by the foregoing analysis, it appears that the century from the close of the Napoleonic era to the outbreak of the World War was one of steady, if not remarkable, progress. Despite recurring internal revolutions and foreign wars between 1815 and 1871, France had been able to develop foreign investments during that period to the extent of from 10 to 12 billion francs. In spite of the cost of the Franco-Prussian War and the heavy burden of the indemnity, her investments abroad were not reduced in the seventies below a net figure of from 6 to 8 billions. And, notwithstanding the huge importations of specie required for the purpose of building up a monetary and banking system of exceptional strength, in the forty years from the conclusion of the indemnity payments in 1873 to the outbreak of the war in 1914 her foreign investments increased by a net amount of more than 30 billion francs.

It may be of interest to note, in passing, how

[7] *Bulletin de statistique et de législation comparée*, October, 1902, p. 450.

the total of French foreign investments at the outbreak of the Great War compared with those of Germany and Great Britain. Germany had a gross total of foreign investments of about 25 billion gold marks, with an offset of foreigners' investments in Germany of about 5 billion marks, leaving a net total of 20 billion marks,[8] equivalent to about 25 billion francs. Great Britain's foreign holdings approximated 4 billion pounds sterling, or 100 billion francs. From the standpoint of geographic distribution, moreover, the investments of Great Britain, as matters turned out, proved to be much better placed than those of either France or Germany.

It has sometimes been contended that this rapid growth of French foreign investments was not altogether advantageous to the nation. In the latter years before the war there was considerable controversy over the relatively slow internal development of industry and commerce, and it was felt by many that foreign investments were being promoted at the expense of domestic enterprises.[9] The use of finance as an arm of diplomacy naturally gave some color to this view. Whatever may be the merits of this contention, it is none the less clear that France had by 1914 achieved a very strong for-

[8] See Moulton and McGuire, *Germany's Capacity to Pay;* Appendix A. The McKenna Committee estimated Germany's foreign investments in 1914 at 28 billions. This figure, which we think is somewhat too high, is obviously for *gross* investments, though the Committee makes no mention of any offset for foreigners' investments in Germany.

[9] But see discussion of the problem of French internal development on pages 296-8 below.

eign investment position. This, coupled with the exceptional strength of her banking and monetary system, was to prove a source of great aid in the disastrous years to follow.

III. EFFECTS OF THE WAR UPON FRANCE'S INTERNATIONAL INCOME

The enormous economic burden sustained by France during the war is nowhere more clearly reflected than in the statistics of international trade and financial operations. The trade deficit was multiplied manyfold. The interest on French foreign investments meanwhile was very greatly reduced, and although the income from other sources, particularly from foreign soldiers and other temporary sojourners in France, was large, the income from services of all kinds was less than half the trade deficit.

The table on page 24 gives the French commodity and specie figures for the eleven-year period 1914-1924, inclusive.

From an economic point of view, the war period may be taken to include the last five months of 1914, the four full years 1915-1918, and the first half of 1919. The enormous deficit in the French balance of trade during these years could not be covered by the income from the invisible sources; hence France was compelled to borrow very heavily abroad. In fact, she borrowed not only to provide funds for meeting the deficiency in the trade and service accounts, but also for the purpose of loaning to some of her allies.

The figures which follow on page 25 (in billions of paper francs) show in concise form the deficit resulting from the trade and service operations of France from August 1, 1914, to June 30, 1919.[10]

TRADE AND SPECIE BALANCE OF FRANCE 1914-1924 *

(In millions of francs)

Year	Trade Balance			Bullion and Specie Balance			Total Adverse Balance
	Imports	Exports	Net	Imports	Exports	Net	
1914..	6,402	4,869	— 1,533 ⎫				
1915..	11,036	3,937	— 7,099 ⎪	Net export of about 1			
1916..	20,640	6,214	—14,426 ⎬	billion francs [a]			61,182
1917..	27,554	6,013	—21,541 ⎪				
1918..	22,306	4,723	—17,583 ⎭				
1919..	35,799	11,880	—23,919	176	37	—139	24,058
1920..	49,905	26,895	—23,010	214	688	+474	22,536
1921..	22,068	19,773	— 2,295	662	874	+212	2,083
1922..	23,931	21,379	— 2,552	125	77	— 48	2,600
1923..	32,689	30,433	— 2,256	65	83	+ 18	2,238
1924..	40,133	41,454	+ 1,321	116	240	+124	+1,445

* Colonies, as in the preceding table, p. 14, are treated as foreign countries. Data are from the *Annuaire Statistique* and from *Documents Statistiques sur le Commerce de la France*.

[a] The French statistics of bullion and specie movements, published as a part of the official trade figures, indicate that in every war year, except 1914, specie imports exceeded the exports, with total net importations for the five years, 1914-1918, amounting to 210 million francs. These figures, however, obviously do not include exportations of bullion and specie on government account. The estimated loss of 1 billion during war years, given in the table, is based on a comparison of the pre-war and post-war figures of the total gold and specie holdings in France.

[10] Discussion of the detailed items making up the totals here given will be found in Appendix A.

Deficit from Trade and Specie Operations.......... 72.4

Net Income from:
  Interest 2.1
  Other services 29.3
                                          ——— 31.4

Net Deficit in Trade and Service Accounts........ 41.0

The figures given below (also in billions of paper francs) summarize the credit operations for the same period, indicating how this deficit was met and the loans to Allied countries made possible. The French debt statements divide the government's foreign debt into two categories, the political debt and the commercial debt. The term political debt is used to mean the borrowings of the French government from the Treasuries of Great Britain and the United States "for strictly war purposes." The term commercial debt is applied to all other borrowings of the French government. This usage is followed here and elsewhere in this book.

Commercial Transactions:
  Government commercial borrowings, less discounts.. 6.8
  Other borrowings (sale of domestic securities, commercial credits, etc.)............................ 12.5
  Sale of foreign securities........................... 3.9
                                                      ——— 23.2

Political Operations:
  Net receipts from government political borrowings.. 24.8
  Net loans to Allies (with deductions for discounts, interest, etc.) 7.0
                                                      ——— 17.8

Net total of receipts from credit operations............. 41.0

Leaving reparation claims out of account, the economic requirements of the war changed France

from a creditor to a debtor nation. Before the
war the gross total of French investments abroad
stood at 45 billion francs, while foreigners had invested in France about 7 billions, the net total of
French pre-war foreign investments thus standing
at 38 billion francs. During the war France extended loans to her allies aggregating about 10 billion francs, but war requirements led to the sale of
about 3.5 billions of foreign securities, while something like 23 billions of the remaining investments
—namely, those located in Russia, the succession
states, and the Levant—have been rendered valueless for many years, if not permanently. At the
same time at least half of the new loans made during the war, namely, those extended to Russia,
Greece, and Poland, have been placed in the same
category. Meanwhile, also, the French government
contracted a foreign debt amounting to about 31.4
billion (gold) francs; 10 billions of French (domestic) securities and property were sold to foreigners;
and about 1.9 billions of additional indebtedness
was incurred through the opening of commercial
credits and the sale of francs.

Drawing these figures together in tabular form,
the effects of the war upon France's international
economic position may be shown by a comparison
of French foreign investments on June 30, 1919,
with the total debt which France owes to foreigners.
In order to make all of the figures comparable, the
figures with regard to French investments abroad

have been converted to paper franc values, on the basis of exchange rates for June, 1919.

FOREIGN DEBT AND INVESTMENT POSITION, JUNE 30, 1919
(Figures are in billions of francs)

In paper, at average
rates for June, 1919 [a]

INVESTMENTS

French-owned foreign investments (at par of exchange):
Total of all investments, June, 1914 ...,.................... 45.0
Less:
  Foreign securities sold during the war 3.5
  Losses on other pre-war investments 23.0   26.5

Total remaining, June 30, 1919 .. 18.5[b] equivalent to 22.2
War loans of France to her Allies (including discounts, interest, etc.) 10.0
Total of investments and war loans, June 30, 1919........ 32.2

DEBTS

Total debt to foreigners, exclusive of political debt:
Pre-war investments .... 3.5[c]
Domestic securities and real estate sold during the war 10.5
Commercial credits, francs held abroad, etc. 2.0
Foreign commercial debt of the French government (6.8 at par) ....: 8.2   24.2

Political debt of the French government including capitalized interest due Great Britain[d] (24.6 at par) 29.6
Interest at 5 per cent on the debt to the United States (56 million francs at par)[d] 7   30.3

Total foreign debt of France, June 30, 1919......   54.5

[a] A conversion ratio of 1.2 paper to 1 gold franc is used throughout the table, this ratio being the result obtained by three dif-

The result of the war from the point of view of foreign investments was in effect to wipe out 38 billions net (1914 gold values) of foreign holdings and replace them by a net indebtedness to foreigners of about 22.3 billions (1919 paper values), equivalent to 6.8 billions in terms of 1914 purchasing power. Such losses, though not visible to the eye of the traveller, are no less real than the physical destruction of property in the territories occupied by the enemy.

IV. INTERNATIONAL INCOME, JULY 1, 1919– DECEMBER 31, 1923

The economic strain upon France did not end with the war years, but has continued with varying degrees of intensity to the present time. The first half of the year 1919 was included in the foregoing

ferent methods of computation: (1) French exchange on 16 important countries; (2) a weighted average of rates in the countries where the commercial debt was placed; (3) a weighted average for the political debt.

[b] Income on about 3 billions, located in South America, was suspended during the war, leaving only about 15.5 billions in the income-paying class.

[c] The total in 1914 was 7.0 billions. This amount has been reduced to 3.5 billions because of the seizure of the investments in France belonging to enemy powers.

[d] The French political debt figure includes capitalized interest in the case of Great Britain, but not in the case of the United States. We have put in a separate item for the accumulated interest on the debt to the United States in order to give uniformity to the general investment and debt statement. It should be added here that the accumulated interest is included in the 10 billions of loans to the Allies.

computation as properly a part of the war period. We shall now consider the four-and-a-half year period from the middle of 1919 to the end of 1923, leaving the year 1924 for separate discussion in the following section.

The second half of the year 1919, and even the year 1920 showed no lessening of the adverse balance of trade. The necessary re-stocking with raw materials, coupled with the inflation of the time, resulted in a great expansion of imports measured both in value and in quantity terms. Exports naturally increased also, but not sufficiently to improve the balance of trade.

As the table on page 24 indicates, the severe business depression of 1921 led to a very drastic curtailment of imports. The inventories of dealers were excessive, French industries were overstocked with raw materials, and a period of retrenchment was in order, in France as elsewhere. While a considerable part of the decline, as shown by the value figures, is attributable to the fall in prices, the tonnage of imports also decreased by 20 per cent. The value of exports also declined, though by no means proportionately to the reduction of imports. In fact, owing to increased exports of heavy materials such as iron ore and excess reparation coal, the tonnage exports actually increased in 1921. In 1922 and 1923 there was a general recovery of French trade leading to an expansion both of imports and exports, but without affecting materially the adverse balance.

The figures which follow reveal in summary form the total deficit resulting from the trade and service operations of France from the middle of 1919 to the end of 1923.[11]

	Billions of paper francs	
Deficit from:		
Trade and specie operations	41.7	
Interest (exclusive of political debt)	2.3	44.0
Net income from services (other than interest) and from reparations		17.1
Net deficit in trade and service accounts		26.9

The figures which follow summarize the credit operations for this period.[12]

	Billions of paper francs	
Receipts from Commercial Transactions:		
Sale of domestic securities, commercial credits, etc.	11.7	
Sale of francs	14.5	
Sale of foreign securities	1.8	28.0
Less repayment of debt and new investments	4.1	23.9
Receipts from Political Operations:		
Political borrowings	6.8	
Less net loans to Allies	3.8	3.0
Net receipts from credit operations		26.9

At the end of four and a half years of reconstruction the French foreign debt was greatly increased. The trade deficit was 41.7 billion paper francs during the period. And in contrast to war and pre-war con-

[11] For the detailed figures see Appendix A.
[12] For details see Appendix A.

INTERNATIONAL INCOME 31

ditions, this deficit was increased by a net outgo on account of interest operations. While France received about 6.5 billions paper on account of interest, she had to meet about 8.8 billions of interest on accumulating foreign debts, thus adding about 2.3 billions to the deficit on account of trade. The large net income from services, amounting to 17.1 billions, was far from adequate to cover this deficit of 44.0 billions on trade and interest accounts; hence a net deficiency of 26.9 billions had to be met through credit operations of one kind or another.

This deficit was covered by receipts from a number of types of borrowing operations. Commercial transactions provided a net total of 23.9 billions, while government political transactions yielded 3 billions. The largest single source of income from abroad was the sale of francs to foreign speculators amounting to approximately 14.5 billion francs for the period. It is indeed an interesting phenomenon that the strained financial and economic condition which accounted for the fall in the franc should have provided large sums with which to meet pressing external obligations. This situation has, of course, found its counterpart since the war in other European countries.

The French international debt situation at the end of 1923 is shown in tabular form below. The figures have been converted to paper francs, this time on the basis of exchange rates for December, 1923.

FOREIGN DEBT AND INVESTMENT POSITION, DECEMBER 31, 1923
(Figures are in billions of francs)

In paper, at average rates
for December, 1923.[a]

INVESTMENTS

French-owned foreign investments
(at par of exchange):
Total, June 30, 1919 .... 18.5
Acquisition of Sarre mines 4

Total 18.9
Less foreign securities sold after
the war 9

Total remaining, December 31,
1923 (gold franc)........ 18.0[b]   Equivalent to   37.8
War and post-war loans of France to neighboring states.... 13.8

Total of investments and loans, December 31, 1923...... 51.6

DEBTS

Total debt to foreigners, exclusive of political debt:
Pre-war investments of foreigners 3.5
War and post-war sales of domestic securities and
real estate 21.0
Paper francs held by foreigners 15.0
Commercial credits (open accounts) 2.0
Municipal and industrial borrowings abroad (face
value .36 at par of exchange) 1.2
Foreign commercial borrowings of the government
(5.3 at par) 18.0   60.7

Political debt of the government including capitalized interest on debt to Great Britain (30.5 at
par) 106.8
Interest at 5 per cent on debt to the United
States (3.5 at par) 12.9   119.7

Total foreign debt of all kinds 180.4

[a] Conversion ratios used are as follows: 2.1 paper francs to 1 franc at par for French-owned foreign securities, based on French exchange rates on seventeen important countries; 3.4 for government commercial debt, based on weighted average of French exchange on countries in which debt was contracted; 3.5 for political debt of the government, also a weighted average for countries concerned; 3.7 for interest on the debt to the United States.
[b] Interest payments on 3 billions of South American securities

V. INTERNATIONAL INCOME FOR THE YEAR 1924

The economic position of France—viewed solely from the standpoint of international income— showed in 1924 a marked improvement over previous years. For the first time since the war, indeed for the first time since 1905 and the second time since 1875, French exports exceeded imports. There was also a considerable net income from the service accounts, so that France showed a substantial net income for the year.

The following figures show in concise form the trade and service operations for the year 1924.[13]

Deficit for interest (exclusive of political debt).......		.6
Net income from:		
Trade and specie operations	1.4	
Services other than interest and reparations	5.8	7.2
Net surplus other than interest and reparations		6.6

The credit operations for the year may be summarized as follows:

Outgo on account of commercial transactions:			
Repurchase of francs from foreigners.........	5.0		
Bankers loans to foreigners	1.0		
New private investments ("flight of capital")	2.5	8.5	
Less receipts from commercial borrowings....		2.1	6.4
Outgo on account of new political loans			.2
Net outgo on account of credit operations.....			6.6

were resumed near the end of this period, though for the most part, paid in paper.

[13] For detailed figures see Appendix A.

By paying no interest on her political debt, France was able to reduce her net foreign indebtedness in 1924. As the foregoing figures indicate, the net income was 6.6 billions.[14] Of this amount, it appears that about 5 billion francs were utilized at the time of the Morgan loan in repurchasing bills of exchange which had previously been sold to foreigners. The net result of other credit operations was to reduce the foreign indebtedness by 1.6 billion francs. Since the francs held abroad did not yield interest, the year's reduction in indebtedness does not help in reducing the payments required on interest account. The repurchase of these francs, moreover, does not necessarily mean a net gain to the nation, viewed as a long run story. They were repurchased in the main when the franc was worth from three to four cents. If the franc ultimately falls below this level, their repurchase at this price will have involved a loss rather than a gain.

The French international debt situation at the end of 1924 is shown in the table on page 35.

The favorable trade balance of the year 1924 is primarily attributable to the fall of the franc. In November, 1923, French exchange began a rapid decline which continued until March, 1924, when it was checked by means of funds provided through the Morgan loan. As had previously been the case when the German mark declined rapidly, the fall of

---

[14] No adjustment has been made for the trade and service operations of the colonies, for reasons which are discussed in Appendix A, pp. 370-2.

the franc precipitated a temporary trade boom.
France became a very cheap market in which to buy,
and foreign orders for French goods were placed in

FOREIGN DEBT AND INVESTMENT POSITION, DECEMBER 31, 1924
(Figures are in billions of francs)

In paper, at average rates
for December, 1924.[a]

INVESTMENTS

French-owned foreign investments:
Total, December 31, 1923 (18. at par of exchange)   39.6
Plus new investments during 1924:
  Bankers loans .... 1.
  New private investments 2.5   3.5   43.1

War and post-war loans of France to neighboring states....   15.1

Total of investments and loans, December 31, 1924.......   58.2

DEBTS

Total debt to foreigners, exclusive of the political debt:
  Pre-war investments of foreigners 3.5
  War and post-war sales of domestic securities and
    real estate 22.0
  Paper francs held by foreigners 10.0
  Commercial credits (open account) 2.0
  Municipal and industrial borrowings abroad (nom-
    inal value about .65 at par) 2.4
  Foreign commercial debt of the government (5.8 at
    par) 20.3   60.2

Political debt of the government including capitalized
  interest due Great Britain (31.3 at par) 109.6
Interest at 5 per cent on debt to the United States
  (4.2 at par) 15.5   125.1

Total foreign debt of all kinds 185.3

[a] Conversion to paper franc values has been made on the basis
of average exchange rates for December, 1924. The ratios—
worked out by the same methods as for 1919 and 1923 (see pp.
27 and 32)—are 2.2 paper francs to 1 franc at par for French-
owned foreign investments; 3.5 for government debt, both commercial and political; and 3.7 for municipal and industrial
borrowings.

unusual volume. British merchants, for example, displaying French wares, advertised, "bargains while the franc is falling."

French exchange during the summer of 1923 had ranged around 6 cents. Then in November the average for the month fell to 5.52; in December to 5.25; in February 1924 to 4.42; and early in March it reached a low point of 3.49, though the average for the month, thanks to the Morgan loan, was 4.68. In April the average rate was 6.16, though it soon fell again to a little above 5 cents where it remained for the rest of the year. The total value of exports, which had ranged around 2,600 million francs per month in the summer of 1923, increased to 2,900 millions in November; to 3,900 millions in February, 1924; to over 4,300 millions in March; and in April, owing to the lag in filling orders, the total was still above 4,000 millions. The table on the opposite page shows the value of imports and exports for each month of 1923 and 1924, respectively.

It will be seen from this table that the large favorable balance in the three months of February, March, and April, when the effect of the fall of the currency was most pronounced, was considerably larger than the net balance for the year as a whole. Figures for other years indicate that large exports in these months are not a seasonal phenomenon. The total exports for these three months was 12,300 million francs, and the total imports were 10,629 millions, giving a favorable balance of 1,671 million francs, as compared with a net favorable bal-

FRENCH FOREIGN TRADE, 1923-1924 *
(In millions of francs)

Month	1923			1924[a]		
	Imports	Exports	Net	Imports	Exports	Net
January	2,136	1,803	— 333	2,888	2,700	— 188
February	2,341	2,378	+ 37	3,714	3,918	+ 204
March	2,479	2,381	— 98	3,623	4,355	+ 732
April	2,550	2,442	— 108	3,292	4,027	+ 735
May	2,524	2,664	+ 140	3,177	3,360	+ 183
June	2,630	2,482	— 148	3,179	2,922	— 257
July	2,632	2,412	— 220	3,100	3,014	— 86
August	2,625	2,486	— 139	3,072	2,967	— 105
September ...	2,604	2,484	— 120	3,157	3,184	+ 27
October	3,060	2,808	— 152	3,398	3,532	+ 134
November ...	3,161	2,941	— 320	3,415	3,433	+ 18
December ...	3,827	3,114	— 713	4,118	4,042	— 76
	32,569	30,935	—2,174	40,133	41,454	+1,321

* Special trade.
[a] Provisional figures.

ance for the year of only 1,321 million francs. The great increase in the value of exports during these months is not to be explained by the fact that prices had risen. There was also a roughly proportionate increase in the physical volume of trade—as shown by tonnage figures and by value figures with the effects of price changes eliminated.

While the favorable balance of trade is thus accounted for by the extraordinary volume of exports during the months of currency decline, it should also be noted that exports held up very well throughout the year and were considerably larger during the last half of the year than during the corresponding period of 1923. This is true of the physical volume as well as of the value of exports.

The maintenance of a large volume of foreign trade—both imports and exports—throughout the year, accompanied as it was by large internal production and trade, was the result of a continuation of the boom period initiated in the earlier months of currency decline. Even after the franc was practically stabilized at a little above five cents France retained some advantage in foreign trade as compared with the preceding year. The stabilization of the German currency at pre-war par of exchange had made Germany a relatively high-priced market in which to buy; and the credit crisis further restricted German competition in foreign markets. At the same time British exchange rose steadily from an average of $4.32 for the month of June to $4.70 for the month of December, and British purchases of French goods consequently continued heavy throughout the year.

In the last month of the year, French exports were again very large, owing primarily to the bulge in shipments of Alsace-Lorraine goods across the German frontier, in anticipation of the expiration early in January, 1925, of the five-year treaty provision governing the free admission of such goods into Germany. The month of December did not, however, show a favorable balance, because of a bulge in imports of high priced foodstuffs and raw materials.

The year 1925 can be expected to show another favorable trade situation, only if the artificial advantage of cheap currency continues. During the

early months of the year the franc was somewhat
weaker and the British pound continued to rise toward par. The French trade figures for the first
five months of 1925 are as follows:

FRENCH FOREIGN TRADE, 1925
(In millions of francs)

Month	Imports	Exports	Net
January	3,172.6	3,562.6	+390.0
February	3,346.4	3,595.1	+248.7
March	3,306.7	3,762.2	+455.5
April	3,051.0	3,557.7	+506.7
May	2,968.7	3,640.2	+671.5

It only remains to point out that a trade boom
based on falling currency does not represent an altogether sound situation. Other things meanwhile do
not remain equal, and these other economic results
of a depreciating currency quickly have their repercussions upon the trade figures themselves. As we
shall see in Chapter VI the trade boom of 1924 was
accompanied by rapidly mounting prices and currency inflation which precipitated before the end
of the year a social and political crisis over the
high cost of living, a banking crisis on account of
the growth of the note currency, and a treasury
crisis because of the inability of the government to
float additional securities in the market.

The results of France's international economic operations from 1914 to 1924, inclusive, as revealed
by the preceding analysis, may now be shown in
tabular form.

SHIFT IN FOREIGN DEBT AND INVESTMENT POSITION, 1919-1924
(In billions of paper francs) *

Classification	June 30, 1919	Dec. 31, 1923	Dec. 31, 1924
Foreign commercial debt	24.2	60.7	60.2
Non-government loans and investments	22.2	37.8	43.1
Net, commercial debt	2.0	22.9	17.1
Government political debt to Allies	30.3	119.7	125.1
Government war and post-war loans to foreign governments	10.0	13.8	15.1
Net, political debt	20.3	105.9	110.0

* For details concerning conversion ratios see pp. 27, 32, and 35.

These figures, it should be observed, include the political war debts owed both by and to France, but leave future reparation claims out of the picture. In other words, the figures merely reveal the changes that have occurred in France's international economic position as a result of war and post-war financial operations to the end of 1924.

The reader will bear in mind also that the figures are all stated in paper francs. While such values give a true picture of the balance of indebtedness on any particular date—at the rates of exchange then current—they do not accurately reveal the real economic changes that have occurred. A considerable part of the increase both in the volume of foreign investments and of new indebtedness is accounted for by the fall in the value of the franc. In the following chart the changes in the French international debt and investment position are shown in terms of 1914 gold prices—both the changes in the world price level and the fall in the value of paper currencies, including the franc, being eliminated. For purposes of comparison, the table on the preceding page is also presented here in graphic form.

SHIFT FROM CREDITOR TO DEBTOR POSITION, 1914-1924.

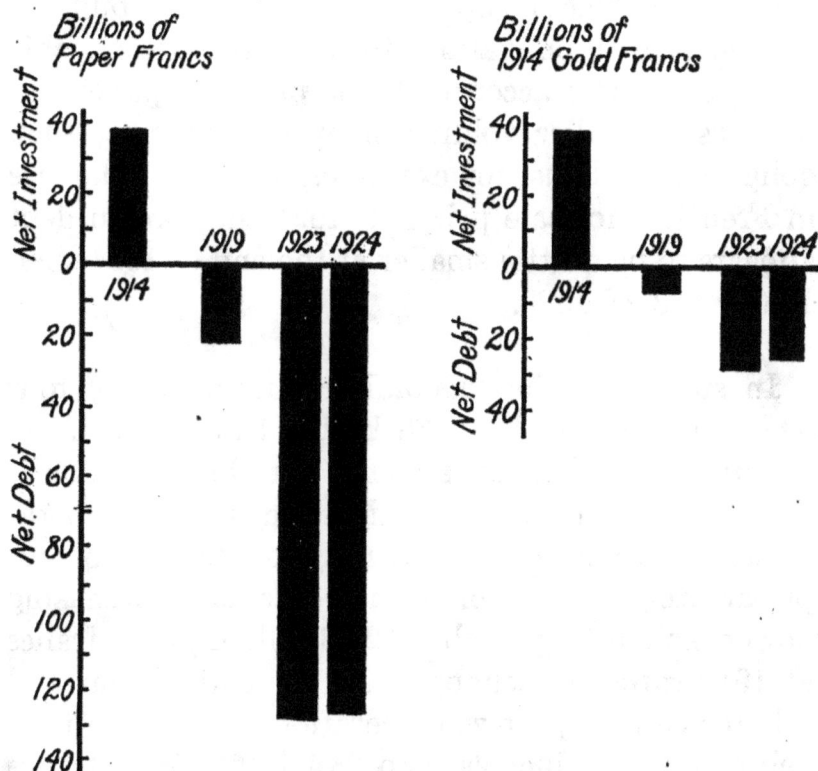

This chart measures, in terms of 1914 gold francs, as well as in paper, the shift that has occurred in France's foreign investment and debt position between 1914 and 1924. That is to say, it compares

the volume of goods due France in 1914 on account
of foreign investments with the volume of goods
that France owed to foreigners in the later years on
account of her accumulated indebtedness.   The
changes from one period to another are the result
of two factors, namely:—borrowing (or repayments) and changes in the price level in France.
The second factor operates because the bulk of
French private obligations to foreigners are payable
in paper francs; accordingly, as prices in paper rise
it takes a smaller volume of exports to meet such
obligations.   Thus, for example, because of the rise
in French wholesale prices in 1924 the foreign debt
appears to be a little smaller at the end of 1924 than
at the end of 1923.

In summary, the economic requirements of four
years of war wiped out 38 billion francs net of accumulated foreign investments that had been built
up during a century of trading and financial operations, and replaced it by a net indebtedness of approximately 6.8 billion francs of equal purchasing
power, amounting to about 22.3 billion paper francs
at 1919 rates of exchange.   At the end of four and
a half years of post-war operations, the foreign indebtedness had increased to 28.1 billion gold francs
of 1914 value, equal to 128.8 billions in 1923 paper
franc values.   The inflationary boom of 1924, however, coupled with especially large income from services, made possible a slight reduction in the debt
during that year.   Leaving interest on the political

debt out of the reckoning, France had thus achieved a favorable balance in her international accounts.

The commercial inflation which had made possible a favorable balance of trade in 1924 had, however, contributed to the development of a cost of living, banking, exchange, and Treasury crisis which France was seeking in vain to control in the early months of 1925. These attending crises not only constituted extremely difficult problems by themselves; at the same time they threatened to result in the not distant future in a severe trade and business reaction which would unquestionably lessen the future balance of trade.

CHAPTER III

GROWTH OF THE PUBLIC DEBT: 1814-1918

THE varying amounts of international income between 1870 and 1924, as has been shown in the preceding chapter, determined the status of France's foreign debt and investment position. Both private and public transactions were included in the analysis; hence the figures indicated the nation's—as distinguished from the government's—international financial position. Many of the changes in the nation's foreign investment and debt position did not involve or directly concern the government treasury. In the present chapter we shall focus attention upon the fiscal operations of the French government, for the purpose of revealing the enormous growth of the public debt, both internal and external.

The expansion of the public debt has long presented a serious problem in France. For many decades prior to the Great War the French national debt had been steadily increasing, and by 1913 it had reached a total considerably larger than that of any other nation, standing at 33,637 million francs—approximately 6,500 million dollars. As a result of the financial exigencies of the past ten years, the French debt has assumed such enormous proportions that the debt problem, both internal and external, now overshadows every other economic consideration in France.

I. THE FRENCH DEBT PRIOR TO 1914

Public as well as private debts arise from unbalanced budgets. If a government's expenditures exceed its taxation revenues, the deficiency must be met by borrowings. An accumulating public debt over a period of years simply reveals the sum of the annual treasury deficits over the period in question. The pre-war budgetary situation of France may thus be succinctly shown by the growth of the national debt.

Large debts had been accumulated in the eighteenth century and earlier, but about two-thirds of the total was repudiated during the period of the French Revolution. The amount that was acknowledged and refunded in 1800 equalled only 926 million francs. Napoleon met the great bulk of his enormous expenditures, not by taxation at home, but by foreign levies. The countries which he conquered were forced not only to support his invading armies, but also to make large contributions in money and property. In consequence, the French national debt increased between 1800 and 1814, the end of the Napoleonic era, by only 340 million francs.

During the 100 years between 1814 and the outbreak of the World War the debt increased twenty-seven fold. The rate of growth during this period is indicated by the chart on the following page.

At the close of the Napoleonic era, France was naturally confronted with budgetary difficulties, and large loans were required for a number of years. But

GROWTH OF THE FRENCH PUBLIC DEBT, 1814-1914.

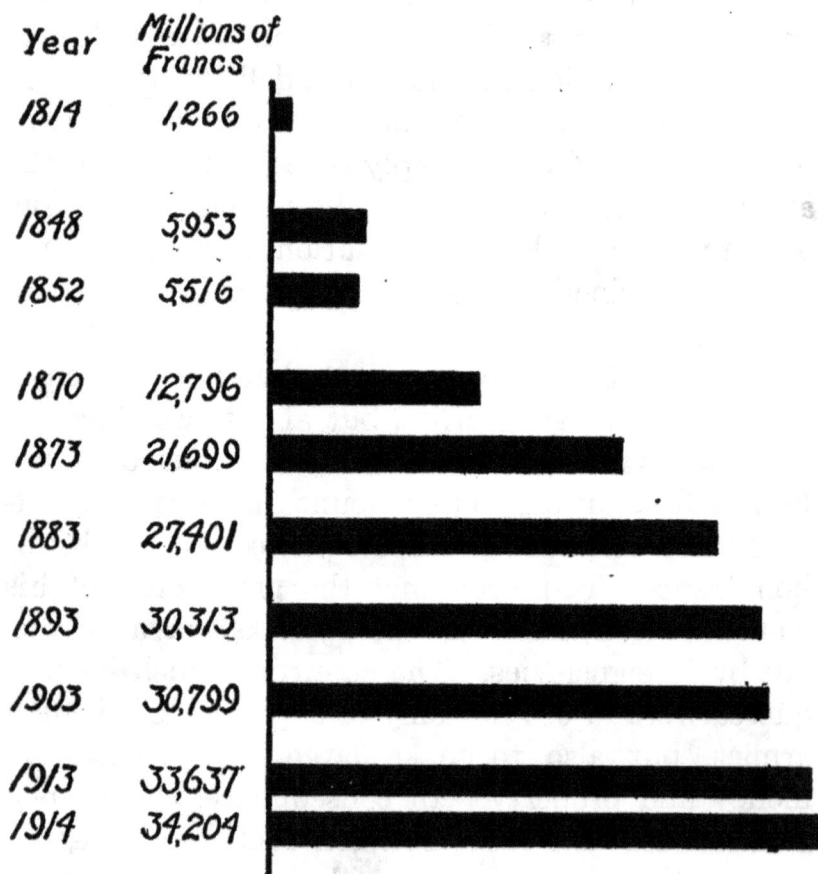

Year	Millions of Francs	
1814	1,266	
1848	5,953	
1852	5,516	
1870	12,796	
1873	21,699	
1883	27,401	
1893	30,313	
1903	30,799	
1913	33,637	
1914	34,204	

in the decade of the twenties, the Bourbon government succeeded in securing a budgetary surplus and in redeeming a considerable volume of debt. During the Orleanist régime, from 1830 to 1848, however, the debt steadily accumulated, and at the end of the period the consolidated debt stood at 5,953 million francs. Large expenditures for public works and for military purposes were a primary cause of the persistent budgetary deficits of the period.

The rapid growth of the public debt of France dates from the period of the Second Empire, 1852-1870. The Crimean and Italian wars and the Mexican and other adventures resulted in an enormous increase in the debt. Four successive national loans increased the public debt to the extent of 3,054 million francs in the fifties, while two smaller loans, amounting to 1,125 millions, were necessary in the sixties to take care of the accumulating treasury deficits caused by continued military outlays and expenditures on public works. At the same time, there was accumulating a large floating debt—consisting of short-time loans, periodically renewed. By 1870 the total debt was 12,796 million francs.[1]

The French public debt was increased by nearly nine billion francs as a result of the Franco-Prussian War. The direct war costs, plus the indemnity imposed by Germany, resulted in a growth of the public debt from 12,796 million francs at the beginning of 1870 to 21,699 million francs in 1873. The war and the indemnity payment were financed by four large bond issues, with a face value of 8,497,708,766 francs, yielding to the French government 6,808,-

[1] Including 11,419 millions of consolidated public debt; 643 millions for annuities to railways, etc.; and 734 millions of floating debt. The factual data in the foregoing paragraphs have been taken from Théry, Edmond, *Conséquences économiques de la guerre,* pp. 300-307.

909,187 francs. At the same time the floating and other forms of government debt increased by 1,897 million francs.[2]

After 1878, the financing of public works by the government steadily enlarged the public debt. With a view to building up the economic resources of the country, France undertook to carry out an extensive program of public works in the late seventies and eighties, particularly the construction of railroads and canals, and telegraph and telephone systems. This accounts for about half of the 12 billions of debt increase between 1873 and 1913. After 1885, there was a virtual budget balance, aside from the annuities for public works.

While some of these economic developments, promoted by the government, proved of great economic benefit to the nation and ultimately paid for themselves, the expenditures upon waterways showed no compensating advantages. In order to induce traffic to move by water it was found necessary to abolish all tolls and dues in 1880; and thereafter the state constantly sustained a heavy deficit, amounting to about 100 million francs a year.[3]

The policy of colonial expansion proved a source of great expense to the French government. From

[2] The indemnity amounted to 5 billion francs. The funds within France were raised by borrowing operations rather than by means of increased taxes. For a full analysis of the methods by which the payment was effected, see Appendix F.

[3] For a detailed discussion of French water and rail transportation see Moulton, H. G., *Waterways versus Railways* (1912), Chapter XII.

1871 to 1880, the net expenditure by the French government on the colonies, that is, over and above receipts from the colonies, averaged about one hundred million francs annually. During the next decade it was much larger, due mainly to military operations in Tunis, Indo-China, and Madagascar, reaching in 1885 a total well over 200 million francs. During the twenty years ending in 1910 the total net expenditure averaged somewhat below 200 million francs annually, but from then until the war it increased rapidly, the military occupation of Morocco bringing the total up to 592 millions in 1914 and 535 millions in 1915.[4]

The lack of a unified budget system also contributed to the increase in public indebtedness. The disjointed character of the French national budget dates far back in French history. During the period between the Franco-Prussian and World wars, for example, the budget consisted of several parts. There was first the general, or ordinary, budget; second, the annexed budgets; third, the extraordinary budget; and fourth, special treasury services. The annexed budgets covered many, though not all, of the enterprises administered by the State, the most important of which were the State railroad administration, and the national savings banks. The annexed budgets were submitted to Parliament along with the general or ordinary budget; hence they gave rise to no confusion.

[4] For these data we are indebted to an unpublished study of French colonial policy, by Constant Southworth.

The extraordinary budget was in theory intended to cover temporary or non-recurring outlays. In this budget were put expenditures for war, public works, armaments, etc. It is apparent that it would often be difficult to distinguish between ordinary and extraordinary expenditures. The door was thus open to loose budgeting practices, and to large expenditures that had to be met by the "extraordinary" method of borrowing.

The special treasury services or accounts were particularly conducive to extravagant expenditures and consequent increase of the public debt. It was not required that they should be submitted to Parliament by the Finance Minister, nor were they submitted to audit. Hence the government was free to launch enterprises in which it was interested, regardless of the immediate budgetary situation. Like the extraordinary budgets, the special treasury outlays went largely for the promotion of public works and for the improvement of the military establishment. As a result of an agitation for a unified fiscal system, the extraordinary budgets were discontinued after 1891; but the special accounts continued to be utilized.[5]

An example of the way in which these special accounts led to an increase in the public debt may prove instructive. In 1898 an account entitled "Perfecting the material of armament and reinstall-

[5] The original purpose of the Special Treasury Accounts was to facilitate the recording of specific transactions that properly belonged outside the regular budget. For a full discussion of the special treasury services, see Appendix B.

ing military services" was created. It represented *extraordinary* expenditures based upon *supposititious* future receipts. The intention was to pay for work on the military establishment, the cost of which should naturally have gone into the ordinary budget. The funds devoted to the purpose were treasury funds which were to be paid back later from receipts secured from the sale of military lands. As might readily have been foreseen, it turned out that the original expenditure had been greatly under-estimated, and the prospective receipts greatly over-estimated.[6]

The results of the loose budgetary methods which prevailed may be realized from the fact that from 1881 to 1891 the net total of extra-budgetary expenses was over five billion francs.[7] The danger in this form of treasury accounting was, however, coming to be appreciated, and at the end of the period under discussion the abuses were being gradually eliminated.

In the last ten years preceding the Great War the French budget was nearly in balance. Accordingly, the increase in the French debt was relatively slow. The figures which follow show the total revenues from sources other than borrowing, and the total expenditures (in millions of francs) during selected years just before the war.

[6] Cernesson, André, *Le principe d'unite budgetaire en France,* 1911, pp. 132 ff.

[7] Hirst, Francis W., *The Credit of Nations* (Report of U. S. National Monetary Commission, 1910), p. 89.

	1904	1907	1910	1913
Total revenues	3,739	3,968	4,274	4,907
Total expenditures	3,639	3,880	4,322	5,072
Net revenues	100	88	—48	—165

The character of French expenditures in the latter years before the war is shown in the following classification.

PRE-WAR GOVERNMENT EXPENDITURES, BY BROAD GROUPS *

(In millions of francs)

Services	1904	1907	1910	1913
Public debt	1,205	1,220	1,257	1,355
Military expenditures	995	1,138	1,278	1,807
General administration	1,439	1,522	1,787	1,904
Total ordinary expenditures ..	3,639	3,880	4,322	5,066
Special Treasury Services	....	....	....	6
Total	3,639	3,880	4,322	5,072

* Data for the years 1904, 1907, and 1910 are from *Bulletin de statistique et de législation comparée*, January, 1914, pp. 56-9; for 1913, from the *Exposé des motifs du projet du budget, 1923*, pp. 10-33.

It will be observed that the charges on account of the public debt were increasing but slowly during these years. The expenses for general administration (*services civils*), however, expanded steadily and out of proportion to the general increase in the population and wealth of the country. The extensive overhauling and improvement of the French military organization following 1910 is reflected in the sharp increase in the military outlays.

The character of the taxation system which had grown up to meet these expenditures is indicated

by the table below which gives the government's
revenues during corresponding years.

PRE-WAR REVENUES FROM SOURCES OTHER THAN BORROWING *
(In millions of francs)

Classification	1904	1907	1910	1913
Direct taxes	549	561	587	634
Indirect taxes:	2,076	2,230	2,447	2,890
Registration	592	646	690	834
Stamp	190	207	239	241
Bourse	7	8	12	10
Stocks and bonds	84	101	108	138
Customs	437	509	586	756
Excise and consumption	766	759	812	911
Other revenues:	1,114	1,117	1,240	1,383
Monopolies [a]	842	882	950	1,035
State properties	62	60	64	62
Receipts by order, etc.	210	235	226	286
Grand Total	3,739	3,968	4,274	4,907

* Data for the years 1904, 1907, 1910, from *Bulletin de statistique
et de législation comparée*, January, 1914, pp. 52-5, for 1913
from *Exposé des motifs du projet du budget, 1923*, p. 39.
[a] These are exclusive of the particular government enterprises
which are covered by the "Annexed Budgets"; see Appendix B.

Of the receipts from taxation, about 82 per cent
in 1913 were derived from indirect levies, of which
excise and consumption taxes, registration fees, and
customs duties were the most important. The direct
taxes were divided into four main groups—popularly
called the "four old women"—and a miscellaneous
group of taxes and fees on carriages, clubs, billiards,
mines, etc., known as the "assimilated" taxes. The
"four old women" comprised taxes on (1) land, (2)

doors and windows, (3) movable property, dwell-
ings, etc. (*contributions mobilières*), and (4) occupations. The French levied no income tax, as such,
prior to the Great War; but interestingly enough
an income tax, which had been discussed for many
years, was provided for in the acts of March 29
and June 15, 1914.

*The French taxation burden before the war was
comparatively heavy.* In 1893 the taxation receipts
of the national government amounted to approximately 12 per cent of the national income, while
in 1913 it amounted to about 11.5 per cent. If the
taxation receipts of the departments and communes
be included, the percentages are approximately 15
for 1893 and 14.5 for 1913.[8] Taxation in France
absorbed a larger portion of the national income
than in any other leading nation. The United Kingdom took about 11.3 per cent of the national income; Germany about 10.5 per cent; and the United
States only about 6.7 per cent—including in each
case the taxation of the states and municipalities.[9]

[8] The taxation figures for the national government (*Annuaire
statistique*, 1919-20, pp. 156-7) include receipts from the direct,
assimilated, and indirect taxes and from the tobacco, match, and
powder monopolies, and exclude receipts from other government
monopolies, from the national domain, etc. The figures for the
departments and communes include the *centimes additionnels*
attached to the direct and assimilated taxes (*ibid.*, p. 167), and
the *octrois* (*ibid.*, p. 173). A brief discussion of national and
local taxation in France is given in Appendix B, pp. 408-423.

[9] See Seligman, Edwin R. A., *Political Science Quarterly*, March,
1924, p. 143. Professor Seligman's figure for France is 14.1 per
cent, the difference from ours resulting from the fact that he has

As a matter of fact, these figures do not fully show the French tax burden as compared with that of the United States and the United Kingdom, since the income per capita of these countries was much larger than that of France. Just prior to the war, the per capita national income of these countries was approximately as follows: The United States, $343; the United Kingdom, $238; France, $178; Germany, $152.[10] It is obvious upon a moment's reflection, that a taxation burden of 14.5 per cent on France's per capita income of only $178 bears more heavily than would a similar rate of tax upon the larger incomes of the United Kingdom and of the United States.

In concluding this discussion of the pre-war growth of the French public debt, it will be of interest to note that the growth of population and national income, in comparison with the growth of the debt, reveals a gradual improvement in the general economic position of France. The figures for national income, page 56, are but rough estimates, particularly for the year 1893. The population and debt figures are from official sources.[11]

not included the communal receipts from the assimilated taxes. The estimate for the United States is for the fiscal period ending June 30, 1914; for England and Germany for the fiscal period ending March 31, 1914.

[10] These figures, which are given by Seligman (*ibid.*), have been compiled from numerous sources. For a discussion of the French figure see Appendix C.

[11] Figures concerning national income are discussed in Appendix C (pp. 424-9). Population and public debt figures are from the *Annuaire statistique*, 1919-20, pp. 12 and 153.

	1893	1913	Percentage Increase
National income	24 billions	36 billions	50
National income (in 1913 prices)	30 "	36 "	20
Population	38.3 millions	39.7 millions	4
Public debt	30.1 billions	33.6 billions	12

It will be observed that the national income increased considerably faster than the public debt, and very much faster than the population. From a military standpoint the negligible increase in French population was a serious matter, but from the point of view of per capita income and average well-being, the slow increase of population was no doubt fortunate. In view of the relatively dense population and restricted resources of the country a more rapid increase of population would probably not have been matched by a proportionate increase in production and in national income.

The general improvement in the economic situation is best shown by the per capita figures, as follows:

Per Capita	1893 [a] (francs)	1913 (francs)	Percentage Increase
National income	627	907	45
Taxation	100	131	31
Public debt	784	847	8

[a] These figures have not been adjusted for price changes. The price level is a factor which directly affects the corresponding figures for taxation receipts and national income, but not the figure for the accumulated public debt.

The national income per capita was growing steadily, and more rapidly than per capita taxation. Thus the burden of taxation, as was indicated on page 54, had declined slightly. Since the debt had increased only 8 per cent, it is clear that the public credit was improving, and that the fiscal situation was being kept pretty well in hand during the latter years before the war.

II. THE PUBLIC DEBT INCREASE, 1914-1918

At the opening of the Great War, the French government was heavily indebted to its own people, but it was entirely free of foreign obligations. The enormous financial requirements of the war years are reflected both in a great increase of domestic borrowings and in the creation of a foreign debt of huge proportions. The explanation of the former is to be found in a succession of unbalanced budgets, and of the latter in a succession of unfavorable trade balances, as shown in the preceding chapter.

The French budget showed a huge deficit from the very beginning of the war. The budget of 1914, after long delay, was passed on July 15, just ten days before the Austrian ultimatum to Serbia. The budget called for ordinary expenditures of 5,192 million francs and extraordinary expenditures on the army and navy of 848 millions, while the estimated ordinary revenues from taxation, government monopolies, etc., was only 4,779 million francs. Thus there was forecast a deficit of 413 million francs in the ordinary accounts of the government, and a special or extraordinary deficit of 848 millions. This large deficit was to be met by three means: First,

by an issue of 3½ per cent, 25-year, amortizable
government bonds, estimated to yield 805 million
francs; second, by the sale of 298 million francs of
short-term Treasury obligations; and third, by
drafts against the Treasury balance.

The outbreak of the war naturally played havoc
with the budget. Not only were expenditures enormously increased in the last five months of the year
1914, but the yields from taxes, government monopolies, and from the loan all proved disappointing. The 3½ per cent government bonds, or *rentes*,
which it had been thought would sell for 97, brought
at the outset only 92.80, owing to a provision that
the income from these bonds should be subject to
a tax, a provision which greatly depressed the market.[12] In consequence of the Austrian ultimatum,
these bonds fell almost immediately to 85.

The following table shows the French budgetary
situation for the war period as a whole. The reader
should bear in mind that since no loans were included among the revenues in this table, the deficit
column represents the amount of expenditures that
had to be provided out of borrowing operations of
one kind or another. The expenditures figures include outlays in connection with the special treasury services as well as ordinary and extraordinary
budget appropriations.

[12] French government bonds had been tax exempt since 1793,
and the provision that the income on this issue should be subject
to tax created great uneasiness in financial circles, lest all future
government securities should be taxed.

FRENCH BUDGET OPERATIONS, 1914-1918
(In millions of francs)

Year	Expenditures [a]	Revenues from Sources Other Than Borrowing [b]	Deficits
1914	10,371	4,196	6,175
1915	22,120	4,130	17,990
1916	36,848	4,932	31,916
1917	44,661	6,186	38,475
1918	56,649	6,791	49,858
Total	170,649	26,235	144,414

[a] *Exposé des motifs du projet du budget, 1913*, p. 39.
[b] *Ibid.*, pp. 10-1, 14-5, 20-1, 30-1, 33.

The nature of French government expenditures for the war years is shown by the following table.

GOVERNMENT EXPENDITURES, BY BROAD GROUPS, 1914-1918 *
(In millions of francs)

Classes	1914	1915	1916	1917	1918	Total
Public debt	1,360	1,818	3,327	4,816	7,021	18,342
Military charges	6,526	14,712	23,853	28,662	36,120	109,873
Civil services	2,005	2,479	2,817	4,119	5,443	16,863
Total, ordinary budget	9,891	19,009	29,997	37,597	48,584	145,078
Expenditures later charged to Germany (Recoverable budget) [a]	372	1,914	2,947	4,081	5,952	15,266
Special Treasury Services	108	1,197	3,904	2,983	2,113	10,305
Total	10,371	22,120	36,848	44,661	56,649	170,649

* Data compiled from the *Exposé des motifs du projet du budget, 1923*, pp. 10-33.

[a] Data taken from Finance Minister Clémentel: *Inventaire de la situation de la France*, 1924, p. 16. For an explanation of the recoverable budget, see pp. 80-84.

Direct military expenditures, including those later charged to Germany, account for 72 per cent of the total outlays. Administrative expenditures comprised about 11 per cent; and outlays on account of the public debt, approximately 10 per cent of the total. Special Treasury services, which provided for a multitude of theoretically non-recurring needs not covered by budget appropriations, equalled about 6 per cent of the total expenditures.

Taxation receipts proved altogether inadequate to meet the enormous financial requirements of the war. The chart which follows shows the total revenues from sources other than borrowing for the

GOVERNMENT REVENUES AND EXPENDITURES, 1914-1918.

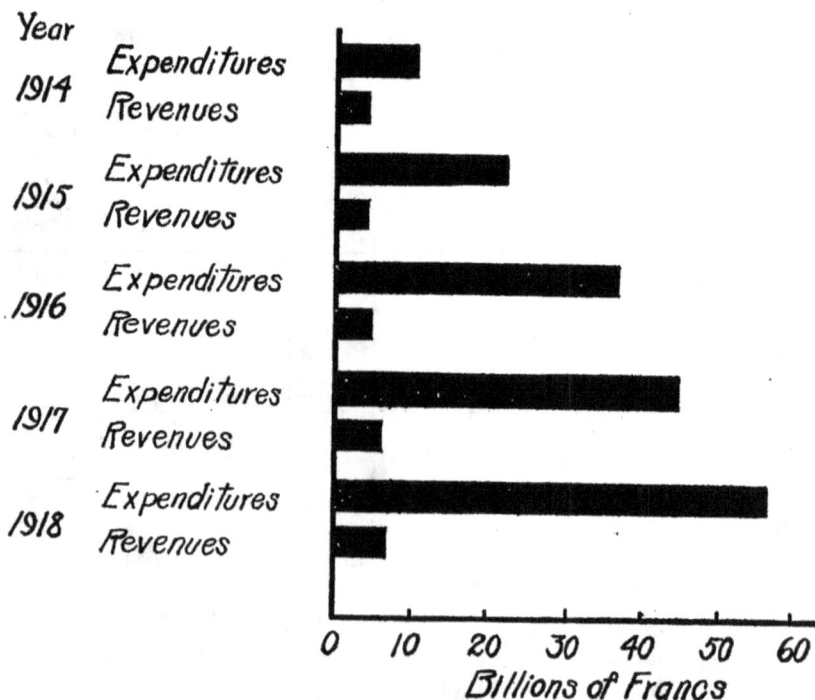

Billions of Francs

war years, 1914-1918, as compared with total expenditures.

The total revenue, excluding that from loans, was sufficient to meet only about 42 per cent of the total expenditures in 1914, 19 per cent in 1915; about 14 per cent in 1916 and 1917; and approximately 12 per cent in 1918.[13]

The way in which the several classes of direct and indirect taxes and other "ordinary" revenues of the government responded to war stimuli is shown by the table below.

FRENCH REVENUES FROM SOURCES OTHER THAN BORROWING, 1913-1918 *

(In millions of francs)

Classes	1914	1915	1916	1917	1918	Total
Direct taxes:	611	547	550	939	1,386	4,033
Old, assimilated, and income	611	547	550	730	696	3,134
Special tax on incomes	....	....	....	....	112	112
War profits	....	....	....	209	578	787
Indirect taxes:	2,310	2,261	2,979	3,667	3,720	14,937
Registration	611	464	525	720	924	3,244
Stamp	198	145	158	173	216	890
Bourse	6	1	2	3	3	15
Stocks and bonds ...	153	157	181	242	253	986
Customs	579	764	1,400	1,511	1,186	5,440
Excise and consumption	763	730	713	1,018	1,138	4,362
Other revenues:	1,275	1,322	1,403	1,580	1,685	7,265
Monopolies	942	853	950	1,116	1,158	5,019
State properties	60	114	110	120	148	552
Receipts by order and Sundry	273	355	343	344	379	1,694
Grand total	4,196	4,130	4,932	6,186	6,791	26,235

*Exposé des motifs du projet du budget, 1923, p. 39.

[13] The revenue and expenditure figures include the income and outgo in connection with the operation of the State monopolies.

The year 1914, as compared with the year 1913, showed a slump in each of the three general classes of ordinary income. Revenue from indirect taxes, and from the miscellaneous group made up of monopolies, state properties, etc., did not reach the 1913 figure until 1916, while it was 1917 before the income from direct taxes equalled and exceeded the 1913 figure. The obvious explanation for the fall in the ordinary receipts of the government in 1914 as compared with 1913 is the fact that the loss of revenue from the devastated departments was only slowly and gradually balanced by increases in revenues from the other departments.

During the war France continued to derive the greater part of her tax revenues from indirect sources. As in pre-war years, excise and consumption taxes, customs duties, and registration fees yielded the largest income. While an income tax had been provided for just prior to the outbreak of the war, it was not to become operative until the year 1915. In fact, its operation was delayed until 1916, and its yield was unimportant until 1918. A tax on war profits also yielded considerable sums in the last two years of the war.

France met the bulk of her war expenditures with the proceeds of loans. There is little to be gained from any post-war discussion of French fiscal policy during the war period. The fact of the case is that the need for funds was imperative, while tax reforms, which had long been under discussion, were necessarily slow of realization. The government, therefore, turned to the Bank of France, to the French public, to foreign investors, and to foreign governments for the funds which it desperately needed, leaving to the future the problem of settling the obligations thus incurred.

During the war months of 1914, over 60 per cent of the government's borrowings were from the banks of issue. Thereafter, the greater part of the total was secured by means of internal bond and bill issues, many of which were, of course, placed with banking institutions. In the latter years of the war, from one-quarter to one-third of the total was borrowed abroad.

The internal loans were of three classes: The first is the *perpetual* or long-term funded borrowings. These long-term obligations mainly take the form of government bonds (*rentes*), although included in the debt statement are also some state railway bonds and the capitalized value of certain "annuities," or annual sums paid by the State to cover deficits on state operated properties. Only ten days before the Austrian ultimatum, a large issue of 3½ per cent amortissable rentes had been authorized. However, owing to the weak and uncertain state of the financial markets in the early months of the war, these bonds were absorbed but slowly, and it was not until November, 1915, that a new issue was authorized. In all, four large loans were authorized during the war period: the 5 per cent rentes of 1915 and 1916; the 4 per cents of 1917; and the 4 per cents of 1918.

The second type of internal loan was the so-called

short-term borrowing, represented by five- and ten-year obligations. Some of these were designated Treasury bonds (*obligations du Trésor*), and the rest National Defense bonds (*obligations de la Défense Nationale*). These bonds played a very unimportant rôle in war financing, the amount outstanding comprising at the end of the conflict less than one-half of 1 per cent of the total internal indebtedness. The short-term treasury bonds which were outstanding at the beginning of the war were soon absorbed in new issues of other types.

The third class was the floating debt, consisting of "advances of the banks [14] of issue," of certain sundry accounts and deposits, and of Treasury bills (*bons du Trésor*) and National Defense bills (*bons de la Défense Nationale*). The "advances of the Bank of France" represented loans procured from the bank—Treasury bills, or *bons du Trésor,* being given the banks as security. The theory of such loans from banks is that they will shortly be liquidated out of the proceeds of loans placed in the regular investment markets. As a matter of fact, however, the financial exigencies of the French government were so pressing that the amount of such advances steadily expanded throughout the war period, reaching a total of 18,800 millions at the time of the Armistice. As we shall see in the following section, the practice of borrowing from the bank did not cease at the end of the war. The effects of this prac-

[14] Mainly of the Bank of France, with the Bank of Algeria contributing small sums.

tice upon the condition of the banks will be discussed in the following chapter.

The Treasury bills were little used during the war; but the National Defense bills played a very important rôle. In fact, a larger volume of these bills was issued during the war period than of any other class of government securities, the total outstanding at the end of the war being over 35 billion francs. These "floating" National Defense bills should be distinguished from the short-term National Defense bonds.

The National Defense bills were intended primarily to absorb the floating funds of the country, and to reach the masses of the people who might be interested in short-term savings plans. They were issued in denominations varying in size from 100 to 100,000 francs and for periods ranging from three months to one year. Interest at 5 per cent was payable in advance, making the effective rate of yield somewhat higher. No record whatsoever was kept concerning the buyers of these bills, which were made transferable without impeding formalities. Their patriotic name was not without its appeal, and the fact that the investor was assured that no attempt would be made to use his purchases as an index of his financial resources—and therefore as a check on his income tax returns—contributed to make them a success. We shall return to a discussion of these bills in the next chapter.

The foreign loans were procured from England and the United States, and from certain other allied and neutral countries. The loans contracted in England fall into two classes: first, the loans of the British Treasury, against which the French Treasury gave its one-year bonds, redeemable at maturity; second, the commercial borrowings of the French government in the London market.

Included in this second class are the loans which were extended to the Bank of France by the Bank of England, as security for which the Bank of France deposited gold with the Bank of England, equal to one-third of the amount of the loan. The loan when first extended amounted to 60 million pounds sterling and the gold deposit to 20 millions; later when the loan increased to the peak figure of 72 million pounds, the deposit increased to 24 millions. Subsequently, as payments have been made against the loan, the amount of gold deposit has been correspondingly decreased.

Loans secured in the United States also fall into two classes. Before the United States declared war on Germany, the French government obtained large grants of credit from American banking and commercial houses. After the declaration of war by the United States, the French government borrowed directly from the Federal treasury. Against these borrowings it gave demand bonds of the French treasury bearing interest at a nominal rate originally of 3½ per cent, but later increased to 5 per cent.

The loans procured from other allied and neutral countries were, for the most part, obtained from banks and commercial houses, against which the Treasury gave collateral in the form of foreign securities which it had purchased in the French market.[15]

The following summary table [16] shows the amounts which the government realized during the war from its various types of borrowing operations.

PROCEEDS OF FRENCH WAR LOANS, 1914-1918

(In billions of francs)

Internal loans:		
Rentes, short-term bonds, bills, etc.	80,389	
Advances of the banks of issue	17,265	97,654
Foreign loans		32,237
		129,891
Repayments of loans		1,745
Net proceeds		128,146

The relatively low taxation and the huge borrowing operations of the war period resulted in an enormous increase in the public debt. The national debt figures, in millions of francs, stood as follows at the beginning and at the end of the war.

It will be seen that the government's domestic debt, already the heaviest in the world, was nearly quadrupled during the war period, and that a for-

[15] Detailed data concerning these loans is given by M. de Lasteyrie, formerly Minister of Finance, in the *Exposé des motifs du projet du budget, 1923*, pp. 62-72. These loans are taken into account in connection with the international accounts of France, Chapter II, and Appendix A, of this book.

[16] For detailed statement of the year to year borrowings, together with the sources from which these amounts were secured, see Appendix D, page 431.

PUBLIC DEBT OF FRANCE, 1914 AND 1918 *

(In millions of francs)

Classification	July 31, 1914	December 31, 1918
Domestic debt:	34,186.0	123,794.3
Perpetual and long-term	32,235.3	67,248.0
Short-term	342.0	531.1
Floating	1,608.7	56,015.2
Foreign debt:		30,598.2
Political	....	23,832.4
Commercial	....	6,765.8
Total	34,186.0	154,392.5

* For the detailed debt statement of the Minister of Finance, see Appendix D, page 432. The total of the annual deficits as shown on page 59 is considerably larger than the increase in the public debt. This is due to the fact that some of the budget figures as given are still provisional. The increase in the debt, therefore, more accurately reflects the total of deficits.

eign debt was incurred nearly equal in amount to the domestic debt of 1914. The effects of this rapid growth of the public debt upon the credit of the French government and upon the rate of interest on loans will be considered in Chapter V.

CHAPTER IV

POST-WAR BUDGET DEFICITS

THE end of the war did not put an end to French economic difficulties. The immediate tasks were to convert the economic plant and equipment from war to peace-time operations; to undertake the physical reconstruction of the devastated departments; and to mitigate so far as possible the human sufferings born of the war. The longer run requirements involved both internal fiscal reforms and international financial adjustments.

Few people realized the gravity of the situation with which France was confronted at the close of the war. The inflation boom of 1919, as the financial literature of the time shows, was quite generally construed as the beginning of a long era of economic prosperity in the world at large. The illusions of the post-war period, no less common in France than in other countries, proved a serious barrier to the carrying out of constructive fiscal reforms. The reluctance to grapple with realities was perhaps more pronounced in France than elsewhere, because of the confident belief that Germany would be forced, in good season, if not immediately, to pay for the damages of the war. Rather than an increased taxation burden, it was hoped that a re-

duction of taxes would shortly be made possible.
It was but natural, of course, that the people who
had sacrificed so much during the war years should
hope that a time of recompense was near at hand.

I. FINANCIAL SITUATION OBSCURED BY BUDGETARY METHODS

The real condition of French public finance since
the war has been concealed by the methods of budgetary accounting that have been employed in the
early part of the post-war period. The budgets
which were passed by Parliament bore little resem-
blance indeed to the ultimate receipts and outlays.
Government departments were repeatedly granted
supplementary credits as the exigencies during the
course of the year seemed to require; and besides
the ordinary budget there was an extraordinary budget, as well as numerous special "Treasury services"
outside. There was also introduced the so-called
"recoverable" budget in which were placed all expenditures which were chargeable to Germany on
reparation account.

Under pressure of criticism both at home and
abroad, the budgetary practice has improved as the
years have passed; but even yet the budget as published to the world is not a completely unified statement covering all revenues and expenditures, and
it does not convey a true picture of the fiscal situation. Year after year the budget statements have
given the impression that the budget was almost, if
not quite, or at any rate was about to become, satis-

factory. But the final deficits at the end of each year and the rapid growth of the public debt have proved that the budget figures as officially presented have year after year been persistently and grossly misleading.

For example, the budget of 1920 indicated that the total outlay would be approximately 47.9 billion francs and the total revenues 21.8 billion francs, with a deficit of only 26.1 billion francs. According to later official figures, however, the total expenditures equalled in fact 58.1 billions, and the revenues 20.1 billions, giving a deficit of 38 billions. Even as late as 1923 the budget estimates created the impression that the expenditures would be 37 billions and the revenues 26.5 billions, with a deficit of only 10.5 billions. But official records—still incomplete—show expenditures of 45.8 billions, and revenues of 23.8, giving a deficit of 22.0 billions. The explanation of such discrepancies is to be found in a number of unsound budget practices.

The proceeds of loans were commonly included in revenue estimates. There has developed a very bad habit in many countries of "balancing" the budget by means of loans. There is, of course, no objection to a resort to loans as a means of meeting budget deficiencies; but it was quite misleading to call the budget "balanced" by the proceeds of loans. If loan receipts of all kinds and descriptions are considered as revenues a budget could obviously never be unbalanced. While there has been much improvement in French budgetary methods since

1919, it is still true, as we shall presently see,[1] that
certain bond issues are counted as revenues.

*"Supplementary" credits and Special Treasury
Services opened the way to enormous increases in
expenditures.* The nature of Special Treasury Services has already been considered and hence no discussion of the problem presented is necessary at this
place. The system of allowing supplementary
credits when the budgetary appropriations have
been used up has persisted throughout the post-war
period. In a speech before the Chamber of Deputies on February 19, 1925, Finance Minister Clémentel, severely criticized this practice in the following terms: [2]

The system of supplementary credits stands in the way of good
administrative control. This system is contrary to sound financial
methods and, in the end, weighs heavily on the Treasury. Because
of it, budgets apparently in balance when adopted, actually result in deficits in the course of their execution.

Even the Budet for 1925 is misleading. This
is true notwithstanding the contention that at
last the government had presented a genuinely honest and a genuinely unified budget, covering everything. It is unified in the sense that the recoverable budget is now included along with the regular
budget; but the totals are still not all inclusive. As
M. Bérenger, budgetary reporter for the Senate remarks in referring to the 1925 "unified" budget: [3]

We have never pretended to look upon capital expenditures
for the liberated regions as items belonging to the budget. How-

[1] See page 79 below.

[2] *Débats parlementaires, Chambre,* Feb. 20, 1925, p. 999.

[3] *Débats parlementaires, Sénat,* Feb. 21, 1925, p. 136.

ever, we have left out of the budget certain outlays properly classified as budgetary, and these we must incorporate there in order to make it a sincere and honest document. Otherwise, we are going straight ahead toward new disillusionment. For example, why is interest on advances from the Bank of France not included in the budget? And, if we have any notion of achieving a real balance, why not incorporate in the budget the advances to the railroads and to the posts and telegraphs which represent annual, renewable expenditures?

Of far more importance than the continuing omissions of items from the budget proper is the method of accounting employed in connection with capital expenditures for reconstruction. The recoverable budget must, therefore, be considered before we enter into a discussion of the net results of post-war fiscal operations in France.

The methods of budgeting outlays chargeable to Germany conceals the true total of outlays for reconstruction. In the first place, the recoverable budget has not, until 1925, been a part of the budget proper, being passed upon separately and subsequently. Accordingly, the regular budget estimates as published have failed to include a large total of outlays. If these had been "recovered" currently from Germany it would not have mattered, but as things stood they were actual French outlays which had to be met from either internal taxes or loans. In the second place, the recoverable budget itself did not include all of the outlays incurred in connection with reconstruction activities. Hence when the recoverable budget is combined with the budget proper, the gross totals are still inadequate.

The recoverable expenditures are of two principal types. The first represent capital outlays on behalf of the so-called *sinistrés* (those who have suffered damages from the war). The second consist of recurring expenditures such as administrative outlays, pensions, etc., and also capital outlays in connection with the reconstruction of public properties, such as buildings, roads, bridges, etc. The practice is to include only the second of these classes in the recoverable budget and to provide for the other outlays by special methods, namely: through the agency of the Crédit National; by direct grants of annuities to the *sinistrés;* and by giving National Defense bonds to those entitled to damages, etc. A short statement about these methods of financing reconstruction is necessary to make the budget situation clear.[4]

A law of April 17, 1919, provided that the "payment of indemnities, of interest, and of loans to the *sinistrés* should be effected directly by the State or under its guarantee, and that, in case the State should turn the work over to a consortium of financial houses, the regulations governing the work of such a body should be submitted to the Chamber for ratification." Believing that in the actual work of reconstruction and in dealings with the *sinistrés* a separate organization would be more flexible than a government department, Parliament, by a law of October 10, 1919, authorized the creation of the

[4] The information given in the following paragraphs is from *Documents parlementaires, Chambre*, 1924, pp. 2109-11.

"Crédit National pour faciliter la réparation des dommages causés par la guerre."

The purpose of the Crédit National, which had a capital of 100 million francs, was two-fold: first, and most important, acting under the authority of the Minister of Finance it should advance funds to the *sinistrés;* second, it might make loans of from three to ten years' duration and to a total of not more than 500 million francs for the purpose of helping industrial or commercial enterprises. It was specifically barred from carrying on ordinary banking operations. The loan resources of the Crédit National are obtained from the issue of bonds and bills, these issues being made under the authority of the Minister of Finance, and controlled by him. Funds obtained from such borrowing operations are, according to the agreement, turned over to the State treasury until such time as they are used for reconstruction purposes. Interest on these loans is paid by the State, and is included among the expenditures of the ordinary budget.

Security issues by the Crédit National began in 1919, and up to the end of 1924 over 25 billion francs in bonds and bills had been floated.

Until 1924 these issues met with a favorable reception by the public and were subscribed without difficulty. The 1924 loan, however, proved a bitter disappointment. A total of three billion francs was offered for sale in bonds of 500 francs denomination, bearing a nominal interest rate of 6 per cent, and sold to yield approximately 7 per cent. The total taken by the public, however, amounted to a face value of only 1,633,413,500 francs. Another two billions was authorized, but after the failure of the first issue they were never offered for sale.[5] As a result the work of reconstruction carried on by the Crédit National had to be curtailed.

The following table gives details concerning the borrowing operations of the Crédit National:

SECURITIES FLOATED BY THE CRÉDIT NATIONAL *

Year	Amount in Millions of Francs	Rate	Term
1919	4,000	5% bonds	5 years
1920	4,000	5% "	5 "
1921	3,000	6% "	15 "
1922 (Feb.)	4,710	6% bills	10 "
1922 (July)	3,290	6% "	10 "
1923 (Jan.)	3,000	6% "	25 "
1923 (July)	2,000	6% bonds	25 "
1924 (Jan.)	1,633 ª	6% "	50 "
Total	25,633		

* Documents parlementaires, Chambre, 1924, p. 2110.
ª Five billions were authorized.

A second special method by which the government has facilitated reconstruction was authorized under a law of February 28, 1923. This law provided that the government should be permitted to pay interest and to make payments for damages to personal property in National Defense bonds. It further provided that at the option of the sinistrés other damages might be met in the same way.

[5] Documents parlementaires, Chambre, 1924, Annexe No. 537. p. 2110.

While this method shifts the actual task of raising funds for reconstruction to the *sinistrés*, the public debt is increased just as though the government itself had sold bonds and turned the proceeds over to the *sinistrés*.

A third method of aiding reconstruction was authorized under the laws of April 30 and July 23, 1921. The government was permitted to make compensation for certain damages to personal property by the delivery of government *rentes*. That is, in lieu of selling *rentes* and paying over the proceeds, the government turned over bonds, which could be kept or sold at the option of the recipient.

A final method of providing reconstruction funds was developed under a law of July 31, 1920. This law provided that the State might grant thirty-year annuities to the *sinistrés*—that is to say, the State would advance a certain amount each year for a period of 30 years. In order that those who received these grants might realize in advance the aggregate of the payments, it was provided that these annuity promises might be put up as security for loans. Forty-four such loans, totaling 12 billion francs, have been issued by the departments, towns, and societies with these annuity obligations of the State as security. The reader will bear in mind that the government's deficit was increased each year only to the extent of the annuities paid.

The results of these methods of handling reconstruction outlays may be illustrated by reference to the recoverable budget bill of 1924. The total

estimated expenditures were set in the draft of the
budget at 11,727,640,000 francs and the revenues at
2,127,640,000, leaving an estimated deficit to be covered by borrowing of 9,600 millions. The total deficit, however, as revealed in the Finance Minister's
own explanation of the recoverable outlays, was 18
billions, made up of the following items: [6]

	Millions of Francs
Deficit in the recoverable budget	9,600
Issues of the Crédit National	5,000
Indemnity payment in National Defense bonds for certain war damages	2,000
Annuity payments	1,000
Indemnity payment in rentes for certain war damages	400
Total	18,000

Since contemplated capital outlays amounting to
8,400 million francs were not included in the budget,
they received no mention in discussions of the budgetary outlook. Only the 9,600 millions which were
budgeted were taken account of in ordinary public
discussions.

As a result of such practices the true condition
of French finances is never revealed in the budget
estimates. The practice of not including capital
outlays in the budget might perhaps be justified;
but, as we have seen, there is no consistency even in
this practice, certain types of capital outlays being
included in the budget.

[6] *Exposé des motifs du projet du budget des dépenses recouvrables, 1924.* No recoverable budget for the year was formally
passed, but the necessary credits were approved from month to
month.

Items which actually represent an increase in the public debt are included as revenue in the recoverable budget. Among the revenues is a general heading called "receipts by order," under which one finds, among other items, "indemnity payments in *rentes* for certain war damages," and "indemnity payments in National Defense bonds for certain war damages." As explained above, the use of *rentes* in meeting certain damage claims was authorized by the acts of April 30 and July 23, 1921, and the use of National Defense bonds by the act of February 28, 1923. These *rentes* and bonds—which afforded a means of meeting claims—have been put down in the budget as revenues, notwithstanding the fact that they represent an increase in the public debt. By analogy, an individual with an income of $5,000 and expenditures of $7,000, who gives promissory notes of $2,000 to "meet" the deficit, would be entitled to include the value of the notes given in "settlement" as a part of his income. Mr. Micawber, it may be recalled, always paid by giving his note.

The *rentes* given in settlement of claims first manifested themselves in the 1922 budget, but no figures of the amounts that were actually delivered have been discovered. In the 1923 and 1924 budgets 1 billion, and 400 millions, respectively, were authorized. •It appears that 200 millions were utilized in 1924.[7] The revenues in the form of National De-

[7] See p. 94. These *rentes* are not actually included in the budget estimates at the beginning of the year, their utilization being authorized separately; but they are included in the final budget totals.

fense bonds were put in the 1923 budget at 3,250 million francs, and in the 1924 budget at 2 billions. A somewhat smaller amount is included in the provisional budget for 1925.

Because of this practice, the summary fiscal statements which purport to show the final results of the year's fiscal operations, understate the deficit by the amount of these fictitious receipts. In the figures given in the next section, showing French government revenues from sources other than borrowing, these bonds have been eliminated from the revenue totals for the years 1923 and 1924. Since we are unable to ascertain the amount of fictitious revenues included in the earlier budgets, we have used for 1919 to 1922 the figures as officially published.

The net result of the whole post-war budgetary procedure is confusion confounded.

II. THE OUTLAYS FOR RECONSTRUCTION

Only about half of the recoverable expenditures has been devoted to the physical reconstruction of the devastated areas. The outlays which are chargeable to Germany are of diverse kinds, and any assertion that France has spent well over a hundred billion francs in the physical reconstruction of the devastated departments is grossly misleading. No small portion has gone for pensions and for relief work of one sort or another.

Although the recoverable budget was not created until 1920, it was in effect retroactive. That is to say, from the beginning of the war certain outlays,

chiefly grants to men on duty and civil victims of
the war, were charged to special accounts on the
theory that in the event of a successful issue of the
war they would be properly assignable to Germany.
These items, as shown on page 59, had reached a
total of more than 15 billion francs by the end of
1918. The total recoverable outlays, including those
that lie outside the recoverable budget, are grouped
in the table on page 82 in three main classes, by
years, since the beginning of the war.

Public debt charges include two main items:
(1) pensions, and (2) interest on bonds issued to
provide funds for reconstruction purposes. The
pensions are to civil victims of the war, granted in
accordance with the law of June 24, 1919. The
total of pension outlays in 1921 was 3,806 millions,
and in 1922, 2,552 millions,[8] comprising in those
years the greater part of the total outlays under
public debt charges. In the later years, as the outstanding total of bonds has increased, the interest
item has become of greater relative importance.

The military service outlays, included under military expenditures, were incurred mainly during the
war years. They included the following types of
expenditures: allowances to families of men on active duty; allowances to civil victims of the war;
advances on pensions; maintenance of prisoners;
the administration of the *Office National des Mu-
tilés et Réformés;* expense of destruction and clear-
ing away of munitions left on the fields of battle;
and the restoration of damaged military establish-

[8] *Exposé des motifs du projet du budget, 1923,* p. 31.

RECOVERABLE EXPENDITURES, 1914-1922 *

(In millions of francs)

Classification	1914	1915	1916	1917	1918	1919	1920	1921	1922
Public debt charges	....	17	107	149	168	186	3,454	4,364	4,973
Military expenditures:									
Military services	368	1,882	2,495	3,233	5,250	3,400	1,994	1,604	453
Special account (maintenance of troops of occupation)	....	....	....	....	....	1,790	644	786	527
Civil expenditures:									
In the liberated regions	4	15	345	689	495	9,604	15,709	13,829	16,162
Other services	....	....	....	10	39	501	478	840	969
Total	372	1,914	2,947	4,081	5,952	15,481	22,279	21,423	23,084

* Exposé des motifs du projet du budget, 1923, pp. 30-1. Classified data for 1923 and 1924 are not available.

ments. The pensions, as indicated in the preceding paragraph, were after 1919 included under public debt charges. These so-called military outlays have naturally been steadily diminishing. The special account, called "maintenance of troops of occupation," was devoted to the expense of the French High Commission in the provinces, as well as to the maintenance of the troops in the Rhineland and the region under plebiscite. The figures do not, however, include the outlays in connection with the occupation of the Ruhr.

The civil expenditures in the liberated regions, it might seem at first glance, would have gone solely for the physical reconstruction of the devastated areas. Such, however, is not precisely the case. A portion has gone for relief work and for other purposes not strictly to be classed as reconstruction of the devastated areas,—although these expenditures were, of course, in the main made necessary by the general damages wrought by the war. For example, in the year 1923, we find under the Ministry of Public Instruction, outlays of 130,000,000 francs for "wards of the State," and under the Ministry of Agriculture another 300,000 francs for scholarships to "wards of the State." Under the special Ministry of Liberated Regions we find items such as the following: 9,500,000 francs for relief work; 14,000,-000 for public hygiene; 2,000,000 for payments of war indemnities to colonies and protectorates; 15,-000,000 for costs in connection with the evaluating of war damages, and about 20,000,000 more for simi-

lar costs incurred by the *arrondissements*.[9] Salaries
and other office expenditures of this Ministry for
the same year amounted to about 7,000,000 francs.

It remains true, however, that the bulk of the
civil expenditures went for actual reconstruction.
The following table shows the recoverable expenditures, classified, to the end of 1924.[10]

	Billions of Francs
Pensions (damages to persons)	36
Damages to property	61
Reconstruction of public domain, railways, and roads..	13
Interest on Treasury loans for reconstruction purposes	19
Total	129

Included in the figure of 61 billions representing
damages to property is approximately 2.5 billions of
interest on Crédit National bonds, annuities, and
rentes. Thus the total of outlays for physical reconstruction has been approximately 58 billions, including, of course, the types of outlays mentioned
on page 83. The State expenditures on public domain, railways, and roads raise the total to roughly
70 billions—a little over half the total outlays.

III. FISCAL OPERATIONS, 1919-1924.

The net results of French fiscal operations for the
six-year period from the end of the war to the beginning of 1925 may now be presented in summary
form. The following table, which shows the budget

[9] The arrondissement is an administrative subdivision of the
department.

[10] These figures are taken from *Documents parlementaires,
Chambre, annexe* 537, 1925, p. 2109. They represent expenditures
made down to October 1, 1924, and estimated expenditures for
the last three months of 1924.

deficites for each year, gives the total expenditures for all purposes and the revenues derived from sources other than borrowing. Total revenues are not identical with tax receipts: first, they include certain miscellaneous revenues, such as reparations, proceeds from the sale of war materials, and sundry rents and profits; and second, the revenues from State enterprises are gross figures—the administrative outlays involved being carried in the expenditures account. A classification of the receipts will be found on page 88, and a separate discussion of the budget of 1924 will be found in Section IV of this chapter. In this table we present only the summary totals.

BUDGET DEFICITS, 1919-1924
(In billions of francs)

Year	Expenditures	Revenues from Sources Other Than Borrowing	Deficits [a]
1919	54.2	11.6	42.6
1920	58.1	20.1	38.0
1921	51.1	23.1	28.0
1922	48.9	24.2	24.7
1923	45.8	23.8	22.0
1924	45.5	29.0	16.5
Total	303.6	131.8	171.8

[a] The summation of the annual budget deficits does not exactly coincide with the figures of debt increase as shown on pages 97 and 98. The discrepancy was attributed in 1923 by Finance Minister M. de Lasteyrie to two causes: (1) some of the accounts, both expenditures and receipts, were still in a provisional stage; (2) because of the steady depreciation of the franc the foreign debt figure does not exactly show what the government received from this source (*Exposé des motifs du projet du budget, 1923*, p. 72).

For the first four years following the war, the revenues from sources other than borrowing were never equal to 50 per cent of the total expenditures. In 1923, however, the revenues increased to 52 per cent of the expenditures, and in 1924 they were about

GOVERNMENT REVENUES AND EXPENDITURES, 1919-1924

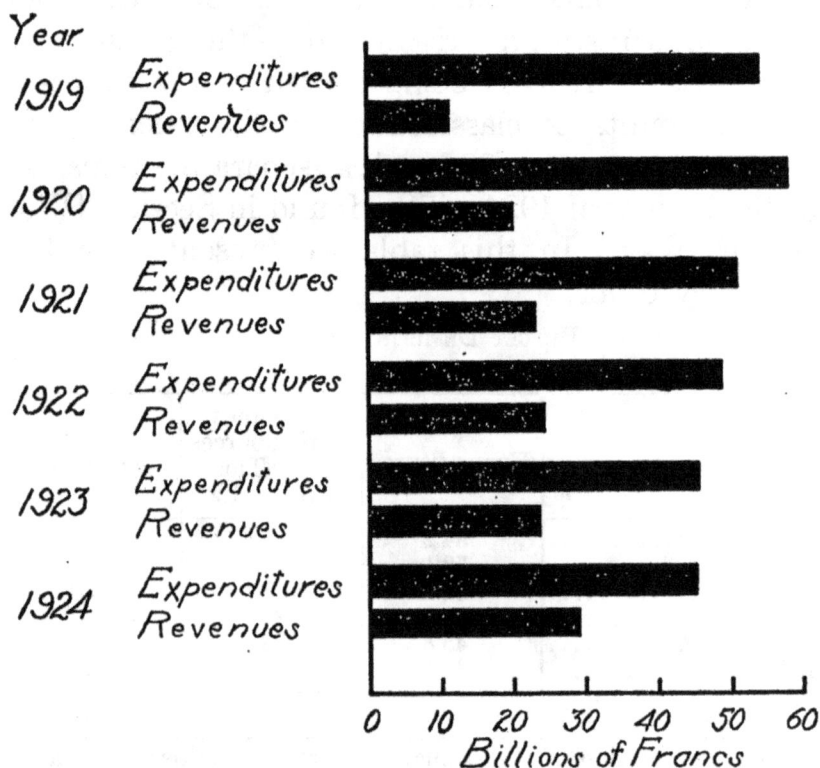

70 per cent. With the exception of the years 1923 and 1924, the expenditures were greatly in excess of the revenues, even with the recoverable outlays eliminated from the picture. The 1924 budget will presently be discussed in some detail.

The following table on page 88 gives the classified revenues from sources other than borrowing. For a discussion of the various classes of receipts shown in the table, see Appendix B, pages 408-18.

Indirect taxes have continued to furnish the larger part of French revenues. The percentages derived from direct and indirect taxes, and from other sources during the six-year period 1919-1924, are indicated in the final column of the table. The figures for the fiscal monopolies (tobacco, matches, etc.) are gross figures. The net proceeds are equivalent to tax revenues, and in estimating the fiscal burden borne by the country they should be so considered. (See discussion in Chapter IX.)

IV. DISAPPOINTING RESULTS OF 1924

The results of the fiscal year 1924 were both disappointing and disillusioning. It had been hoped that the sixth year following the war would definitely mark a turning point in French fiscal affairs, if indeed complete budgetary equilibrium were not established. While there was much concern at the time of the "franc crisis" early in the year, after the Morgan loan was granted conditions were regarded as extremely promising. It was expected that the 20 per cent increase in direct taxes,[11] provided by the law of March 22, would go far toward establishing budgetary equilibrium. At the same time the appointment as Finance Minister of M. Clémentel,

---

[11] This did not apply to the taxes collected for the benefit of the departments and communes.

REVENUES FROM SOURCES OTHER THAN BORROWING, 1919-1924 *

(In millions of francs)

Classification	1919	1920	1921	1922	1923	1924	Total	Percentage
Direct taxes:								
Old, assimilated, and income	1,741	5,153	6,664	6,427	5,477	7,156	32,618	24.6
	1,069	1,929	3,495	3,377	4,143	5,825	19,838	
War profits	672	3,224	3,169	3,050	1,334	1,331	12,780	
Indirect taxes:								
Registration	6,387	9,736	10,607	12,299	13,859	17,653	70,541	53.2
Stamp	1,874	2,718	2,705	2,960	3,391	4,656	18,304	
Bourse	314	517	565	617	697	906	3,616	
Stocks and bonds	7	25	19	26	53	93	223	
Customs	290	568	926	1,018	1,166	1,704	5,672	
Excise and consumption	1,477	1,596	1,197	1,615	1,609	1,624	9,118	
Special tax on payments	2,156	3,056	3,284	3,762	3,912	4,510	20,680	
Luxury and turnover	269	314					583	
		942	1,911	2,301	3,031	4,160	12,345	
Other revenues:								
Fiscal monopolies	3,458	5,371	6,030	6,049	4,419	4,171	29,498	22.2
Posts, telegraphs, and telephones, etc.	1,052	1,582	1,711	1,803	1,971	2,275	10,394	
State properties	589	1,051	1,206	1,285	1,319		5,450	
Receipts by order, etc., and sundry receipts	155	151	113	166	230	400	1,215	
Sale of war materials	455	938	1,499	2,295	699	1,443	7,329	
	1,207	1,649	1,501	500	200	53	5,110	
GRAND TOTAL	11,586	20,260	23,301	24,775	23,755	28,980	132,657	100.0

* Sources of the data are as follows:

For the years 1919-1924: Direct and indirect taxes and fiscal monopolies are from M. Clementel, *Inventaire de la situation financière*, 1924, p. 105. Posts, telegraphs, and telephones for 1919 are from the *Exposé des motifs du projet du budget, 1923*; and for 1920-1924, from M. Clementel, *ibid.*, pp. 100-1. State properties, receipts by order, and sundry proceeds, are from M. de Lasteyrie, *Exposé des motifs du budget de 1923*, pp. 38-9.

For 1923: War profits tax is from *Journal Officiel, (Lois et Décrets)* Jan. 16, 1924, p. 513. The receipts by order item included from the recoverable budget is from *Exposé des motifs du projet du budget des dépenses recouvrables de 1924*, p. 17. All others are from the *Journal Officiel, (Lois et Décrets)* Jan. 17, 1925, pp. 717-27.

For 1924: See p. 95.

former President of the International Chamber of Commerce, inspired much confidence and led to the expectation that an improvement in administrative methods would result in curtailing expenditures as well as in increasing revenue.

There was a substantial increase in taxation revenues as compared with the previous year. The taxation yields for the years 1923 and 1924 are shown in the following table. The returns from public utilities (posts, telegraphs and telephones) are excluded from this table, since they are more than offset by expenditures in connection with their administration. Certain miscellaneous receipts are also excluded. The fiscal monopolies, however, yielded a net revenue which is properly included along with taxation receipts.[12]

	1923	1924
Direct taxes	5,477	7,156
Indirect taxes	13,859	17,652
Fiscal monopolies	1,971	2,275
Total	21,307	27,083

The increase in revenue amounted to nearly 27 per cent. Interestingly enough the increase in the proceeds of indirect taxes was nearly equal to the increase in direct taxes, amounting to about 26 per cent as compared with 30 per cent for the direct

[12] The figures for the fiscal monopolies as given in the tables are, however, gross returns. In 1923 the cost of administration for the tobacco and match monopolies was 580 million francs. Data for the powder monopoly are not available. At the time of writing the cost of administration of the monopolies in 1924 had not been made public.

taxes. This fact suggests the principal explanation of the generally good showing that was made.

The year 1924 was one of extraordinary business activity, owing primarily to the temporarily stimulating effects of low exchange rates and the continuance of credits for reconstruction purposes. Not only was there no unemployment, but over 190,000 foreign workers were imported. A tourist trade of exceptional proportions also contributed to the maintenance of "prosperity" at an unprecedented level. At the same time prices were steadily rising, averaging for the year 17 per cent higher than in 1923, so that in terms of monetary value the volume of business transactions and earnings was enormously increased.

All this was naturally reflected in tax receipts. Even the direct taxes yielded more, because increased business at higher prices meant larger incomes. But it was in the indirect taxes that the results were most strikingly manifested. The yield of most of the indirect taxes varies directly with the volume and value of business transactions. Thus the registration tax increased 36 per cent; taxes on stocks and bonds 44 per cent; stamp taxes 28 per cent; excise and consumption taxes 14 per cent; and the luxury and turnover taxes 36 per cent. Customs on the other hand, showed virtually no increase.

In passing, attention must be called to the fact that, contrary to commonly accepted economic notions, large tax receipts are not typically accompanied by reduced spending and consumption on the part of the populace; on the contrary the larger the purchases, the greater is likely to be the yield of taxes. While this is particularly true in France, where indirect taxes play so large a rôle, it is a generalization that may safely be made for all countries—with tax systems constructed as they are.

The inflationary boom of 1924 temporarily increased revenues faster than expenditures. In the light of recent German experience it has become a commonplace that a rapidly falling currency and mounting prices disorganizes the budget system. By the time the taxes levied have actually been collected their paying capacity, or power in meeting obligations, is greatly reduced,—this because the expenditures required increase in monetary terms from week to week as prices rise. In the early stages of such a period, however, the reverse is true—expenditures increase less rapidly than revenues. Interest on the accumulated public debt is fixed, for a period at least; and it is only the additions to the debt that bear higher rates. Pensions and payrolls, including those for the military establishment, need not be increased immediately. Accordingly, it is the expenditures that lag, and the budget is temporarily benefited.

The word *temporarily* is used advisedly, for before the end of the year 1924 a fiscal crisis in France was already at hand. On Armistice Day an army of war victims paraded the streets of Paris demanding an increase of pensions to compensate for the rising cost of living, while government employees of every class were equally insistent that compensating wage increases should be granted them. The attempt of the government to control the price of bread was conceived as a palliative measure.

The budget of 1924 was aided in another, and unexpected, manner. The issue of 5 billion francs of Crédit National bonds for reconstruction purposes was contemplated. But because of the growing realization that the mountain of public debt that had been piling up in connection with reconstruction activities would probably have to be mainly shouldered by France herself, the public lost confidence in these securities and only 1,633,000,000 could be marketed, yielding 1,552,000,000 francs to the government. The reconstruction activities were accordingly curtailed, the total outlay of the Crédit National for the year being 2,064,000,000 francs.[13] The amount in excess of 1,522,000,000 was advanced by the Treasury. This curtailment of reconstruction made the budget deficit about 3 billion francs less than would otherwise have been the case.

In spite of exceptionally favorable conditions, the year 1924 closed with a deficit of about 16.5 billion francs. The general impression, even in the French Parliament, is that the deficit for 1924 was only about 4 billion francs. Accordingly, it is necessary to present the data on which we base our conclusion that the deficit is still in excess of 16 billion francs.

In the table on page 85 the expenditures were put at 45.5 and the non-borrowed revenues at 29.0

[13] M. Bérenger, *Documents parlementaires, Sénat*, 1925, pp. 10-1.

billions, leaving a deficit of 16.5 billions. These figures have been derived from data published by the
French government.

1. *Expenditures:* The latest data published with
regard to expenditures for 1924 shows the following
budget credits, or grants, voted by Parliament: [14]

	Millions of Francs
General budget	27,730.8
Recoverable budget	12,344.1
Special account (maintenance of troops of occupation)	818.8
Total	40,893.7

This is not, however, the whole story about expenditures. On the one hand, deductions must be
made for credits that have been cancelled or carried
forward to the year 1925. On the other hand, additions must be made for expenditures not included
in the budgets.

The cancellation of budget grants (March 31,
1924, and July 13, 1924) amounted to 104.3 millions,
and grants carried forward to 1925 amounted on
January 27, 1925, to 697.8 million francs. These
deductions reduce the budget expenditures from
40,893.7 million francs to 40,091.6 millions.[15]

[14] *Journal officiel (lois et décrets)*, April 9, 1925, p. 3646.
[15] M. Bérenger, *Documents parlementaires, Sénat,* 1925, p. 8.
M. Bérenger, the *Rapporteur Général* of the Senate Finance Committee, deducts 908.7 millions francs from the general budget and
503.7 millions from the recoverable budget for credits carried
forward from preceding years; and also 550 millions for an adjustment in the old special treasury accounts of Agricultural and
Industrial Reconstruction (O. R. A. and O. R. I.). If such deductions are made from 1924 expenditures, equivalent additions

The additions that must be made on account of extra-budgetary expenditures of the government amount to a large total. The discussion of the budget system in this chapter points out the fact that numerous items of expenditure are not included in either the general or the recoverable budget, but these items must be included in a statement of the government's total expenditures. The figures below indicate the approximate totals of these extra-budgetary accounts.[16]

	Millions of Francs
Crédit National	2,064
Securities turned over to the *sinistrés*	790[a]
Amortization of external debt	1,200
Advances to railways	667
Interest to the Bank of France (over and above that shown in the budget)	696
Total of extra-budgetary expenditures	5,417

[a] This item is explained as follows: among the recoverable expenditures approved in the credit grants during the year are 3,200 millions of securities turned over to the *sinistrés*, but according to M. Bérenger's figures the total turned over was 3,990 millions, consisting of National Defense bonds, 3,300 millions; 6 per cent rentes, 200 millions; annuities, 490 millions.

Adding together the total budgetary expenditures of 40,091.6 million francs and extra-budgetary expenditures of 5,417 million francs, gives a total of

should be made to the expenditures of preceding years, while similar adjustments in 1925 would later throw other items back into 1924. For this reason we have made no allowance for the three items given above.

[16] M. Bérenger, *ibid.*, pp. 10-1. Aid in interpreting the data furnished by M. Bérenger is obtained from an earlier Senate document—*Documents parlementaires, Sénat*, 1923, No. 896, p. 281.

45,508.6 million francs as the inclusive expenditures
of the government in the year 1924.

2. *Receipts:* The figure for revenues is quoted
directly from M. Bérenger.[17] On January 27, 1925,
the actual non-borrowed revenues of the year 1924
had amounted to 27,593.2 million francs, a figure
which M. Bérenger estimated would reach 28,747.1
millions by the time the books are finally closed.
Adding to this the receipts shown in the recoverable
budget, 233 million francs, gives the total for all
real receipts of 28,980.1 million francs given in the
table.[18] The deficit is, therefore, approximately 16.5
billion francs.

If the figure at which we have arrived is not precise, it is because of the inadequate methods of budgetary accounting employed by the French government rather than because of any lack of earnest desire on our part to arrive at an exact statement of
the fiscal situation. We feel reasonably confident,
however, that the figure is not seriously in error.

A discussion of the factors involved in bringing
the French budget eventually into balance must be
postponed until certain other aspects of France's
economic, political, and social structure are considered.

[16] *Ibid.*, p. 9.
[18] For 1924 posts, telegraphs, and telephones are included in an
annexed budget, the net deficit being carried into the general
budget as an expenditure. See Appendix B, pp, 398-9.

CHAPTER V

POST-WAR GROWTH OF THE PUBLIC DEBT

THE preceding chapter has shown the nature of post-war fiscal practices and the extent of the budget deficits that have resulted. The huge excess of expenditures over ordinary revenues in the annual budgets have made necessary the continuance of credit operations scarcely less stupendous than those of the war period. In this chapter we shall consider the extent and the economic significance of the enormous increase in the public debt that has occurred since the war.

I. CHARACTER AND EXTENT OF THE DEBT INCREASE

The foreign debt of the French government—apart from accruing interest charges—has increased very little since the war. It is true that a considerable number of new foreign obligations have been incurred since the end of 1918; but other foreign obligations have been liquidated. It is unnecessary, and it would prove wearisome, to relate here the details of the external borrowing operations of the French government since the war. It will suffice for the present purpose to show the net results from December 31, 1918, to November 30, 1924—the last date for which official data are available. The figures in the following table are at par of exchange; hence they do not reveal the effects of exchange depreciation. Accumulating interest charges on the political debt are not included in the figures, the purpose of the table being to show the extent of the increase due to new borrowing operations.[1]

FOREIGN DEBT OF THE FRENCH GOVERNMENT, 1918 AND 1924

(In millions of francs)

Classification	December 31, 1918	November 30, 1924
Political debt	20,694.8	26,618.4
Commercial debt	6,765.8	5,017.4
Total foreign debt	27,460.6	31,635.8

It will be observed that the commercial debt of the French government has diminished by about 1,750 million francs. It should be recalled in this connection, however, that the decrease in this commercial debt of the government has been accompanied by an increase in private obligations abroad, and that the total foreign indebtedness of the French nation as distinguished from the government, was very much larger in 1924 than in 1918.[2]

[1] For a detailed classification of the foreign debt, see Appendix D, p. 435. In the official debt figures published by the Minister of Finance, arrears of interest on the war debt to Great Britain are each year added to the principal of the debt, but the debt due the United States is shown exclusive of interest (see Appendix A, pp. 351-2). Calculation of the capital amount of the political debt to Great Britain in the table given above is based on M. Clémentel's statement in the *Inventaire*, p. 70.

[2] See discussion on pp. 28-43.

The enormous increase of the domestic debt is the direct result of the huge post-war fiscal deficits. The flotation of domestic loans since the war has followed the general lines laid down during the war period,—long-term, short-term, and floating obligations all showing great increases. The growth of the internal debt from the end of 1918 to November 30, 1924, is shown by the following table:

DOMESTIC DEBT OF FRANCE, 1918 AND 1924 *
(In millions of francs)

Classification	December 31, 1918	November 30, 1924
Perpetual and long-term	67,248.0	153,716.9
Short-term	531.1	39,845.0
Floating	56,015.2	90,688.4
Total	123,794.3	284,250.3

* For a detailed classification of the domestic debt see Appendix D, pp. 432-4.

The long-term debt on November 30, 1924, included about 26 billions of Crédit National bonds and annuities to *sinistrés,* the rest of the post-war increase being represented by three issues of *rentes,* a 4 per cent issue put out late in 1918, a 5 per cent issue in 1920, and a 6 per cent issue in the same year. It was the theory immediately after the war that the needs of the government should be provided by these long-term obligations. But the accumulating financial difficulties and the fall of the franc caused the people by 1920 to lose confidence in long-time government obligations, the security of which obviously depended upon the uncertain fate of the franc. Hence the discontinuance after 1920 of long-term loans—except in connection with the reconstruction of the devastated areas—and the resort to shorter term borrowing.

The short-term debt proper, as distinguished from the floating debt, consists of Treasury obligations maturing in from two to ten years. These obligations, which had played a rôle of some importance before the war when they were sold mainly to banks, were scarcely used during the war period. They were revived after the war, however, and nearly 26 billions have been issued since the end of 1918. The National Defense bonds of five and ten years' duration, also but little used during the war, have since been issued to the extent of 7 billions. Over 6 billions of Crédit National bills are also included under the short-term debt, notwithstanding the fact that they run from 10 to 25 years.

The floating debt consists chiefly of three types of obligations: advances of the Bank of France; ordinary Treasury bills (bons du Trésor); and National Defense bills. The advances of the Bank of France decreased steadily from the end of 1918 to the end of 1924, when the government found it again necessary to resort to the bank for funds with which to meet operating expenses. These advances will be discussed more fully in Chapter VI, where they will be considered in relation to the currency problem. The bons du Trésor were issued direct to the banks and are largely held by them. The total outstanding on November 30, 1924, was 2,855 million francs.

The National Defense bills have played an important rôle in post-war finance. As shown in Chapter III, these bills were first issued during the war period, with a view to absorbing the floating funds of the country. At the end of the war the total outstanding was about 35 billions, and on November 30, 1924, the amount stood at 57 billions, an increase of 22 billions. These bills were heavily resorted to in 1920-1921, when the public was beginning to lose confidence in the safety of long-term bonds. Since the National Defense bills, which are of only a few months' duration, were more or less continuously redeemed and reissued, one could purchase them without running the risk of any great depreciation in their value. As a matter of fact they have been continuously at par. The extensive purchase of these bills by banking institutions has, however, given rise to a serious financial problem, which will be discussed in Chapter VI.

II. TEN YEARS OF GOVERNMENT BORROWING

For purposes of exposition it seemed advisable to break up the discussion of French fiscal operations into several periods, and to treat the post-war era as a separate unit. It will prove helpful now, however, to bring together the war and post-war periods, revealing by means of a chart the growth of the French public debt from the beginning of the war to the end of 1924.

In the chart which follows, the domestic or internal debt is expressed in terms of paper francs, and

is shown by the first part of each black bar. Since
the external debt is payable in foreign currency, it
is expressed in official French publications at par of
exchange. In the chart the black area to the right
of the division line represents the foreign debt in
gold values; while the full length of the bar, to
the right of the division line, including the white
area, indicates the volume of paper francs required
to liquidate the foreign debt on the dates in
question.[3]

GROWTH OF THE PUBLIC DEBT, 1914-1924

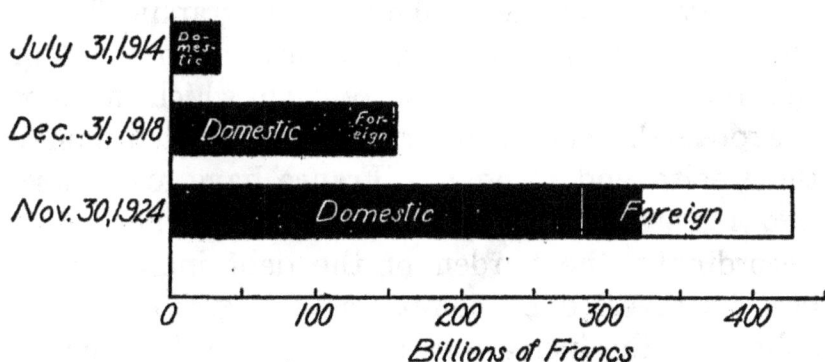

The growth of public indebtedness in France since
the beginning of the war is not fully measured by
the increase in the debt of the national government.

[3] The foreign debt for 1924 includes the capitalized interest due
to Great Britain; and accumulated interest at 5 per cent on the
debt to the United States. Five per cent is taken simply because
that is the rate which the bonds nominally bear. Any subsequent adjustment of the interest charge will of course change the
total.

For the precise figures on which the chart is based see Appendix D, pp. 432-5.

Rising prices and wages have so disorganized the fiscal operations of the Departments and Communes that they also have found it necessary to resort to borrowing operations as a means of meeting operating expenses. The debts of the 87 Departments of France aggregated 1,153 million francs in 1914; 1,223 millions at the end of 1918; and 3,164 millions at the end of 1921. During the same period the Communal debts increased from 4,892 million francs to 7,424 millions.[4] The data for other years are not as yet available.

The growth of the public debt, as graphically indicated above, is somewhat misleading because of the changing value of the currency in which the debt is expressed. Stated in terms of depreciated money the wealth and income of France have, of course, also registered an enormous increase since 1914. Accordingly, the burden of the debt increase can best be revealed by comparing the growth of the debt with the increase in national wealth. Such a comparison nullifies the factors of price changes and currency depreciation, and also brings into focus with the debt situation the general economic changes that have occurred.

The first of the accompanying charts reveals the growth of national wealth [5] and public debt, respectively, from 1914 to 1924, as measured in changing currency values. The second shows the debt as a

[4] *Annuaire statistique*, 1923, pp. 350 and 352.

[5] For the estimates of national wealth for both 1914 and 1924 see Appendix C, pp. 424-9.

percentage of the national wealth for the years in question.[6]

COMPARISON OF NATIONAL DEBT AND NATIONAL WEALTH, 1914 AND 1924

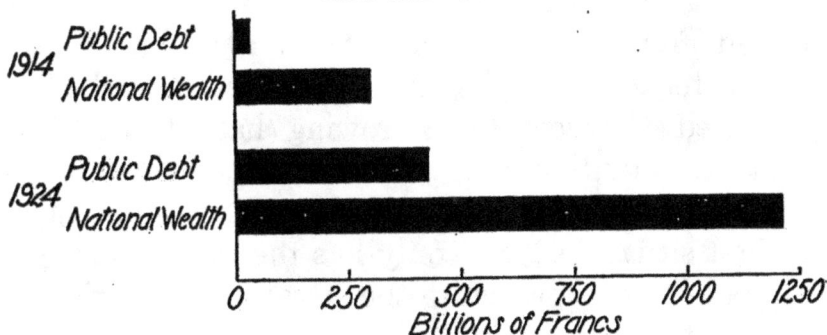

In 1914, the public debt of France—the largest in the world—equalled about 12 per cent of the total national wealth; in 1924 the debt was approxi-

PERCENTAGE RELATION OF NATIONAL DEBT TO NATIONAL WEALTH, 1914 AND 1924

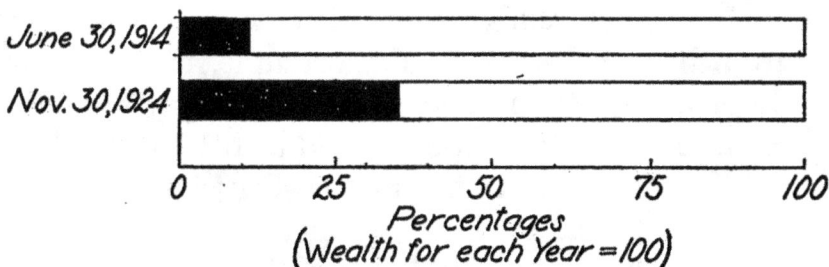

mately 37 per cent of the wealth. In 1914 the debt was entirely domestic; in 1924 the foreign debt

[6] The foreign debt figure for 1924 includes the capitalized interest on the war debt to Great Britain and accumulated interest of 5 per cent on the war debt to the United States.

alone was equal to approximately 13 per cent of the national wealth.[7]

III. THE PUBLIC DEBT AND THE PUBLIC CREDIT

The growth of the public debt has seriously impaired French credit both at home and abroad. As loan after loan has been floated and as the debt has mounted the cost of borrowing has steadily increased, notwithstanding the efforts that have been made to conceal the gravity of the French financial budget situation. Not only has the rate of interest on long-time loans had to be advanced, but what is of much greater significance, increasing difficulty has been encountered in marketing such securities at any price.

Prior to the Great War the standard form of government bond in France was the 3 per cent *perpetual rente*. For a long period of years, notwithstanding the persistent growth of the public debt, the 3 per cent *rente* was quoted on the Bourse at only a little below par. For example, the effective rate of the *rente* in 1890 stood at 3.43 per cent; in 1900 at 3.03; in 1910 at 3.02; and in 1913 at 3.30 per cent. In 1871, during the Franco-Prussian War, the effective rate had risen as high as 5.96 per cent.[8]

The chart on page 105 shows the increased cost of borrowing in the domestic market from 1913 to the end of 1924. The rate in 1913 is obtained from the market price of outstanding 3 per cent *rentes*.

[7] In these rough figures the capital value of reparation claims are not included.

[8] *Annuaire statistique*, 1919-20, pp. 86-7.

The cost of borrowing in the later years is based on the effective rate of the following issues: for 1918, the 25-year 4 per cent loan authorized just after the armistice; [9] for 1920, the 10-year 6 per cent loan of October; for 1921, the 2-year 6 per cent issue of Treasury bonds put out in June; for 1922, the 5-year 6 per cent Treasury bonds of November; for 1923, the 10-year 6 per cent Treasury bonds of November; and for 1924, the 10-year 5 per cent Treasury bonds of November.

THE RISING COST OF BORROWING

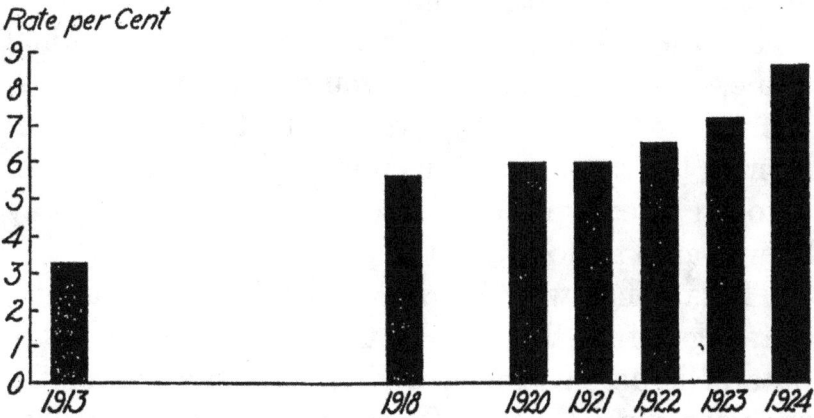

Rate per Cent

These effective rates do not show the increasing cost of borrowing with absolute accuracy, since the different issues carried special provisions of differing degrees of importance to the investor. The chart, however, does illustrate very concretely the results of post-war borrowing operations on the credit of the government. The reader should compare this chart with the one on page 101 showing

[9] For 1919, no issue was put out.

the increase of the public debt during the same period.

The 5 per cent loan of November, 1924, requires special consideration. It was floated at a time when the market price for 5 per cent bonds was around 67.[10] If issued, redeemable at par, these bonds would have sold at a price of approximately 67, and it would have required an issue of about 6 billion francs to have yielded the 4 billions which were needed to meet budgetary requirements. The Finance Minister finally decided to put out the issue with a provision that the bonds would be redeemable with a bonus of 50 per cent of the nominal value,—that is, that they would be redeemable at 150 francs for every 100 francs purchased. The return on the bonds was thus increased from a nominal 5 to an effective 8.62 per cent rate. In this way he was able to float them at par.

These bonds were made redeemable by periodical drawings after the end of the fifth year from the date of issue,—so much a year until the end of the ten-year period. The Treasury further agreed to buy each year on the Bourse, at par or below, bonds to the extent of 3.5 per cent of the total subscribed, thus helping to sustain the market. These bonds, like other government issues, are practically exempt from taxation.

Notwithstanding the high effective rate of 8.62 per cent and the attractive provisions of the issue, the bonds did not yield the cash required. In fact,

[10] *Journal officiel, Sénat,* Dec. 30, 1924, p. 1697.

although 4,920 millions were issued they yielded only about 1 billion in cash,[11] the rest being paid for by outstanding Treasury or National Defense bills. It was the failure of this issue to yield the cash required which gave rise to one of the main difficulties that confronted the Treasury at the beginning of the year 1925.

Further evidence of the increasing cost of borrowing in France is found in connection with the issues of the Crédit National, the securities of which, it will be recalled, are guaranteed by the French government. The following table shows the effective rate of borrowing for each year since 1919:

Cost of Borrowing Through the Crédit National *

Year	Rate Per Cent
1919	5.50
1920	5.81
1921	6.52
1922	6.21 to 6.76
1923	6.48 to 6.71
1924	6.99

* M. Clémentel, *Inventaire*, 1924, pp. 36-7. These rates apparently do not indicate the full cost of borrowing through the Crédit National. They indicate rather the yield to the subscriber. To obtain the inclusive cost to the government one would have to make allowance for the commissions charged by the banks. No data bearing on this point are available for 1923 and 1924. The Société de Banque Suisse, Monthly Bulletin, 1923, No. 1, p. 9, however, gives the average cost of borrowing to the Crédit National in 1919 at 6.60; in 1920, at 7.00; in 1921, at 7.87; and in 1922, from 7.72 to 8.38. This report also shows the yields to the subscriber, and they vary but slightly from those given by M. Clémentel.

[11] *Journal officiel*, *Sénat*, Dec. 31, 1924, p. 1697. See also article by M. Gaston Jèze, *Revue de science et de législation financières*, 1924, pp. 713-24.

These figures again do not reveal the change in the cost of borrowing with entire accuracy, for the reason that the different issues carried lottery provisions and other special privileges of varying attractiveness. In connection with the 50-year 6 per cent loan of 1924, the significant fact has already been noted that although the rate was approximately 7 per cent, only 1,633 millions out of a total authorized issue of 3 billions could be sold.[12]

Since November, 1924, the market price of the issues outstanding has fallen appreciably and if the government had floated an issue in say, May, 1925, it would have had to bear a correspondingly higher rate. The 3 per cent *rentes* were quoted at the end of October (after several weeks of decline) at 49.95 francs, and on June 29, 1925, at 42.90 francs. The 5 per cent issue of November, 1924, put out at par (500), was quoted on June 29, 1925, at 432, equivalent to only 86.2 per cent of par. The 1924 issue of Crédit National bonds was quoted at 411 for bonds of 500 francs denomination—equivalent to 82.2 per cent of par—on October 31, 1924; and at the end of June, 1925, they had fallen to 300 francs, or 60 per cent of par.[13]

Interestingly enough the French government borrowed abroad late in 1924 at a lower rate than prevailed in the domestic market. The Morgan loan

[12] See p. 76.

[13] In January, 1925, the city of Paris borrowed 100,000,000 francs at a cost of 10.5 per cent (Statement of M. Clémentel in Chamber of Deputies. *Journal officiel, débats, Chambre,* Feb. 18, 1925, p. 976).

of November, 1924, bore a nominal rate of 7 per cent, and cost the French government 7.87 per cent.[14] The explanation of this situation is two-fold: first, the foreign commercial debt is of moderate proportions as compared with the internal debt, and French financial authorities regard the maintenance of their foreign credit of such paramount importance that foreign obligations in a sense constitute a first charge against government resources. In the second place, they are floated in terms of foreign money, and thus the individual purchaser escapes the risk of fluctuations in the value of the franc. Of course, if pressure is brought to bear for the payment of the external political debt the soundness of the commercial debt will scarcely remain unaffected.

Public debt charges absorb a large portion of the taxation revenues. The results of the great increase in the French public debt are, of course, directly manifested in the French budget in the growth of the annual interest charges. The French budgetary accountants include under the general heading of charges on the public debt, the so-called pension charges as well as the interest on the debt proper. This is on the theory that pensions, like interest, constitute a fixed obligation, the only difference between the pension debt and the public debt being

[14] The issue price was 94, while a 5 per cent banking commission reduced the amount which France received to 89. *Journal officiel, Sénat débats,* Dec. 30, 1924, p. 1688. At the end of June, 1925, the quoted price in the New York market was 89, the low since January 1 having been 86; and the high, 92⅞.

that the former is not capitalized. Of the total debt charge of a little over 20 billions in 1924, about 3.6 billions represented the pension debt and about 16.5 billions interest obligations.

The inclusive debt charges have increased during the last six years as follows: [15]

Year	Billions of Paper Francs
1919	8.1
1920	15.2
1921	15.5
1922	18.6
1923	17.8[a]
1924	20. +

[a] There could not in fact have been any decrease in 1923, since there had been a huge deficit carried over from the preceding year on which interest had to be paid.

In the year 1924 approximately 80 per cent of the total receipts from taxation were required to meet interest and pensions. The percentage thus absorbed is, however, slightly less than it was two or three years ago. On the one hand, taxes, as shown on page 88, have increased materially in monetary terms, partly because of rising prices. On the other hand, there is a considerable lag in the adjustment upward, as prices rise, of the rate of interest [16] on the public debt, which makes expansion of the debt burden less rapid than otherwise would be the case. In this connection it must be noted, however, that

[15] Compiled from M. Clémentel, *ibid.*, p. 21; M. de Lasteyrie, *Exposé des motifs du projet du budget, 1923*, pp. 30-1; and M. Bérenger, *Journal officiel, Sénat débats*, Feb. 20, 1925, p. 134.

[16] Rising prices are followed by rising market interest rates simply because of the growing scarcity of loanable funds.

the increased cost of borrowing affects the accumulated debt more quickly than one might assume, for the reason that the successive bond issues carry a provision that they may be exchanged for subsequent issues. Hence a more or less continuous refunding process at higher rates of interest has been in operation. To illustrate what occurs, the issue of 5 per cent amortizable *rentes* of 1920 yielded the Treasury a total of 15.9 billion francs, but of this amount only 7 billions represented new capital—8.2 billions being received in the form of National Defense bills, and the rest of the receipts representing sundry other refunding operations on the part of the public.[17] We have already seen that four-fifths of the loan of 1924 was paid for by outstanding securities. In 1925 new budget deficits will further increase the annual interest obligations.

IV. DOES AN INTERNAL DEBT MATTER?

In concluding this discussion of the French public debt the question must be raised whether an internal debt is in any sense an economic burden. This economic issue has been a source of much confusion ever since post-war discussions of European finance began. On the one hand, international bankers in analyzing conditions preparatory to floating European securities in foreign markets have sometimes contended that a huge internal debt does not matter at all, since it is, so to speak, all within the family. On the other hand, the reparation experts who drew

[17] M. Clémentel, *ibid.*, p. 29.

up the Dawes plan insisted—a part of the time [18]—that the virtual elimination of the internal debt of Germany, both public and private, has made possible a proportionate increase in the nation's capacity to make reparation payments.

If one were to ask any recent French Minister of Finance whether a domestic debt is in any sense a burden, he would unquestionably reply that it is a veritable nightmare. The domestic debt in truth lies at the very center of the budget problem in France, and the major purpose of the recently proposed levy on capital was to make possible a reduction of the public debt charges. In the world of reality the internal debt obviously matters a great deal. The explanation is not difficult to find.

The process of internal debt payment is commonly said to be strictly analogous to that of a transfer of money by an individual from one pocket to another. Now it is unquestionably true that before the French people in the aggregate can receive from the public treasury, say, 16 billion francs as interest they must first contribute 16 billions to the Treasury in the form of taxes. The practical results of such a transfer are, however, fundamentally different from changing money from pocket to pocket.

The people who pay the taxes are by no means identical with those who receive the interest on government bonds, and in the process of transferring tax receipts to bond holders a considerable redistribution of wealth may be effected. Moreover, the

[18] See analysis in Moulton, *The Reparation Plan*, pp. 15-17.

receipt of 16 billions of interest by the *rentier* class of France in no sense means that 16 billions more of revenue can be collected than would otherwise be possible. The bonds are held in large quantities by the peasant class from whom it is difficult to collect direct taxes. Large quantities are held by the lower middle classes who contribute relatively little in the way of direct taxes. Large amounts are also held by banks, insurance companies, savings banks, co-operative societies, etc., and the taxes paid by such institutions are not in proportion to their holdings of government securities.

The indirect taxes, which yield the larger portion of French revenues, fall upon all classes of the public in proportion as they purchase commodities on which such taxes are levied. Thus the consumption taxes paid by the agricultural classes, for example, obviously bear little relation to their holdings of government bonds; and there certainly is no close relation between the indirect consumption taxes of the middle classes of the cities and their ownership of government securities. A moment's reflection will, moreover, suffice to convince one that the yield of such indirect taxes as the stamp tax, registration fees, and the tax on stock exchange transactions is little affected by the fact that the French people as a whole receive 16 billions of interest each year on government bonds.

The point is not that the taxes are *no* larger than they would be if there were no receipts of interest on the public debt; it is only that they are by no means larger in proportion to the interest received. The equilibrium that is commonly assumed could be established only by requiring every receiver of interest to pay the precise amount received back to the government in taxes; and as a practical proposition that is impossible.

The fact that those who receive interest on government bonds do not necessarily pay taxes of the same amount gives rise to grave social and political issues whenever any attempt is made to find a way out of the dilemma presented by the internal debt. Those who receive interest on the bonds object to a scaling down of interest rates or a cancellation of principal. Those who pay the larger taxes groan over present rates and resist as strongly as possible any higher levies. The difficulty is in no wise mitigated by the fact that the majority of individuals both hold bonds and pay taxes and that many of them are as much interested in taxes as in interest receipts. It is difficult—particularly where indirect taxes are so important—to weigh the balance of interests; and hence one finds it hard to classify himself as mainly a tax-payer or mainly a *rentier*. In fact, everyone wants to see his interest payments continued, for they represent his savings; and his taxes reduced, for they stand in the way of future savings, and even of present consumption.

Incidentally, the proposition that interest on the internal debt constitutes no burden, if sound, would be equally applicable to all other forms of domestic expenditures. The pension money is received from

Frenchmen and paid to Frenchmen; the outlays of the Civil Departments and the military establishment come from Frenchmen and go to Frenchmen. Even the vast outlays for reconstruction would have given rise to no fiscal burden, for did not the funds come from Frenchmen only to be turned back to Frenchmen? It is sometimes necessary to carry a plausible argument to its logical conclusion to reveal its shortcomings.

CHAPTER VI

THE EXCHANGE AND CURRENCY SITUATION

THE general disorganization of a nation's economic life is directly mirrored in the financial markets, being revealed particularly in a falling ratio of bank reserves to outstanding currency and in the depreciation of the foreign exchanges. At the same time the disorganization of the banking and exchange system contributes toward further maladjustments in the general economic system. All this has come to be vaguely understood even by the layman—as is evidenced by the widespread apprehension over each new "crisis of the franc" and the genuine uneasiness that is manifested over the reported "four billions of currency inflation" at the Bank of France. A survey of exchange and currency movements and an analysis of their interrelations with both public and private financial operations is therefore necessary to a complete understanding of the present French situation.

I. THE FALL OF THE FRANC

In discussing the fall of the franc it is unnecessary to enter into a technical discussion of foreign exchange. It will prove sufficient for the present purpose to note that the decline of the exchanges since the beginning—and particularly since the end—of the Great War is a reflection of two primary economic conditions: first, the status of international trade and financial relations; and second, the internal value, or purchasing power of paper currency as compared with gold, which is directly affected by the state of both public and private finance. These conditions, of course, act and react upon each other.

It may be added that the fluctuations of exchange rates from time to time are to some extent affected by phychological factors and also by exchange operations on the part of the government. It is not our present purpose, however, to appraise the weight of the various influences that bear upon the exchange market. We shall merely indicate the general trend of exchange rates during and since the war and point out the primary reasons for the major changes that have occurred.

The par of exchange between the franc and the dollar is 19.3, which means that the gold franc is worth 19.3 cents in United States money. During the financial vicissitudes of the early seventies there was a slight depreciation of French exchange, but thereafter until 1914 it was continuously quoted around par,—within the limits of the so-called "gold points," determined by the cost of shipping specie for the settlement of balances.

The charte on page 119 shows the monthly fluctuations in exchange rates from the beginning of 1914 to May, 1925. It will be observed from the chart that French exchange rose in terms of dollars during the first three months following the outbreak of the war. This purely temporary phenomenon was due to the sharp curtailment of purchases of American cotton and other raw materials and the sale of American securities by French holders.

The exchange was artificially controlled during the latter part of the war. In 1915 the trade situation was sharply reversed and in the latter part of the year exchange rates fell rapidly. As France began to buy great quantities of war supplies from the United States the demand in France for American currency became very strong. By April, 1916, the rates were down to 16.5 cents to the franc, a depreciation of nearly 15 per cent.

Huge extensions of credit by Great Britain were employed to stabilize or "peg" the exchange. These loans gave to the French government the means of going into the market and increasing the demand for exchange whenever the rate sagged. After the United States entered the war, our government through large credits co-operated with Great Britain and France in the stabilization program. The results are shown in the chart in the actual rise in French exchange in the latter part of the war period.

The trend of the franc has been persistently downward since the war. The first precipitous decline of French exchange began in March, 1919, when the franc was "unpegged." That is to say, the government decided that the time had come when exchange must be freed from artificial control and allowed to take its normal course as determined by

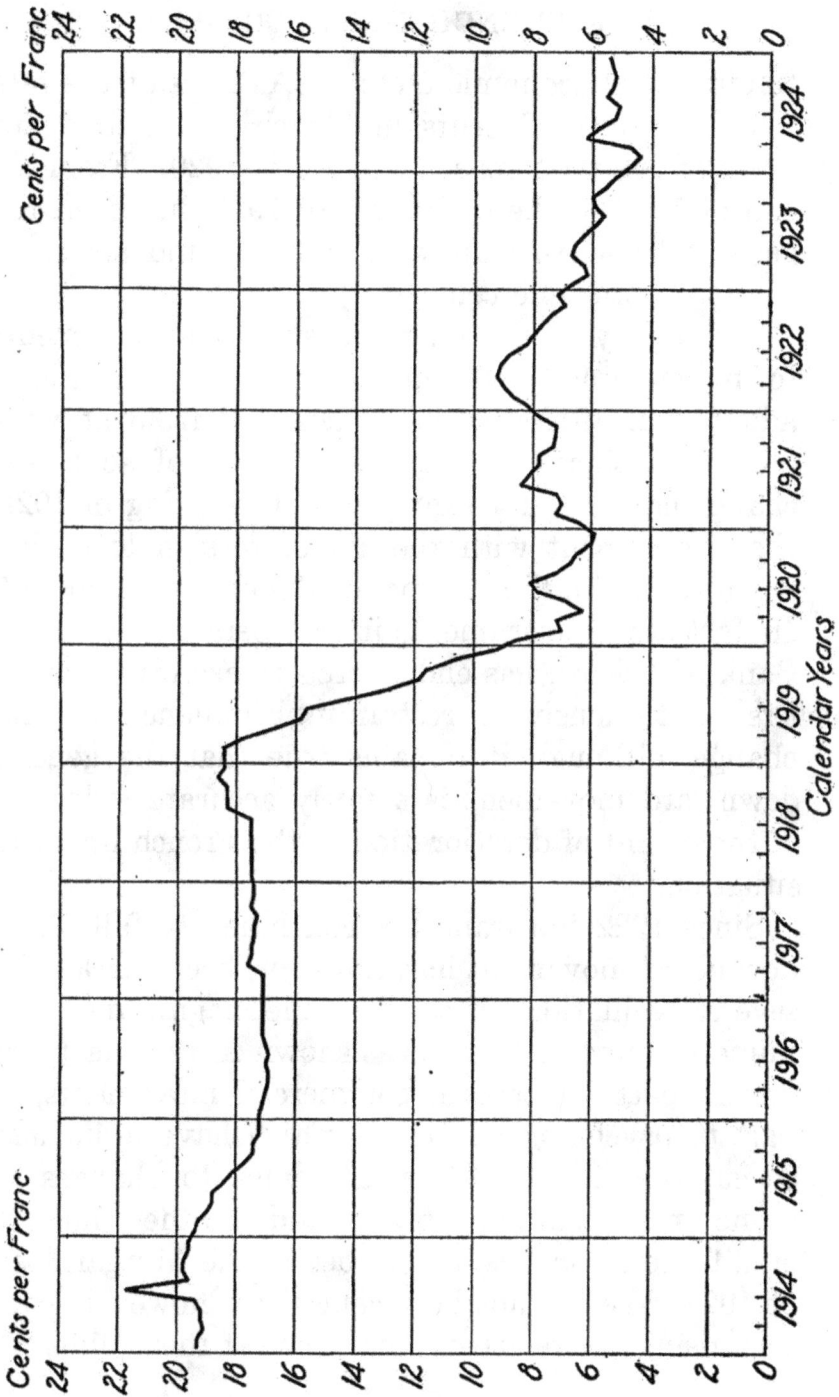

DOLLAR EXCHANGE VALUE OF THE FRANC, 1914-1924

Cents per Franc

Cents per Franc

Calendar Years

119

fundamental economic factors. As a result the rate
fell from over 18 cents in March, 1919, to a low
point of less than six cents in April, 1920. From the
end of 1920 to the early part of 1922, however, the
general trend was upward, from around six cents
to more than nine cents.

The policy of allowing the exchange movements
to be governed by general economic conditions,
adopted in 1919, has been departed from at various times since the war. In periods of acute exchange crises as, for example, in the spring of 1924,
the government with the aid of foreign loans has
again rallied to the support of the exchange market.
In fact, the government, in co-operation with the
Bank of France, has endeavored to exercise more or
less continuously a restraining influence on exchange, although it remains true that the general
downward movement is a fairly accurate reflection
of the extent of deterioration of the French financial
situation.

Since 1922 the franc has continued to fall. The
downward movement has, however, been marked by
several oscillations of considerable magnitude. The
numerous ups and downs as shown in the chart, are
due in part to seasonal commercial movements, in
part to psychological factors which have influenced
speculation in the franc, at times to changes in
money rates and bond prices, and at other times to
credit operations, as in the case of the Morgan loan
of 1924. We are not here concerned, however, with
appraising the relative importance of these different

factors in connection with the numerous minor fluctuations. The general downward trend is our chief interest.

Internal price movements are closely related to fluctuations in exchange rates. As exchange rates fall, commodity prices in France rise in rough proportion, or in other words the franc shrinks in purchasing power. Whether the depreciation of exchanges causes the rise in prices or vice versa, or whether they are interacting forces, need not here be discussed. It suffices that the rates of exchange and the price level are closely interrelated phenomena. The relationship is shown in the chart on page 122. In order to make the two lines on the chart easily comparable, the exchange rates are expressed as percentage of par and the price changes are expressed in terms of the falling purchasing power of the franc since 1913. A decline in the purchasing power of the franc from 100 to 50 of course means the same thing as a rise in prices from 100 to 200.

The figures showing the annual changes in the purchasing power of the franc from 1913 to 1924 are given in the table on page 123.

It will be observed that during the war period and up to March, 1919, the purchasing power of the franc fell steadily (in other words, prices rose), while the exchange was held, by means of gold exports and foreign credits, at a point slightly below par. With the release of artificial control in 1919, the dollar exchange rate, that is, the value of the franc as

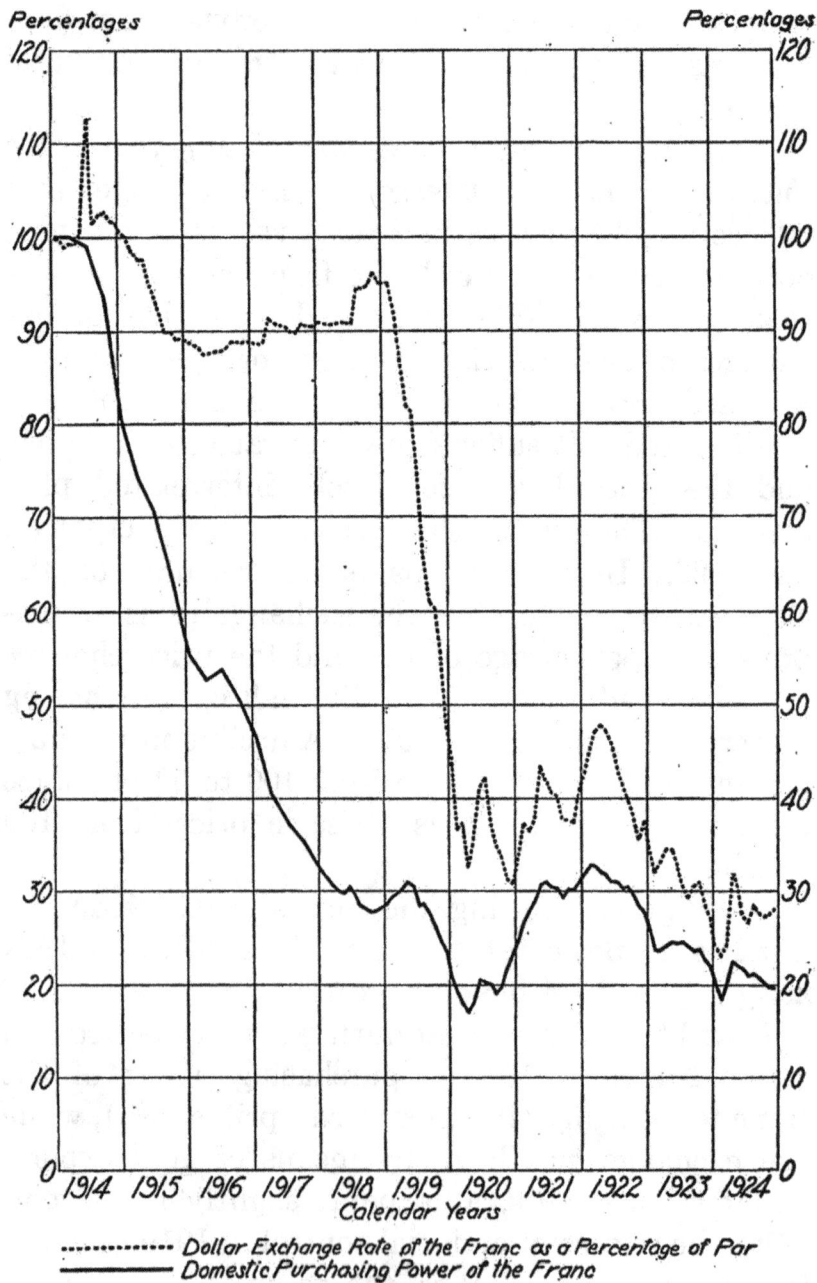

The Falling Value of the Franc

.... Dollar Exchange Rate of the Franc as a Percentage of Par
—————— Domestic Purchasing Power of the Franc

FRENCH PRICE CHANGES, 1913-1924 *

	Purchasing Power of the Franc	Wholesale Price Index
1913	100	100
1914	97	103
1915	71	141
1916	53	190
1917	38	263
1918	29	341
1919	28	357
1920	20	510
1921	29	345
1922	31	327
1923	24	419
1924	20	489

* Calculated from the index numbers of the *Statistique Général de la France.*

compared with the dollar, fell precipitately. Since 1920 the internal price level and the dollar exchange rate of the franc have moved more or less together.[1]

II. THE BANKING AND CURRENCY CRISIS

For a long period of years prior to the Great War the French banking system had been universally recognized as one of extraordinary strength and stability. Conservative and far-seeing administration of the Bank of France, which possessed the sole power of note issue and constituted the financial reservoir of the nation, had enabled the banking sys-

[1] The reader should bear in mind that this chart is not intended to show the purchasing power of the franc in the domestic market as compared with its purchasing power in the external market. The dollar has itself fallen in purchasing power by some 50 or 60 per cent, and hence the dollar exchange rate of the franc, without reference to price changes in the United States, does not show the purchasing power of the franc abroad.

tem to pass through a long series of political and economic crises during the nineteenth century with a very minimum of dislocation. The Bank was founded by Napoleon in 1800 as a privately owned and nominally independent institution. But it soon became and has ever since remained a financial agency of the State—"a private corporation, indeed, as regards the legal ownership of its property, but a public office as regards the actual employment of the property."

The Bank of France has rendered great aid to the government in times of financial stress, notably, of course, in the period of the Franco-Prussian War, in 1871-1873. In general, however, the central bank's primary function has been to acquire and hold adequate reserve funds for the varying needs of commerce and industry and through its control of the discount rate and the issue of currency to regulate the financial system of the country. If the successive managers have erred at all in the performance of their public trust in times past it has been on the side of conservatism.

The strong position of the Bank of France in pre-war days is most clearly revealed by a comparison of the volume of specie reserve and the obligations of the Bank in the form of outstanding note issues. This is because the maintenance of the value of the paper currency at a parity with gold depends upon the ability of the Bank whenever requested to give specie in exchange for its outstanding notes. Experience has shown that under ordinary conditions a central bank is reasonably safe in this regard when its specie reserve is equal to 40 or 50 per cent of its outstanding obligations.[2]

For many years the ratio of specie to outstanding note issues in France was above 80 per cent, although the Franco-Prussian War and the indemnity requirements reduced it to 26.7 per cent in 1873. The redemption of notes in specie was suspended from August 12, 1870 to December 31, 1878. The table below shows the specie reserves and the note issues of the Bank of France for certain years before the Great War.

RESERVE POSITION OF THE BANK OF FRANCE

(Average for the year, in millions of francs)

Year	Specie Reserve	Notes	Percentage Reserve
1850	457.8	485.6	94.3
1860	513.5	749.6	68.5
1869	1,189.8	1,354.5	87.8
1873	762.8	2,856.6	26.7
1880	1,974.1	2,305.4	85.6
1890	2,513.2	3,060.4	82.1
1900	3,237.3	4,034.1	80.2
1910	4,261.6	5,197.8	82.0
1913	3,972.1	5,665.3	70.1

Since 1913 the reserve of the Bank of France has declined from over 70 to less than 10 per cent. As previously indicated, France exported a large amount of gold during 1916.[3] The loss of this gold was, however, largely offset at the Bank of France as a

[2] There have been numerous cases where banks have gotten on for long periods of time with much smaller reserves than this.

[3] See Chapter III, p. 66.

result of the mobilization in the central bank of specie previously used in the channels of ordinary circulation.

Since the end of 1918 the amount of specie holdings has increased a little, but in consequence of a very considerable expansion in the volume of notes outstanding the reserve ratio has continued to decline. At the end of 1918 it stood at 12.42; at the end of 1924 at 9.82; and on June 18, 1925, at 9.28.[4] The following table shows the changes by years from the beginning of the war to the middle of 1925.

RESERVE POSITION OF THE BANK OF FRANCE

(In millions of francs)

Date (End of December)	Specie Reserve	Notes	Percentage Reserve
1914	4,514.5	10,042.9	44.95
1915	5,367.4	13,309.9	40.33
1916	3,677.7	16,678.8	22.05
1917	3,562.1	22,336.8	15.95
1918	3,758.8	30,249.6	12.43
1919	3,868.3	37,274.5	10.38
1920	3,818.2	37,901.6	10.07
1921	3,855.6	36,487.4	10.57
1922	3,959.9	36,359.3	10.89
1923	3,972.6	37,905.4	10.48
1924	3,986.5	40,604.0[a]	9.82
1925 .... (June 18)	3,996.1	43,053.8	9.28

[a] The total of note issues for December, 1924, is probably understated as a result of the falsification of the report. See discussion, pp. 142-3.

[4] Assuming the paper franc to be redeemable in gold only at current rates of exchange, the reserve at the end of 1924 would have amounted to about 35 per cent. See discussion, pp. 219-20.

The explanation of the great expansion of the note issues since the beginning of the war is to be found in part in commercial or general business factors, and in part in the fiscal operations of the government. A brief discussion of the way in which both private and public financial operations led to an expansion of note issues is necessary if one is to understand the currency crisis of 1925.

Business requirements account for much of the expansion of note issues. In France, as in other countries, the enormous demand for war supplies led to sharp advances in prices in a considerable range of commodities, including foodstuffs. The rising cost of living, accompanied by rising wages and increased costs of production generally, resulted in due course in an ever-widening series of price advances. All this, of course, required a larger volume of currency with which to finance business operations,—currency which could come only from the central bank of issue. The process was simple enough: individual business men borrowed from private banking establishments, and the private banking establishments in turn borrowed from the Bank of France, thus expanding the volume of currency.[5]

After the war this expansion process was continued during the boom period of 1919 and 1920.

[5] There is disagreement among economists as to whether the increase in the currency was mainly the cause or mainly the result of the price changes that occurred. This issue cannot, however, be discussed here, and the answer to the question is immaterial for the purpose in hand.

Then, following a business depression of approximately two years, it was renewed in the boom year of 1924. We shall presently discuss, in some detail, the extent of these post-war fluctuations in the supply of currency. Attention must first be given, however, to the relation of the unbalanced government budget to bank note issues.

Both during and since the war the government has borrowed from the Bank huge sums with which to meet treasury deficits. Reference has already been made to the "advances of the Bank of France" to the government,[6] in the discussion of government deficits. These loans to the government are of such vital importance in connection with the currency problem that they must be more fully considered at this place.

During the war when the government treasury was in pressing need of funds with which to meet current expenditures, the Bank of France was appealed to for aid. The Bank issued new bank notes, —which constitute the paper currency of the country,—and turned them over to the Treasury for its use. In turn the government gave to the Bank its promise to pay the loan with interest at a later period. Thus the process resulted, on the one hand, in an increase of the Bank's assets, because it had received promises to pay (treasury bills) from the government; and, on the other hand, it increased the Bank's obligations in the form of outstanding bank notes, which are promises of the Bank to pay

[6] See pp. 63-4 and 99.

cash on demand. However, the general shock to confidence caused by the war and the danger of hoarding, or exporting, specie was such that the Bank from the very beginning of the war decided that it would be the part of wisdom not to undertake to meet its note obligations in cash for the time being. In more technical language, specie payments were suspended for an indefinite period.

The following table shows the amount of loans, or advances, of the Bank of France to the government at the end of each year from 1913 to 1924.

LOANS OF THE BANK TO THE GOVERNMENT *
(In millions of francs)

1913..........	0	1920..........	26,600
1914..........	3,900	1921..........	24,600
1915..........	5,000	1922..........	23,600
1916..........	7,400	1923..........	23,300
1917..........	12,500	1924..........	22,600
1918..........	17,150	1925 (June) ...	25,650
1919..........	25,500		

* Exclusive of a perpetual loan of 200 million francs.

It will be seen that the loans of the Bank to the government increased rapidly until 1920, after which they declined until the end of 1924. Before discussing the means by which the government was enabled to repay some of the loans of the Bank, notwithstanding the fact that its budget was still unbalanced, we must first reveal an *indirect* process by means of which budget deficits react upon the Bank of France.

Meeting government deficits by bond issues usually results indirectly in an expansion of bank note issues. For example, during the war period, the issues of government bonds and short-term obligations in France, as in other countries, were in no small degree absorbed by means of credit operations. Individuals who had no ready cash bought bonds on funds borrowed from the banks; and the private banking establishments themselves bought government securities on funds borrowed from the central bank. Moreover, the funds which the banking houses loaned to their customers for the purpose of buying bonds were also in turn mainly borrowed from the Bank of France. No adequate figures are available to indicate the extent to which the successive bond issues during the war were purchased on borrowed funds, but no small percentage of the total issues floated in the market during the war years was in the last analysis undoubtedly paid for with funds which came from the expansion of note issues. This process as we shall see, has continued since the war.

The deflation of 1921-1923 released funds from commercial uses and made them available for government fiscal purposes. A recognition of the truth of this proposition and a realization of the process involved is fundamental to an appreciation of what has been occurring in France in the last few years and of the gravity of the present financial situation. It is indeed a remarkable phenomenon with which we are here concerned.

The first fact that needs to be pondered is that in the years 1921-1923 the government not only ceased to borrow from the Bank of France, but paid off some of its previously contracted loans. Late in 1920 an agreement was reached between the Finance Minister and the Bank of France that "in order to effect progressive deflation" the Treasury should annually pay off 2 billion francs of its debt to the Bank. This was accomplished in 1921; but in 1922 only 1 billion, and in 1923 only 800 million francs were paid off.[7] The total reduction in three years was thus 3,800 millions. This reduction in the loans of the Bank to the government was almost universally pointed to as complete evidence that France had finally turned her back on the devil inflation and had entered once more upon the broad highway which leads toward financial stability. A gradual return of the franc to par was envisaged by many as the ultimate goal of this policy.

The second fact to consider is that this large reduction in the obligations of the government to the Bank of France was accomplished in spite of the persistence of enormous Treasury deficits. This means that the Treasury had to borrow elsewhere than at the Bank of France the sums required to cover the budget deficiencies, and that it also had to borrow the 3.8 billion francs which were used to reduce the loans from the Bank.

Now the government, as we have seen, borrowed the bulk of the funds required through the flotation of bonds and short-term bills in the domestic market.

[7] In 1924 the amount nominally repaid to the Bank was 1.2 billions.

The absorption, in the financial markets, of billions upon billions of securities during this period was looked upon by most financial and economic writers as renewed testimony to the remarkable thriftiness and saving capacity of the French people. It was regarded as conclusive evidence of the ability of the French to carry on, however onerous the present burdens might appear to be.

Seldom has a more egregious misunderstanding of financial processes been manifested than in this conception of the French situation. The truth of the matter is that a large part of the bonds and bills sold in the domestic market have not come out of increased savings on the part of the French people, but have been purchased with bank credit. Fiscal inflation was still occurring in France, though the process had become an indirect instead of a direct one. The funds which were utilized to pay off government loans from the Bank of France and to cover budget deficits in reality still came from inflation of the note issues of the Bank of France. What is the explanation of this seeming paradox?

In the autumn of 1920, just before the beginning of the period of reducing the government's loans from the Bank, the post-war trade boom collapsed and a period of commercial deflation began in France as in other countries. Now in a period of business liquidation business men may be expected gradually to reduce loans from their banks, and in turn the banking establishments may be expected to pay off the loans which they have previously contracted at the central bank. This is simply because as the volume of trade transactions declines and the cost of conducting business is reduced it takes less money to finance the business requirements of the country than before. A very great decline in the volume of business occurred during the deflation period in France and there was a drop in the level of wholesale prices from 588 in April, 1920, to 306 in February, 1922, a decline of about 50 per cent. As a result, the volume of bank loans required by the business community for commercial purposes was very greatly reduced. But this commercial deflation found no reflection whatever in the outstanding note issues of the Bank of France. And thereby hangs the tale.

The statement was made above that the deflation of 1921-1923 released from commercial operations the funds which went into the purchase of new government securities. Instead of being returned to the bank of issue for redemption and retirement as the volume of loans for business purposes declined, the outstanding note issues were used by business men and by the banks themselves in buying government securities. The evidence on which this statement is made is to be found both in the financial statement of the Bank of France and in the records of the private banking establishments.

The expansion of note issues at the Bank of France during the inflation boom following the war reached its height in September, 1920, at a figure of 39,207,-944,000 francs. The decline from that month continued with minor fluctuations until March, 1922, when a low point of 35,528,005,000 francs was reached. The maximum decline was thus 3,679,-939,000 francs. Now during these very months the government reduced its loans from the Bank of France by 5,100,000,000 francs.[8] As a result of government repayments the note issues during this period should have been reduced by 5.1 billions; but as a matter of fact the reduction amounted to only 3.7 billions. The evidence shows that the outstanding note issues declined by a total considerably less than the amount of the government's repayments to the Bank.

Had the funds released from business uses during the period of commercial defiation not been absorbed in purchasing government securities issued to cover budget deficits, the outstanding note issues of the Bank of France would have automatically declined by many billions, even without any repayments of government obligations. Since the reduction in note issues was less than the amount of government repayments, it is clear that not only did all of the funds released by commercial deflation go into the absorption of government securities, but additional borrowings from the Bank of France were also absorbed in purchasing securities.

Let us now turn to the evidence afforded by the financial records of the banks themselves. The pri-

[8] 2.1 billions were, however, renewed later in the year so that the reduction at the end of 1922, as previously noted, amounted to only 3.0 billion francs.

vate banking establishments of France are not compelled to submit periodical reports to the government, as is the case in some countries, and hence it is impossible to reveal the total increase of government security holdings by the French banks. Reports are, however, made by some of the principal banking institutions, and the figures clearly support the contention that we are making. The combined statements of the Crédit Lyonnais, Comptoir d'Escompte, Société Générale, and Crédit Industriel et Commercial show a steady expansion of an item called *Portfeuille et bons du Trésor*. We are reliably informed that under this general heading are included the National Defense bills, which were so extensively employed by the government in raising funds. The reports do not, however, separate in the portfolio account the National Defense bills from ordinary loans; hence it is impossible to reveal the situation with entire accuracy. The following table gives the amount of portfolio and treasury bill holdings of the four large banking corporations mentioned above for the years 1918 to 1924 inclusive. The figures in millions of francs are for the end of each year.[9]

1918	4,817
1919	8,746
1920	9,261
1921	10,308
1922	10,963
1923	11,899
1924	11,900

[9] For the quarterly figures of the principal items of these banks from 1913 to 1924, see Appendix E.

During the period of commercial deflation one would have expected the ordinary loan portfolio to decline as commercial business contracted. As a matter of fact, however, the portfolio item steadily increased, indicating that the deflation of commercial loans at the banks was more than counterbalanced by purchases of government securities.

The total of outstanding National Defense bills, as shown in Chapter V, is now about 60 billion francs. No one knows the precise amount of these bills that are held by the banks of the country; but conferences with French bankers, business men, and economists have led us to the conclusion that one-third of the total is a very conservative estimate. With the larger banks it is believed that 50 or 60 per cent of the portfolio account consists of government securities. Besides those held by the banks directly, a considerable volume has been purchased by individuals on funds borrowed from the banks.

At the beginning of the period of commercial deflation, the banks were by no means reluctant to purchase these government bills, since they were the source of a very decent profit. It paid better to buy these bonds than it did to liquidate loans at the Bank of France, and so long as their regular customers were not requiring the funds, the banks were satisfied to let the government have the money.[10] As we shall see, the latter part of 1923

[10] The phenomenon of a period of commercial deflation giving a great stimulus to the bond market is not confined to France. It manifests itself in greater or less degree in all countries in connec-

and 1924 brought a great change in this situation and precipitated a crisis alike for the banks and for the business community.

The deflation of 1921 indirectly strengthened French exchange. The liquidation of business loans and the shift of funds to the security markets quickly led to a rise in the price of both public and private securities. With French credit thus apparently improved, foreign investors were quick to buy larger quantities of French bonds and this materially raised the price of French exchange. At the same time the curtailment of purchases of raw materials in foreign countries that resulted from the business depression lessened the demand for *foreign* bills, thus further strengthening French exchange. The rise once begun was of course accelerated by the activities of speculators desirous of anticipating further advances. (See the chart of exchange rates, p. 119.)

Did the National Defense bills serve the purpose of currency? This is a convenient place to raise the question whether these bills, which were issued by the government in small denominations and which possessed many of the attributes of money, did not in reality constitute an addition to the currency supply of the country. It has frequently been contended by foreign observers that the Defense bills were in fact merely a substitute for bank notes.

tion with private as well as public securities. In the United States, for example, the year 1921 was one of great activity in the bond markets. Banking institutions and business men alike bought securities with funds which would otherwise have been idle.

The answer to the question is that they do not appear to have directly served to any great extent as media of exchange. They are not legal tender and they are not quite as convenient as bank notes for ordinary currency transactions; accordingly the holder of bills usually either sells them to the bank for cash when he needs money with which to meet his obligations, or borrows upon them as collateral. While not performing the direct functions of a medium of exchange, they have nevertheless provided the basis for a ready expansion of currency.

The commercial expansion of 1923-1924 reversed the bond market situation and precipitated a crisis both at the Treasury and at the Bank of France. To those who clearly understand financial processes it has been evident all along that the contraction of the total outstanding bank notes could not be permanent so long as the budget remained unbalanced. In a year or so commercial deflation would naturally run its course, and even without a recurrence of business and price expansion the total of outstanding notes would in the end register a new advance. The successive bond and bill issues of the government could not be fully subscribed without further borrowings by the private institutions from the central bank of issue. Even though the government might not borrow directly from the Bank of France, it would have to borrow indirectly from that source just as soon as no further supply of loanable funds was being released as a result of commercial deflation. The amount of *real* savings on the part of the public available for government loans was wholly inadequate to absorb the volume of government and other securities being offered in the market.

From the low point of 35.5 billions in March, 1922, the note issues increased to 36.6 billions at the end of 1922. Then as soon as business recovery and renewed commercial expansion began in earnest in 1923, the bank note circulation expanded rapidly. As in the war years and as in the boom period of 1919-1920, an increased volume of business conducted at rising prices necessitated an expansion of currency for ordinary commercial needs. Business men once more enlarged their borrowings from the banks and the banks in turn increased their borrowings from the Bank of France. Even if the government had not at the same time continued to float loans in the financial markets the note issues would necessarily have increased so long as the business expansion continued. As things stood there was a double pressure for accommodations from the Bank.

The volume of the note issues at three-month intervals from June, 1923, to May, 1925, is shown below.

	Millions of Francs
1923	
June	36,689
September	37,626
December	37,905
1924	
March	39,950
June	39,665
September	40,339
December	40,604

1925
March 40,892
June 43,000

The total of note issues that the Bank of France could legally issue had been fixed by a law of September, 1920, at 41 billion francs. As this limit was approached in the late autumn of 1924, the managers of the Bank naturally became concerned lest the pressure for loans would necessitate an issue in excess of this total. The discount rate was raised, in the hope that borrowing might be somewhat restricted, and at the same time credits were extended much more sparingly. Meanwhile, a currency shortage, threatening a business reaction, had developed.[11] Efforts were made to relieve this shortage by replacing French currency in the Saar by a new currency substitute, and it is stated that plans were also under way for instituting a similar policy with respect to some of the colonies.

The absorption of liquid funds by commercial operations dried up the market for government bonds. As we have seen from previous chapters, it proved impossible in 1924 to derive either from bond issues by the Crédit National or from the Government's direct loans more than a fraction of the sums re-

[11] It has been contended that the hoarding of banknotes has assumed large proportions, some estimates running as high as 7 billion francs. It is very doubtful, however, if hoarding has been extensive, for bank notes are not a safe thing to hoard when a further decline of the franc is threatened. A "shortage" of currency is always popularly attributed to hoarding, whereas, it is usually the result of active business at rising prices, the "shortage" being due to an increased demand rather than a curtailment of supply.

quired. It was not a question of the rate of interest, for the rate, as we have seen, had become very high. The inability to sell the bonds was primarily due to the lack of floating funds in the market. Business men now needed all the money they could lay hands on for their business activities; while the masses of the people, whose incomes had not advanced as prices had risen, found themselves with reduced saving capacity. The private banks, already loaded with government securities, were not only anxious to reduce rather than to expand their holdings, but they were also being asked for more loans for commercial purposes than they could handle. Moreover, their capacity to borrow at the Bank of France was limited by the fact that the Bank was itself approaching the maximum issue permitted by law. At the same time the raising of the discount rate to 7 per cent tended to lessen the possibilities of a profit on investments in government securities.

As a result of this glut of the investment markets with existing securities and the general scarcity of liquid funds, the Treasury found itself for the first time since 1920 in a position where it was unable to meet its current expenditures without resorting to further borrowing direct from the Bank of France. The deflation process which had released the funds necessary for the absorption of government issues for two or three years, had run its course; and new direct borrowing from the Bank had become a necessity.

At the beginning of 1925 the Bank of France again resorted to direct inflation. The Bank was reluctantly forced once more to follow the policy that carried the German financial system into complete disintegration. Under powerful pressure from a government which found itself without money for operating expenses the Bank finally yielded, and without legal authority "advanced" about two billion francs to the government, and then endeavored to conceal the fact by entering the transaction on the balance sheet under the heading "miscellaneous." The reader should understand that the transaction required, on the liability side of the Bank's accounts, an increase of the note item, and on the assets side an increase of advances, or loans, to the government. Not only was the limit of note issues exceeded, but the limit of loans to the government (22 billions) was also illegally exceeded.

In this connection it should be understood that the 41 billion note issue maximum permitted by law constitutes no sacred figure; and an increase of the total is nothing new in French financial history. It may be interesting to note some of the other occasions in which the total circulation of the Bank of France has been increased by law. In December, 1871, the Bank was authorized to issue a maximum of not more than 2,800 millions; in July, 1872, this limit was raised to 3,200 millions; during the period of commercial expansion in 1884, to 3,500 millions; then, between 1884 and 1904, it was raised four different times to a maximum of 6,800 millions.

During this period of gradual business expansion an increased volume of currency gave rise to no serious problem, particularly in view of the fact that the gold reserve held against the notes was increased even more rapidly than the outstanding notes. After the outbreak of the Great War, the maximum was extended from time to time until a limit of 33 billions was reached in 1918. In the inflation period of 1919-1920, it was raised three times,—to 36, to 40, and finally, on July 21, 1920, to 43 billions, this total being reduced to 41 billions just after the deflation period began. The policy has always been to raise the limit before it is reached; and there has been a good deal of discussion as to the significance of a limit which was certain to be raised before it could be reached. The most that can be said for the practice is that the setting of the limit necessitates a reconsideration of financial policy from time to time.

The gravity of the present situation lies in the conditions which necessitated the advance at this time and in the deception with which the transaction was carried through. When the Bank of France, in the light of its long record of conservative and honest financial administration, will falsify its official report—no matter under what pressure—conditions have indeed become serious. The subsequent act which establishes a legal maximum of 45 billions for note issues and 26 billions for advances to the government in no wise mitigates the economic crisis; it merely officially recognizes it.

Such an expansion, it is feared by many, foreshadows a further and perhaps an uninterrupted decline of the franc—a repetition if you please of the German debacle. Coming at a time when a very strong group in France was hopeful that the franc might be gradually restored to par, the situation has naturally produced a crisis of tremendous import. The actual issue of additional notes direct to the government for fiscal needs, and the setting of a new note issue limit of 45 billions, mean that advocates of sound currency have had to bow before economic forces which they could not control.

Whether these limits will be adequate for more than a few months will depend upon two factors: first, whether a period of business expansion and rising prices continues; and second, upon the success of the Treasury in bringing the budget into balance.

CHAPTER VII

PRODUCTION AND TRADE

IN previous chapters we have been studying the French economic situation mainly from the evidence afforded by the records of the financial markets. It will serve to round out the picture if we now turn to a survey of the condition of trade and industry. Here we shall find the story a more cheerful one. As we shall show in the following chapter, however, the relatively favorable trade situation has been attained, not in spite of an unsound financial situation but in a very real sense because of the financial methods that have been employed.

The material will be presented under the following headings: (1) the reconstruction of the devastated areas; (2) the economic importance of the acquisition of Alsace-Lorraine; (3) agricultural production; and (4) the status of industry.

I. RECONSTRUCTION OF THE DEVASTATED AREA [1]

The population of the devastated area—which included a large part of the ten northern departments of France—was 4,690,000 in 1914, or almost 12 per cent of the total population of the country.

[1] This section is based in part on personal observation and in part upon published official data.

At the end of the war the population had been reduced to 2,075,000; 741,993 houses had been entirely destroyed and a great many others seriously damaged; about 22,900 factories and workshops had been more or less completely wrecked; 8.2 million acres [2] of land, approximately 7 per cent of the area of France, had been devastated, including about 4.75 million acres of arable land which were rendered unfit for cultivation. The coal mines of the Nord and Pas-de-Calais had been flooded and otherwise seriously damaged; bridges, canals, highways, and railroads had been torn up; and cattle, horses, and other farm animals had practically disappeared from the region. [3]

Reconstruction was begun almost immediately after the war, and by the middle of 1924, when the lack of funds caused an appreciable slowing down of the work, much the larger part of the task had been completed. Concretely, the following results had been accomplished: [4]

7.3 million acres, or 89 per cent of the devastated area, had been reconstituted.

4.43 million acres, or 93 per cent of the arable land that had been laid waste, were again under cultivation.

606,000 houses, or 81 per cent of those destroyed, had been rebuilt, while another 183,000 had been repaired and 42,000 temporary homes had been constructed.

[2] 2.471 acres = one hectare.

[3] *Documents parlementaires, Sénat*, No. 276, April 2, 1924, p. 260.

[4] See (1) *Journée Industrielle*, April 19, 1924, Feb. 1-2, 1925; (2) Cahill, J. R., *Economic Conditions in France*, 1924, pp. 24-5, 60-1; (3) M. Clémentel, *Inventaire*, 1924, pp. 88-9.

20,872, or 91 per cent of the factories and workshops had
   been restored.
Coal production in the damaged mines of the Nord and
   Pas-de-Calais was equal to 94 per cent of the output
   in 1913.
The railways had been entirely reconstituted, and about
   95 per cent of the public highways had been rebuilt.
The number of livestock had increased to a little more
   than 50 per cent of the 1914 total.

The land is, on the whole, apparently quite as
productive as before the devastation. The factory
capacity is, moreover, now considerably greater than
it was before the war. The more important factories and workshops were the first to be rebuilt, and
those that remain unrepaired are typically small
establishments and of little moment from the standpoint of total industrial output. In the main, new
and larger plants with up-to-date machinery and
equipment now stand in the place of the smaller
and more or less antiquated establishments of pre-
war days. Many of the coal mines are more productive than before the war, although the Lens mines,
which were the most seriously damaged, will not be
fully restored before 1927 at the earliest.
   The visible contrast between the devastated area
of 1919 and 1924, as has been noted by many observers, is truly amazing. A dreary waste with mile
after mile of gaunt trees, shell holes, barbed wire
entanglements, deserted fields, demolished towns—
with no cattle, no horses, no living beings anywhere
except in an occasional oasis where a town had in

some miraculous way escaped destruction—had been replaced by fields of waving grain, by new roads and highways, and by whole new villages and towns full of life and energy.

Not that the ruins were all gone. Here and there, to be sure, the ruins of a small village had been left untouched—forever to commemorate the Great War. Now and then the scars which the earth had suffered seemed beyond repair, as at Berry-au-Bac, where a ragged, chalky plain marked the site of the vine-covered hills of pre-war days. Some concrete imbedded iron posts still stood where the barbed wire entanglements had been, and a few historic dugouts were left to excite the imagination of the tourist. The cathedral town of Rheims still showed the marks of war on every hand, with new houses and garish hotels rising in haphazard fashion among the tottering walls of unrestored neighbors. But Rheims and Berry-au-Bac were the exceptions and not the rule. On the whole, the work of reconstruction has largely obliterated the evidences of the occupation.

All this has been accomplished, as we have already seen, by means of credit. Through processes of inflation, money in practically unlimited quantities was made available by the national treasury to the *sinistrés*. With no necessity of counting the costs involved, the way was opened for the most intensive period of building activity known to the history of France, or probably any other country. While we are not here interested in appraising the economy and the efficiency with which the work of reconstruction has been carried out, it is perhaps permissible to call attention to the fact that wholesale graft has been charged in the French Parliament. Excessive claims, padded bills, and extravagant outlays were no doubt inevitable. In any country, whenever the government foots the bills, claims and charges are notoriously exorbitant. Where the bills are to be presented for payment to an enemy country, one can hardly expect greater restraint.[5]

II. ECONOMIC IMPORTANCE OF ALSACE-LORRAINE

With the acquisition of Alsace-Lorraine, the area of France was increased by 5,600 square miles, and the population by 1,700,000 people.[6] The acquisition of this territory has been of some importance from the standpoint of agriculture, and of enormous importance from an industrial point of view.

[5] A French commission was appointed in 1924 to investigate the extravagance connected with the awarding of claims. While this commission has made no official report, much material bearing on the problem is to be found in the *Journal officiel, documents parlémentaires, Chambre,* 1925, particularly pages 130-1, and 267-8. The nature of the fraudulent transactions may be illustrated by the following cases. A certain farmer obtained 21,000 francs for his property, including claims for damages, from a *concessionnaire,* who in turn obtained 548,678 francs from the government. A certain sugar refinery was sold to a *concessionnaire* for 336,000 francs, and the latter was awarded a claim for 7 million francs. Two octogenarians sold their chateau with 200 hectares of land and timber for about 300,000 francs cash, plus a *rente viagère* of 80,000 francs; the *concessionnaire* obtained 5 million francs as the replacement value of the property.

[6] The pre-war population of Alsace-Lorraine was 1,900,000 but the estimate for 1924 is only 1,700,000. *Journal officiel, annexe,* March 22, 1925, p. 107.

The following table shows the cereal crops and livestock holdings of Alsace-Lorraine as compared with France as a whole in 1913.

AGRICULTURAL COMPARISON OF ALSACE-LORRAINE AND FRANCE, 1913 *

Index	Figures in Thousands		Alsace-Lorraine Figures as a Percentage of French
	Alsace-Lorraine	France	
Important crops: (metric tons)			
Wheat	237	8,692	2.7
Oats	210	5,183	4.1
Barley	109	1,044	10.4
Rye	92	1,272	7.2
Potatoes	127	13,586	9.3
Livestock holdings: (number of head)			
Horses	137	3,222	4.3
Cattle	523	14,788	3.5
Sheep	46	16,131	.3
Hogs	431	7,036	6.1

* Compiled from the following sources: (1) Théry, M. Edmond, *Les richesses économiques de l'Alsace-Lorraine,* 1920, pp. 180 and 192; (2) *Journal officiel (lois et décrets),* July 23, 1924, p. 6623.

Alsace-Lorraine has an area equal to only 2.7 per cent of that of the rest of France, but her population is 4.5 per cent of the rest of France. The table indicates that the agricultural production of Alsace-Lorraine is proportionately greater than that of the other departments of France. But in view of the denser population of Alsace-Lorraine, the per capita production of breadstuffs and meat is smaller than for France as a whole. Accordingly, the food import requirements of the country have been increased somewhat because of the acquisition of this territory.

The rich potash deposits of Alsace represent the greatest agricultural gain from the acquisition of this territory. Before the war, France had to depend almost entirely on imports for supplying her need of this important mineral salt, which is one of the three chemicals required in abundance for large crop yields. In 1913, Alsace produced approximately 65,000 tons of potash,[7] or about one and one-half times the quantity which France imported in that year. It is estimated that these mines are capable of a yield of more than 700,000 tons, or more than the 1913 consumption of the entire world outside of Germany. The agriculture of France will undoubtedly profit greatly from the future development of this resource.

The industrial resources of France were enormously increased by the recovery of Alsace-Lorraine. The most important gain, of course, came from the acquisition of Lorraine ore, which increased the metallic iron reserves of France by more than 45 per cent. The relative industrial importance of Lorraine is perhaps best shown by a comparison of production figures for 1913—the slowing down of production since the war making post-war comparisons show less strikingly the extent to which the iron industry had been developed in Lorraine.

[7] Tonnage figures used in this paragraph are for pure potash (K_2O).

LORRAINE AND FRENCH IRON PRODUCTION, 1913

Classification	In Thousands of Metric Tons		Lorraine Production as a Percentage of French
	Lorraine	France	
Iron ore	21,136	21,918	96.4
Pig iron	3,864	5,207	74.2
Steel (ingots and castings)	2,280	5,058	45.1

Although possessed of but 45 per cent of the iron resources of France, Lorraine was producing before the war almost as much iron ore, three-fourths as much pig iron, and about 45 per cent as much crude steel. As a result of the war, therefore, France not only increased enormously her natural resources, but she came into possession of the plant and equipment of a very highly developed industry.

Of almost equal importance with the iron industry of Lorraine is the textile industry of Alsace. This industry is one of the oldest and most important of the Alsace-Lorraine country. The fabrication of cotton goods occupied a position of preeminence before the war. In 1913, for example, for every 1,000 inhabitants there were 1,013 cotton spindles at work in Alsace as compared with only 185 in France and 143 in Germany. Alsace also has porportionately more cotton looms than France or Germany. The spinning, weaving, and finishing of woolen goods was also of considerable importance and there was some manufacture of silks and linens. Comparative figures with regard to the cotton and woolen textile industries of pre-war Alsace and France, respectively, are shown in the table which follows.

ALSATIAN AND FRENCH TEXTILE EQUIPMENT, 1913 *

| Spindles and Looms | Figures in Thousands | | Alsatian Figures as a Percentage of French |
	Alsace	France	
Cotton spindles..	1,898	7,230 [a]	26.2
Cotton looms....	44	150	29.3
Wool spindles...	699	3,090	22.6
Wool looms.....	10	46 [a]	21.7

* Compiled from figures given by Théry, Edmond, *Les richesses économiques d l'Alsace-Lorraine*, 1920, pp. 150-5.

[a] According to the *Annuaire général de la France et de l'étranger*, 1923, pp. 366-7, and 1924, pp. 303-5, the number of French cotton spindles in 1913 was 7,571 thousand, and the number of looms for weaving woolens was 55 thousand.

On the whole, the acquisition of Alsace-Lorraine has more than offset the losses sustained in the devastated areas. Now that the devastated areas have been practically reconstituted, the economic—particularly the industrial—resources of France are considerably larger than before the war. One may estimate that the acquisition of Alsace-Lorraine increased the agricultural output of France by 4 or 5 per cent, making no allowance for the future agricultural importance of the rich potash deposits; and the industrial resources as a whole somewhere from 25 to 50 per cent. This needs to be kept in mind in connection with the figures of agricultural and industrial production given in the sections which follow.

III. THE AGRICULTURAL SITUATION

While French agriculture as a whole has steadily improved since the end of the war, the output in 1924 is still considerably below that of 1913. The following table shows in some detail the area planted and the total yield of the principal crops in 1923 and 1924 as compared with 1913.

AREA AND YIELD OF CERTAIN IMPORTANT CROPS FOR 1923 AND 1924 COMPARED WITH 1913 *

Crops	Area Planted (in thousands of acres)			Production (in thousands of metric tons)		
	1913	1923	1924	1913	1923	1924
Cereals:						
Wheat	16,165	13,672	13,413	8,692	7,500	7,684
Meslin	304	274	255	149	132	130
Rye	2,906	2,216	2,150	1,272	928	1,013
Barley	1,878	1,683	1,715	1,044	980	1,000
Buckwheat	1,114	850	857	556	325	423
Oats	9,832	8,458	8,560	5,183	4,891	4,293
Maize	1,132	845	823	543	322	460
Vegetables:						
Green beans	57	54	...	78	56	...
Dry beans	348	358	334	145	62	101
Green peas	74	69	...	126	82	...
Potatoes	3,825	3,585	3,578	13,586	9,919	15.512
Jerusalem artichokes.	274	301	314	1,779	1,299	2,118
Forage Crops:						
Beets	1,789	1,683	1,717	25,220	17,587	22,865
Rutabagas and turnips	457	415	450	3,456	2,506	3,826
Cabbage fodder	623	561	531	8,275	5,708	6,768
Clover	2,898	2,829		4,872	4,245	
Lucerne	2,896	2,735	7,009	5,818	4,998	12,141
Sainfoin	1,898	1,549		2,953	2,156	
Meadow and grazing land	27,250	29,724	...	45,361	38,214	
Industrial Crops:						
Sugar beets	615	403	457	5,939	3,683	5.138
Distilling beet root..	128	62	59	2,050	654	740
Wine (production in million gallons)...	3,830	3,798	3,566	1,171	1,523	1,778

* The figures for 1913 and 1923 are from a report by the Minister of Agriculture, published in the *Journal officiel*, July 23, 1924, p. 6623; for 1924 the figures are from the *Bulletin de la statistique générale*, January, 1925, pp. 116-7.

In 1924, only four crops showed an increase over 1913; namely, Jerusalem artichokes, potatoes, rutabagas and turnips, and wine. It is in these crops that Alsace-Lorraine is particularly important as a producer, and the output there more than offsets the decreased production in other parts of France. All other crops show a smaller total yield in 1924 than in 1913, including such important commodities as beets and cereals. The 1924 production of wheat, by all odds the most important food product, was only 88 per cent of the 1913 crop.

The agricultural decline has been due to reduced acreage rather than decreased per acre yields. The most striking fact revealed in the table is the decline in the area planted in every crop in the list except Jerusalem artichokes. This, the reader will bear in mind, is true despite the acquisition of Alsace-Lorraine which increased the land area of France by 2.6 per cent.

For certain crops the per acre yield was even larger in 1924 than in the pre-war period. The yield of wheat per acre in 1924 was 21 bushels as compared with 19.8 bushels in 1913, with an average of 19.6 for the five years preceding the war. For barley, the yield per acre was 26.8 bushels in 1924, as compared with 25.5 bushels in 1913 and 26.6 for the five-year average 1909-13. The yield of potatoes showed a remarkable increase over the pre-war period, the output per acre averaging 159.3 bushels in 1924, as compared with an average of 127.4 for the five-year period 1909-13, the improve-

ment being due to the excellent crops of Alsace-
Lorraine. Oats, however, show a slight decrease per
acre, the figures being 34.6 bushels in 1924, as compared with 36.3 in 1913 and 36.2 for the five years
1909-13.

It may prove of interest in passing to note that
the yields per acre in France before the war were
low as compared with those of other European countries. For the purpose of putting the figures for
French agriculture into their proper perspective,
comparative figures for certain of the important
agricultural countries of Europe are given in the
table below.

AVERAGE BUSHEL-PER-ACRE YIELD IN CERTAIN EUROPEAN COUNTRIES,
1909-13 *

Country	Wheat	Oats	Barley	Potatoes
France	19.6	36.2	26.6	127.4
Germany	31.8	55.2	38.8	203.9
Great Britain......	31.4	49.9	34.2	218.1
Austria	20.2	39.9	28.1	147.5
Belgium	37.0	78.6	44.2	272.4
Denmark	40.9	48.8	40.7	203.9
Holland	35.7	58.3	52.8	219.9

* *Sénat commission des finances, Rapport,* No. 322, *portant fixa-
ion du budget général de l'exercice* 1923. Conversions were made
s follows: 2.471 acres = 1 hectare; 220.46 lbs. = 1 quintal; 60
bs. = 1 bushel of wheat; 32 lbs. = 1 bushel of oats; 48 lbs. = 1
bushel of barley; 60 lbs. = 1 bushel of potatoes.

The explanation of the decline in acreage is pri-
narily the rural exodus that has occurred. Accord-
ng to the census of 1911, 55.8 per cent of the popu-
ation of France was classified as rural; but in 1921

this figure had fallen to 53.7 in the 87 old departments of France, and to 53.6 with Alsace-Lorraine
included. The causes of the movement from the
farms to the towns—and for that matter from the
small villages to the larger towns—are numerous.
The most important are the restlessness and discontent resulting from the war, and the rising standards of living and working conditions in the industrial centers resulting from the intensive industrial
development to which reference has previously been
made. The slowing down of industrial activity with
the completion of the work of reconstruction will
undoubtedly send many workers back to the farms
with a resulting increase of agricultural output.
Even so, however, it is not anticipated that there
will be a return to full pre-war agricultural output
for some time to come.

The present unfavorable agricultural situation of
France is also shown by the decrease in livestock
holdings. A great loss in livestock holdings, of
course, resulted directly from war conditions. After
the war, particularly in 1919 and 1920, the apparently high prices that were prevailing in France
led many of the farmers to sell off livestock and
invest the proceeds in securities or mortgages, an
illustration of the far-reaching effects of a government budgetary deficit. The eagerness of the farmer
to take advantage of what appeared to be a "great
opportunity" in buying government bonds yielding
5 or 6 per cent is easily explained when one considers how very small his margin of profit was—

and is—in France. As one French writer describes it: [8]

> I know a number of farming families who, from very early times, have continued to live on the same large farms in Berry. One family, for example, has exploited the same farm for five generations. But in spite of the century-long labor of this family, in spite of the technical ability of those who have thus followed the same calling from father to son, the position of the person who was cultivating the soil in 1914 did not perceptibly differ from that of his ancestor who cultivated it in 1811. Agriculture has permitted these families to maintain their social status (here we are speaking of farms of 100 to 200 hectares), but it has never yielded them profits sufficient to lift them from the bourgeois class.

A comparison of the figures for 1913 and 1923 show that five years after the close of the war, livestock losses had still not been made good, even with the livestock holdings of Alsace-Lorraine included in the 1923 figures. This comparison is shown in the table below.

LIVESTOCK HOLDINGS IN FRANCE, 1913 AND 1923 *

(In thousands of head)

Kind	1913 (Pre-war area)	1923 (Present area)
Horses	3,222	2,848
Mules	188	192
Donkeys	357	284
Cattle	14,788	13,749
Sheep	16,131	9,925
Hogs	7,036	5,406
Goats	1,435	1,353

* Documents parlementaires, Sénat, No. 417, 1924, p. 531. Figures for 1924 were not available at the time of writing.

[8] La Journée Industrielle, July 18, 1923, p. 2.

The decrease in livestock holdings has naturally resulted in a shortage of meat production in France. In consequence the French government has removed restrictions standing in the way of the importation of frozen pork from the United States, Canada, Argentina, Brazil, and Uruguay. Imports of fresh and frozen beef are also increasing. The United States Department of Agriculture states that "competent French observers attribute the increase of (meat) imports to both decreased domestic production and to a tendency to greater consumption of meat . . . (the latter being) a common tendency noted in practically all European countries since the war." [9]

Milk production in France is also below the prewar figure, though gradually increasing since the armistice. The total production of cows' milk in 1923 amounted to 3,091,910 thousand gallons as compared with 3,383,406 thousand in 1913. The uses to which this was put in 1923, as compared with 1913, are as follows: The quantity used for feeding calves in 1923 was 674,636 thousand gallons as compared with 765,752 thousand in 1913; used for butter, 1,029,589 thousand gallons in 1923, as compared with 1,145,722 thousand in 1913; that used in cheese manufacture, 589,914 thousand in 1923, as compared with 385,412 thousand in 1913; that remaining for use as milk or cream 797,771 thousand in 1923, as compared with 1,086,520 thousand in 1913.[10]

[9] *Foreign Crops and Markets* (U. S. Department of Agriculture), May 21, 1924, p. 433.
[10] *Journal officiel,* March 14, 1924, p. 2525.

On the whole, French agriculture in 1924, the best
year since the war, was not yet back to the position
it had attained before the war. Even with the production of Alsace-Lorraine included, the agricultural output of the country in 1924 was only about
90 per cent of that of 1913. The prosperity of the
country about which so much has been said and
written, has evidently not been a prosperity based
on a great increase in the production of foodstuffs.
On the contrary, the period since the war has been
marked by increased imports of both grain and
meat.

IV. THE STATUS OF INDUSTRY

The recovery and expansion of industry has been
perhaps the most gratifying phase of post-war economic developments in France. Thanks to the acquisition of Alsace-Lorraine, French industry is on
the whole considerably more productive now than
it was in 1913. We present below the significant
data with reference to coal, iron and steel, machine
manufacture, and textiles.

*In 1924, French coal production, for the first time
since the war, exceeded the output of 1913.* This
noteworthy achievement has been the result of several factors as follows: (1) the acquisition of Lorraine coal; [11] (2) the rehabilitation of the mines of
the Nord and Pas-de-Calais; (3) the innovations in

---

[11] The figures of coal production in the Saar are not included in
this account, because the Saar is not strictly speaking a part of
France.

plant and equipment that had been effected during the last five years; and (4) the changes in the business and financial organization of the industry since the war. The gradual recovery of the industry to a production higher than that attained in 1913 is shown by the annual production figures [12] (in thousands of metric tons).

1913	40,848
1920	25,260
1921	28,980
1922	31,920
1923	38,544
1924	44,952

This recovery of French coal production does not, however, mean that France can get on henceforth with smaller imports of coal. The acquisition of Lorraine ore and the expansion of the metallurgical industry has increased French needs for coal to such an extent that even with coal production above that of 1913 her import requirements will be considerably larger than before the war.

French iron and steel production in 1924 was considerably in excess of the 1913 output. The increase is wholly due to the acquisition of Alsace-Lorraine, the production of the rest of France still being considerably less than it was before the war. The table on page 162 shows the production of iron ore, pig iron, and steel in 1913 and in 1924, with the figures for Lorraine shown separately.

[12] *Bulletin de la statistique générale de la France.* (These figures include a small percentage of lignite.)

COMPARISON OF FRENCH IRON AND STEEL PRODUCTION,
1913 AND 1924 *

(In thousands of metric tons)

Classification	Pre-War France		Lorraine		Present France	
	1913	1924	1913	1924	1913	1924
Iron ore........	21,918	(a)	21,138	(a)	43,056	28,994
Pig iron........	5,207	4,025	3,864	2,980	9,071	7,005
Steel (ingots and castings).	5,058	3,974	2,280	2,365	7,338	6,339

* Figures from the *Bulletin de la statistique générale de la France* and from *l'Journée Industrielle,* Feb. 1-2, 1925, p. 1. Where the two sources failed to agree the figures of the *Statistique Générale* were used.

(a) Separate data for Lorraine iron ore production in 1924 are not available.

The recovery of the iron and steel industry since 1920 has been noteworthy. Iron ore production in that year amounted to 13.9 million metric tons, pig iron production to 3.4 million metric tons, and steel ingots and castings to 3.0 million metric tons. The increase since 1920 amounts to 57 per cent in the case of iron ore, 53 per cent in the case of pig iron, and 70 per cent in the case of steel ingots and castings.

The metal working and machine manufacturing industries are also more productive than in pre-war days. The plant and equipment of the metal working industry suffered comparatively little damage from the pillage and destruction of the war, because only a small part of these industries was located in the North. In 1913, to be sure, the manufacture of electrical machinery was beginning to concentrate in the Nord, about 20 per cent of the industry being located there at the outbreak of the war. On the whole, however, the great centers of manufacture of machines were Paris and Lyons, which lay outside the devastated areas.

To a large extent the expansion of these industries since the war has been due to the acquisition of the iron and steel resources of Lorraine. It is also partly due, however, to the growth of the industry in the rest of France, a development stimulated by the enormous demands resulting from reconstruction operations.

Production figures for these industries are not published; hence it is necessary to turn to the foreign trade statistics for information concerning the condition of the industry in 1924 as compared with 1913. The table on page 164 shows imports and exports of machinery for the years in question.

With the exception of printing presses and sewing machines, France exported a larger tonnage of all kinds of machinery in 1924 than in 1913. In many lines the expansion of exports has been quite remarkable. At the same time there has been a decrease in the tonnage of imports of all classes except agricultural machinery, printing presses, and automobiles.

Three classes of machinery products show an increase of net exports; four classes show a decrease of net imports; and seven classes show net imports replaced by net exports. Apparently France is not only supplying a larger volume of goods for foreign

IMPORTS AND EXPORTS OF MACHINERY, 1913 AND 1924

(In thousands of metric tons)

Classification	Imports		Exports		Net Imports (−) Net Exports (+)	
	1913	1924	1913	1924	1913	1924
Agricultural machinery	34,827	47,514	12,311	13,653	−22,516	−33,861
Textile machinery....	21,406	14,558	1,968	10,726	−19,438	−3,832
Electrical machinery..	6,224	4,203	2,948	9,526	−3,276	+5,323
Electric lamps and electrical machine parts.	12,069	11,852	14,636	31,216	+2,567	+19,364
Parts for other machines	33,029	14,941	12,837	37,501	−20,192	+22,560
Motors, engines, locomotives, hydraulic machinery, etc.........	26,236	9,606	5,897	12,133	−20,339	+2,527
Milling and hoisting apparatus	14,901	7,543	6,863	23,409	−8,038	+15,866
Boilers of all sorts...	15,727	11,549	4,021	7,380	−11,706	−4,169
Machine tools and other tools	28,533	17,585	11,177	20,783	−17,356	+3,198
Printing presses and accessories	2,565	2,970	811	732	−1,754	−2,238
Sewing machines	8,555	5,354	391	265	−8,164	−5,089
Railway cars, including street cars	20,929	3,839	5,783	25,625	−15,146	+21,786
Automobiles, carriages and parts	3,345	19.763	27,772	64,234	+24,427	+44,471
Bicycles and motorcycles	963	715	1,344	5,529	+381	+4,814
Aircraft and parts....	...	...	544	1,398	+544	+1,398

markets, but she is also supplying a larger share of her own machinery requirements.

Owing to the acquisition of Alsace, the textile industry is now producing as much as before the war. Next to agriculture and the State services the textile trades afford employment for more people than any other industry in France. From the point of view of the foreign trade balance this industry is also of paramount importance. Cotton, wool, and silk goods are the principal textiles, although there is some manufacture of linen, hemp, and jute products. An important adjunct to the textile industry in France is the manufacture of men's and women's clothing.

The spinning and weaving of cotton was seriously crippled as a result of the war, owing to the fact that the industry was centered in the departments where the devastation was greatest—in the Vosges, Meurthe-et-Moselle, and the Nord. About 30 per cent of the cotton spindles and looms were destroyed or transferred to Germany. The restoration was apparently not quite completed at the end of 1924.[13]

As an offset to the losses, however, France acquired the very important textile industry of Alsace, and the net result has been a considerable increase in textile producing capacity. The number of cotton spindles in Alsace was about 26 per cent and the total of cotton looms nearly 30 per cent of the number in pre-war France.

In the absence of published data as to the volume of cotton production, the state of the industry as a whole must be sought in the import and export trade statistics. Figures showing the foreign trade in raw cotton, yarn, and cloth for 1913, 1919, and 1924 are given on the following page.

The consumption of raw cotton by the industry in 1924, as indicated by the net import figures in the table, was about 16 thousand tons greater than

[13] J. R. Cahill, in a report of the British "Department of Overseas Trade" on *Economic Conditions in France* in 1924, p. 75, indicates that the industry was entirely reconstructed, his figures being identical with those which the *Statistique général* reported in 1922 as the total equipment when the work of reconstruction should be entirely accomplished. M. Clémentel in his *Inventaire*, however, reports that in the middle of 1924 the work of reconstructing the devastated areas still lacked 9 per cent of completion. It is probable that some textile plants had not been rehabilitated or rebuilt.

in 1913. At the same time net exports of cotton yarn increased by 6.5 thousand tons; and net exports of cotton cloth, by nearly 14 thousand tons.

COTTON IMPORTS AND EXPORTS, 1913, 1919, AND 1924
(In thousands of metric tons)

Trade	Raw Cotton			Cotton Yarn			Cotton Cloth		
	1913	1919	1924	1913	1919	1924	1913	1919	1924
Imports	329.1	218.7	302.0	3.2	28.5	4.2	4.9	18.2	2.9
Exports	60.9	18.1	18.0	8.5	7.9	16.0	55.4	30.3	67.1
Net....	−268.2	−200.6	−284.0	+5.3	−20.6	+11.8	+50.5	+12.1	+64.2

Apparently domestic consumption of cotton fabrics had been somewhat reduced.

The woolen industry was also concentrated in the northeastern part of France, and in consequence suffered severely from the war. About 35 per cent of the spindles and 60 per cent of the looms were destroyed or carried away during the war. Much has been done since then to replace and restore these losses, but even so it is only by the addition of Alsace that the plant and equipment of the French woolen industry in 1924 was equal to that of 1913.[14] And the volume of production had not yet attained the pre-war level.

As in the case of the manufacture of cotton goods, the raw materials for the woolen industry are in

[14] Statistics with regard to the plant and equipment of the woolen industry are contradictory and unsatisfactory. Our general conclusions are based, however, upon studies of the *Bulletin de la statistique générale*, January, 1922, p. 166; *Annuaire général de la France et le l'étranger*, 1923, p. 365; Cahill, J. R. *Economic Conditions in France*, 1924, p. 75; and Finance Minister Clémentel's *Inventaire*.

large part imported. Net imports of raw wool together with net exports of yarn and fabrics, therefore, are a fairly good index of the activity of the industry. The figures for 1913, 1919, and 1924 are given in the following table.

FOREIGN TRADE IN WOOL AND WOOL MANUFACTURES, 1913, 1919, AND 1924
(In thousands of metric tons)

Trade	Raw Wool, Washed and Unwashed			Woolen and Worsted Yarn			Woolen Fabrics		
	1913	1919	1924	1913	1919	1924	1913	1919	1924
Imports	285.6	165.9	234.7	1.0	6.8	.8	4.3	22.6	1.2
Exports	80.7	10.9	52.1	14.9	1.8	15.8	23.4	5.5	31.5
	−204.9	−155.0	−182.6	+13.9	−5.0	+15.0	+19.1	−17.1	+30.3

The import figures indicate that the woolen mills consumed 21 per cent less wool in 1924 than in 1913. The fact that there was at the same time an increase in net exports of yarn and fabrics, however, is not offsetting evidence of increased production, but is an indication of decreased domestic consumption of woolen goods.

The silk industry was little affected either by the devastation or by the acquisition of Alsace-Lorraine. France produces only about 6 per cent [15] of the raw silk that she requires; hence a production index for the industry is furnished by the figures for net imports of raw silk and silk waste together with exports of silk fabrics.

The net import figures for raw silk and silk waste indicate that the product of the silk industry in 1924 was about 17 per cent larger than in 1913.

[15] Exclusive of silk waste for which no figures are published.

IMPORTS AND EXPORTS OF RAW AND MANUFACTURED SILK, 1913, 1919, AND 1924

(In thousands of metric tons)

Trade	Raw Silk and Silk Waste a			Silk Yarn			Silk Fabrics		
	1913	1919	1924	1913	1919	1924	1913	1919	1924
Imports..	19.5	14.0	15.0	.3	.7	3.1	.9	.6	.3
Exports..	8.8	4.4	2.5	1.4	.6	.5	6.2	6.0	8.6
Net......	−10.7	−9.6	−12.5	+1.1	−.1	−2.6	+5.3	+5.4	+8.3

a Tonnage figures for cocoons have been divided by 4 to convert them to raw silk equivalents.

Increased exports of wearing apparel in 1924 also indicate increased activity in the textile industry. Since 1919, there has been a steady increase in these exports and a steady decrease of imports, with the year 1924 showing both in terms of volume and of value a greater export surplus than 1913 or any intervening year. The figures follow:

NET EXPORTS OF WEARING APPAREL, 1913, 1919, AND 1924*

Trade	In Thousands of Metric Tons			In Millions of Francs		
	1913	1919	1924	1913	1919	1924
Imports	709	3,689	376	10.9	140.0	31.6
Exports	7,844	3,235	9,737	252.6	809.2	3,254.7
Net	7,135	−454	9,361	241.7	669.2	3,223.1

* These figures, for goods classified as "vêtements" in the French trade statistics, cover, men's and women's clothing made from silk, linen, and other textiles; cravats and collars; jute bags; and a miscellaneous class.

Among the other important industries the building and leather trades showed greater activity in

1924 than in 1913, but the manufacture of papeꞁ
fell much below the pre-war output. For the first
half of 1924, according to a special French study
published in October, 1924,[16] the index for building
construction was 125 as compared with 100 in 1913
for France and Alsace combined, and the index for
leather about 120. The paper index, on the other
hand, was below 75 per cent. A comparison between
the production within the present area of France
and that of pre-war France—such as we have been
making for the other industries—would increase
these indexes only a little, inasmuch as these industries are not particularly concentrated in Alsace-
Lorraine.

It is extremely difficult to derive from the foregoing data a general index of production. At best
only a rough computation can be made. Our analysis, however, leads to the conclusion that the present
production of France including Alsace-Lorraine,
compared with pre-war production exclusive of
Alsace-Lorraine, is approximately as follows: agriculture 90, coal 110, iron ore, pig iron, and steel,
130; metal trades 115, cotton goods 106, woolens 79,
silk 117, leather 120, building 125, paper 75. A
rough weighting, in accordance with the relative
importance of the industries, gives a general index
of production of about 105.

While these production data obviously leave much
to be desired from the standpoint of statistical precision, one may nevertheless safely conclude from

[10] *Bulletin de la statistique générale,* October, 1924, pp. 73-109.

the foregoing analysis that the total volume of production in France was greater in 1924 than in 1913. Thanks to the acquisition of Alsace-Lorraine and to the fact that the work of reconstruction in basic industries has been almost completed, the productive capacity of the country has been materially expanded. Industry in general, it may be recalled, has been given new impetus, while agricultural production has declined. It should also be borne in mind that 1924 was a year of extraordinary business activity, while 1913 was a year of relatively normal conditions. As we shall see in later chapters, there are reasons for believing that the high peak of production recently reached in industrial lines will not be continuously sustained.

CHAPTER VIII

THE ECONOMIC DILEMMA

THE failure of so many economic observers to appraise correctly the drift of economic conditions in France since the war has resulted in large measure from an inability to view the situation as an interrelated whole. There has been a common tendency to pick out some one particular index of conditions to prove the observer's contention that all is fundamentally well. Great skill has been acquired, moreover, in shifting from one index to another as the exigencies of the situation required, with a view to maintaining always a cheerful demeanor.

Thus, during the boom period of 1919-1920, it was a common practice to point out that, although there might be currency inflation and falling exchange rates, production was rapidly increasing—and increased production, it was observed, is of paramount importance. Then, during the deflation period of 1920-1921, little was heard about the decline in production; but the decrease in the circulation of the Bank of France and the rise in exchange rates were pointed to as definite evidences of improved conditions. During the depressed period of 1921-1922, the large absorption of securities by the financial markets was proclaimed as evidence of the inherent thriftiness and permanent solvency of the French nation. When the trade boom of 1923-1924 began, little mention was made of the renewal of inflation and of the increasing difficulty of floating securities in the bond market; but the production and trade figures were once again seized upon as evidence of the fundamental soundness of French economic conditions. Always, it seems, when one is looking for hopeful auguries, he can find some index that will serve the purpose.

Those who have pretended to make a more thoroughgoing and scientific appraisal of conditions have commonly scrutinized one index after another and then attempted to strike a balance. The economic system of a nation is however not made up of a group of independent parts; it is rather an organism. Moreover, the system as a whole is not the sum of its parts. That is to say, after making a separate appraisal of the budget and debt situation, of the condition of agriculture and industry, of the state of international trade and finance, and of the movements of prices, currency, and exchange, one can not add up the results or strike a balance and thus arrive at a correct diagnosis. As well might a physician conclude that inasmuch as two out of three of a patient's vital organs are reasonably sound, his general condition may be regarded as satisfactory.

Now the interesting and at the same time perplexing feature of the situation has been the fact that the various indexes of economic conditions have not simultaneously pointed in the same direction. When trade has been thriving, the volume of currency has expanded and exchange rates have fallen. When business and trade have been depressed, the banking situation has improved, foreign exchange has risen, and the market for government securities has been capacious. But in periods of commercial inflation the supply of liquid funds has been absorbed in business activities, the bond market has dried up, and the Treasury has had to resort to the Bank of France for money with which to meet current operating expenses.

These perplexing phenomena have not been confined merely to alternate periods of active and depressed business. A fundamental paradox has been evident throughout the post-war period. On the one hand, except for a relatively short interval, France has had practically no unemployment, and has witnessed a period of business expansion of almost unparalleled proportions; on the other hand, her financial situation has gone from bad to worse. Unsound financial conditions and good business have marched hand in hand. The necessity of restoring the devastated area appears to have been a blessing from an industrial point of view. In the work of reconstruction, millions of people have been given employment at good wages, business interests have reaped enormous profits, the industrial life of France has been restored, a new spirit of enterprise has been generated, and the material wealth of the country has increased since 1919 in a very remarkable way.

But these constructive developments have left a heritage of debt and currency disorders which now threaten the political and social as well as the financial stability of the country. If, somehow, the financial problems could be automatically wiped off the slate, the results of five years of post-war developments in France might be regarded as highly gratifying. Unfortunately, however, the financial factors are real, not imaginary, elements in the situation, and they can not be got around by any act of legerdemain.

The foregoing account of the perverseness of economic phenomena, of the apparent refusal of economic laws to operate as they are supposed to operate, explains in part why it has been so difficult for European statesmen to find a solution of post-war problems. What is one to do in the face of a situation where sound fiscal and banking policies and a return of exchange to pre-war parity is accompanied by business stagnation, as in England, while increased production and an industrial renaissance, as in France, leads to currency inflation, the fall of the exchanges, and general financial and economic instability?

The truth of the matter is that in all Europe statesmen have been confronted since the war with a baffling economic dilemma. Whichever way the harassed statesman has turned he has found himself confronted with difficulties. Whatever policy he has pursued developments of an untoward nature have followed. Each of the several possible alternatives has possessed its seamy side.

The dilemma is well illustrated by reference to the French problem at the beginning of 1924. If reconstruction activities were suspended in the interest of the government budget, and if business credits were curtailed in the interest of a sound banking situation, there would ensue a severe business depression, which would affect adversely both the budget and the international trade balance. On the other hand, if reconstruction activities were continued, and if abundance of credits were furnished to meet the requirements of the business boom, a currency crisis was certain to develop before many months, bringing in its train both trade and fiscal difficulties. In the early months of 1924 the dark side of the latter alternative was not clearly perceived by most people. Rather they noted merely the great activity of business, the absence of unemployment, and the "remarkable improvement of French trade conditions." But by the end of the year the chickens had come home to roost, and the dilemma could no longer be blinked.

Since every European country has in greater or less degree been confronted since the war with the same dilemma, it may prove helpful to compare very briefly post-war economic policies and developments in France, England, and Germany. While conditions differ materially in certain important respects in the several countries, the problems have been sufficiently alike to make comparisons fruitful.

*France has sought her way out of post-war diffi-
culties through the medium of credit.* The uses of
credit during the war period quite turned the .heads
of the statesmen of most countries. By means of
foreign borrowings and by internal credit inflation,
the belligerent nations of Europe were unexpectedly
able to maintain throughout the war a great volume
of business activity and for a considerable time reasonably good standards of living for the masses of
people as well. If credit could accomplish so much
during a period of destruction, what might it not
accomplish in connection with reconstruction activities? Little wonder that at the close of the war,
credit should have been looked upon as pretty much
the source of all economic power.

Since the war, France has in fact resorted to the
use of credit to an extent never dreamed of in pre-
war days. Not only has the government undertaken
to finance the reconstruction of the devastated areas
on credit, but it has employed its credit as a means
of carrying out many other national policies as well.
Not merely has the *national* government borrowed
on a greatly expanded scale, but the departments
and cities generally have borrowed large sums both
at home and abroad. Not only have *governments*,
national and local, proceeded to utilize credit for
the accomplishment of results that were deemed
economically desirable, but French industries have
borrowed for expansion, both by groups and as individual entities, in a way and to a degree that
would not have been considered for a moment in

former days. A striking result of this changed attitude about credit is found in the transformation of French banking practice, involving a much larger participation by French banks in financing industrial expansion than before the war.

In short, French reconstruction and industrial expansion have been accomplished, not in spite of unsound financial conditions, but by means of a vast orgy of credit and inflation. The greatest building boom in history has been carried through in the devastated areas almost entirely on credit, and one of the greatest periods of industrial expansion ever known in Europe has been financed largely on the basis of borrowed money, the bulk of which has come from domestic currency inflation. The reader will here recall the analysis of the preceding chapter showing that the greater part of the funds used have come indirectly from the Bank of France.

So long as an individual's credit is good, it is easy to keep up appearances. The casual observer will note that Mr. X has built a new house; that he has enlarged his store or factory; that he has recently purchased a new automobile; and that his wife and children are well dressed and move in the best of circles. Not until his credit is exhausted and no one will any longer accept his I.O.U's does the painful process of readjustment begin.

While the problems are not identical, the situation of a nation which for a time soars on the wings of credit is similar to that of an individual. The foreign borrowings of the nation are strictly analogous to the borrowings of the individual. But with domestic credit inflation the situation is different in that the wealth that is temporarily enjoyed is not procured at the expense of other countries. What happens is that the expansion of currency provides funds for carrying out domestic enterprises which could not otherwise be financed, and thus for a time increases the production of the country. Business activity is stimulated, and the full energy of the country is employed, and so long as the day of financial settlement can be postponed everything is outwardly satisfactory.

The post-war era has accordingly thus far not been economically very painful to France. There was temporary suffering, to be sure, for a year or so after the war, and at no time have conditions been such as to promote tranquillity of heart and peace of mind; but it is nevertheless true that French business as a whole has been prosperous since the war, with employment abundant and wages and earnings reasonably good. Despite complaints over high taxes and high costs of living generally, the average well-being in France, together with the industrial development, has been a source of much general satisfaction.

Great Britain has steadfastly resisted all temptation to resort to further borrowing. Except for a brief interval immediately after the war Britain has followed a policy of financial conservatism, even though it has meant a prolonged period of business depression and the grave social evil of a huge volume of unemployment. To be sure, the problem of balancing the budget was much easier in England than in France,[1] and it is true that England was not confronted with the problem of physical devastation. Accordingly, the British government was not under as much pressure to utilize credit as was the government of France.

Great Britain was, however, in great need of restoring her productive capacity, of expanding her foreign trade, and of raising the standard of living of her people, and no little pressure has been brought to bear upon the government to help promote these ends. Notwithstanding the disorganization of world markets, if the British government had been willing to utilize credit as the French government has done it would have been possible to avoid practically all unemployment during the past five years and to stimulate enormous business activity, accompanied by great constructive industrial developments. Concretely, it would have been possible, by floating government bonds and by borrowing bank notes from the Bank of England, to construct a tunnel under the British channel, to carry through a vast housing scheme for the laboring classes, and, through the aid of government subsidies, to place British industries in a greatly improved condition. Who can not think of innumerable ways in which economic improvements might have been instituted, if only funds had been avail-

[1] The tax burden in France has not been lower than in England as is commonly assumed. See discussion on pp. 55 and 191-2.

able for the purpose, and if the costs for the time
being could have been completely ignored?

Great Britain chose, rather, the painful method
of paying her way as she went. Though difficulties
enough remain, the brighter side of the picture is
that Britain now finds herself in a position of financial solvency, with the gold standard restored, with
exchange at par, and with her financial position in
the world pretty well re-established. Her general
economic condition may be expected to improve as
world conditions improve.

Let it be repeated again that it was much easier
for the British government to follow this policy
than it would have been for the French; and if England had been confronted with the problem of
devastated area, she too might have resorted to
credit as a means of providing rapid reconstruction,
whether or not ultimate reimbursement by Germany
was expected. We are not concerned with making
any invidious comparisons; we are merely interested
in explaining why in the one country business and
employment conditions have temporarily been good
while in the other country they have been bad.

*The German story resembles that of France rather
than that of Great Britain.* Hard pressed at the
close of the war, both on account of internal financial requirements and reparation obligations, the
German government followed a policy of credit and
currency inflation. While in the early post-war
years Germany could not borrow abroad through
the sale of bonds, she found available a great credit

resource in the desire of foreign speculators to purchase her paper money. In addition, she borrowed constantly from the central bank in the form of currency notes and thus provided funds to cover ordinary fiscal deficiencies and to stimulate industrial and trade recovery.

For a time business was very active, unemployment was negligible, and Germany was almost universally pointed to as the most prosperous nation in Europe. The optimistic financial literature of 1920-1922 and the glowing comments of tourists "just returned from Germany" make illuminating reading now. The most striking thing perhaps is the similarity to more recent discussions of the "wonderful prosperity" of France. In the end, the whole German financial and economic system was demoralized.

Thanks to the huge volume of new foreign credits which have been extended since the institution of the Dawes Plan, Germany appears once more to be in a reasonably good position—that is, if one ignores the acute difficulties that lie ahead in meeting, besides the reparation obligations, the interest on the new external debts that have been contracted. But we must return to the problem of France.

From the analysis that we have been making in this and preceding chapters, one thing ought to be entirely clear, namely, that the French financial problem is not to be solved by means of more credit. It is perhaps necessary to labor the point, however, in view of the fact that there is a strong possibility that an easy way out may still be sought through the medium of additional foreign loans. Austria has been granted large foreign loans for purposes of financial reconstruction. Germany has procured huge credits, both public and private, for the rehabilitation of her financial system. Various other continental countries have received loans of greater or smaller amounts. Great Britain has recently been granted credits amounting to $300,000,000 to be used, in case of need, in connection with the restoration of the gold standard. France herself has since the war been repeatedly tided over difficult financial crises by means of foreign loans. Why should she not therefore seek large additional foreign credits at the present time with a view to putting her finances on a solid foundation?

The answer is that France has been made sick by overdoses of credit, and additional doses can not now be expected to make her well. Each additional loan, whether foreign or domestic, adds to the annual interest obligations and increases the burden to be borne in subsequent years. Instead of going ever more deeply into debt, the French government must by some means or other reduce the debt charges.

Further foreign credits, unaccompanied by far-reaching fiscal reforms, would do more harm than good and only prolong yet a little the evil day ot reckoning. As a part of a program of exchange and currency stabilization, however, France may still need some small additional foreign credits; but further loans will not be merited, or forthcoming at moderate rates of interest, unless and until French fiscal affairs are put upon a secure foundation. The problem involved in stabilizing French finances is the subject of the following chapter.

CHAPTER IX

THERE IS A WAY OUT

WHILE it has not always been clearly appreciated, it has now come to be quite generally recognized that the balancing of the budget is the heart of the French problem. In whatever direction other indexes of conditions may temporarily point, there can be no real solution of French financial and economic difficulties until the government's revenues from non-borrowing sources are at least equal to the total of expenditures, ordinary, extraordinary, and extra-budgetary. That curious notion that the people can be permanently prosperous, even though the government be financially insolvent, is now fortunately dissipated. It has at last become reasonably clear to everyone that so long as large budget deficits remain, currency and exchange will be unstable and the whole financial, economic, political, and social life of the country will be in periodic upheaval. Accordingly, the one primary test for French statesmen to apply to alternative lines of policy is the effect upon the government budget.

The problem has both immediate and long-run phases. First, there is the preliminary task of mitigating the currency, exchange, and cost of living crises during the current year, when one can hope for no real improvement of the budget. Second, there is the constructive task of effecting a genuinely balanced budget in 1926 and subsequent years. These requirements will be considered in turn and the chapter will close with a discussion of the problem of stabilizing the foreign exchange and restoring the gold standard.

I. PRELIMINARY STEPS

Two major alternatives are open to French statesmen in the preliminary period: (1) to allow currency and credit inflation to continue in the interest of active business; or (2) to check inflation by means of high interest rates and the outright restriction of loans, both by banks for business purposes and by the government for reconstruction activities. Before indicating which of these alternatives is preferable, some of the more important results of each policy must be pointed out.

If inflation were allowed to continue, business would for a time remain active, foreign trade would be good, and taxation revenues would be relatively large. But the bond market would not be able to absorb the necessary flotations of government securities, and the Treasury would have to increase its direct borrowings from the Bank of France. All this would be accompanied by mounting prices and costs of production, wage and income maladjustments, and increasing disorganization of the whole financial system. The exchanges would be prevented from declining only by means of additional foreign loans, and then only temporarily.

The second alterative, namely, the contraction of credit, both public and private, would also, *for a time*, inevitably produce a very difficult situation. Certain definite results of a policy of credit restriction must be clearly envisaged. First, it would reduce the volume of internal production and business profits. Second, it would lessen the aggregate volume, and reduce the favorable balance of foreign trade, though it would not wipe out completely the present net income from trade and invisible items.[1] Third, it would result in unemployment. Finally, it would, for the time being, reduce government taxation receipts more than it would reduce expenditures.

The final point perhaps needs a word of explanation. There can be little doubt that a substantial curtailment of the volume of business, together with a fall in the level of prices of, say, 30 per cent, would immediately reduce the receipts from taxation by several billion francs, just as the opposite conditions increased them in 1924. Meanwhile, expenditures would not at once be automatically decreased by a like amount. While it might be possible in a period of falling prices to cancel the recent increase in pensions and in salaries of government employees, on the other hand it might prove necessary to increase outlays for relief work and to enlarge the subsidies to certain State enter-

[1] See table of international income, p. 33.

prises, the income from which would be reduced as a result of the business depression.

Hard and painful though the latter alternative may appear to be, it is undoubtedly the less painful horn of the dilemma. If France wants to go the road that Germany traveled in 1922-1923 and witness the obliteration of all public and private bond investments, with attending economic and social demoralization, the responsible officials have only to allow the forces that have been in operation during the past year to continue to operate for another year or so. All that is necessary for the government to do is to continue to resort to the Bank of France for the money with which to meet its ordinary deficits and to carry on the work of reconstruction.

The policy of putting the brakes on business by the contraction of credit [2] is the constructive alternative—notwithstanding the temporarily bad effects upon the budget—for the reason that it alone creates an opportunity to effect the changes that are necessary to bring the budget subsequently into balance.[3] The process of commercial deflation, as in 1921, would relieve the banking and currency crises,

[2] A business depression may, of course, come, as it did in 1920, without a vigorous policy of contraction being instituted by the government and banking officials. But if the policy of resorting to the Bank of France for funds with which to meet government deficits continues, such a business reaction is likely to prove of only moderate proportions, as was the case in Germany in 1921. Rising prices and falling exchanges will stimulate an active though increasingly unhealthy, state of business.

[3] For a discussion of the amount that could be cut off from the "recoverable budget," see p. 190 below.

increase the supply of floating funds, and lower interest rates. The resulting improvement in the market for securities would strengthen the government's credit position and reduce, if not eliminate, the necessity of further recourse to the Bank of France for advances in the form of note issues.

While this program in no sense constitutes a solution of the French financial problem, it offers the best possibility of arresting for the moment the process of currency and exchange depreciation, and of affording the Finance Minister an opportunity to attack the budget problem in a more fundamental way. The immediate phases of the program suggested are designed primarily with a view to giving the harassed statesmen an opportunity to turn around and formulate a longer time program. We turn now to a consideration of the problems involved in effecting a balanced budget the following year.

II. CAN THE BUDGET BE BALANCED?

It must be recalled at the outset that the deficit to be covered is not, as commonly supposed, a matter of three or four billion francs. In 1924 it was over 16 billion francs. In 1925, assuming that no important changes in fiscal policy become effective during the year, the deficit is likely to be somewhat increased, because of an expansion of government expenses—for payrolls, pensions, interest, and military outlays in Africa,—and a possible slight reduction of tax receipts in the event that the slackening of business activity noted in the early months becomes pronounced and general. Curtailment of expenses incident to reconstruction activities during the present year are not likely to counterbalance the increased outlays in other directions. On the whole, it would appear that a deficit of 18 billion francs for the year is not altogether improbable.[4]

In 1926, assuming that the preliminary policies suggested above are carried out, the deficit would still be at least 12 billion francs. The practical cessation of the work of physical reconstruction would cut off about 8 billion francs, but the decline in prices and business activity might easily reduce the

[4] While this book is in proof, the budget bill for 1925—after more than nine months of discussion—has finally been enacted into law. The figures presented show a nominal balance; but, as in previous years, many items of expenditure are omitted. In announcing the final figures, M. Bérenger, the Rapporteur Général of the Budget in the Senate, stated that: "The Budget is sincere in the form in which it has been presented; but between the Treasury and the annual Budget there is still a difference of several billions, including not only certain capital expenditures which do not belong to the Budget, but also certain disbursements which should be included in the Budget, which are still extra-budgetary." (Quoted in the *London Economist*, July 18, 1925.) According to the correspondent of the *Economist*, "Chief among these are of course the expenditure which still has to be faced in regard to the reconstitution of the devastated regions, and a large proportion of the necessary expenditure on war pensions." In other words, the French are still maintaining a budget fiction; and there is no reason to believe that the total government deficit for the year 1925 will not be quite as large as in 1924. (For a discussion of the various ways in which the 1924 budget proper came to be exceeded in the course of the year, see pp. 93-95.

yield of present taxes by two or three billion francs. At the same time necessary expenses for relief might be somewhat increased.   If the deficit did not exceed 12 billion francs—assuming no repudiation or cancellation of the domestic debt—the Finance Minister could consider himself fortunate indeed.[5]

A word of explanation is perhaps necessary for the estimate that the practical cessation of the work of physical reconstruction would reduce the "recoverable" expenditures by only 8 billion francs. It is commonly assumed that just as soon as the devastated areas have been restored, recoverable expenditures of some 16 billion francs a year will be completely eliminated.   The reader will, however, recall from the analysis in Chapter IV that the recoverable outlays include war pensions and interest on the accumulated reconstruction debt, as well as a large miscellany of relief outlays and certain administrative expenses of a continuing nature. These items, together with the costs of the troops of occupation, amounted in 1924 to approximately 8 billion francs.   The great bulk of such outlays will have to be continued indefinitely.

A. MISCELLANEOUS FISCAL REFORMS

Turning now to the possibilities of eliminating the remaining 12 billions of deficit, we must first consider what can be done by effecting miscellaneous fiscal reforms.   From a theoretical point of view, it is possible to bridge a gap of 12 billion francs, either

[5] See the discussion of the Caillaux program in Appendix G.

by increasing taxes 12 billions, by reducing expenditures 12 billions, or by working from both ends toward the middle. We shall take up each angle of the problem in turn, beginning with the possibilities of an increase in taxes.

There is no truth whatever in the prevalent assumption abroad that the French people do not and will not pay taxes. The facts completely contradict this contention, which has been repeated so often that it has come to be almost universally believed. The French tax burden was relatively heavy before the war as compared with other countries,[6] and it has been very heavily increased since 1913. We refer to collections and not merely to the rates that are levied. The revenues derived by the national government in 1924 from taxes and fiscal monopolies equalled 27.1 billion francs, and the taxes of the departments and communes amounted to about 3 billion francs, making a total of 30 billion francs. Since the national income in that year was only 145 billion francs [7] it will be seen that the French people paid in taxes fully 20 per cent of their income. National taxes alone represent nearly 19 per cent of the national income.

This compares not unfavorably with Great Britain, where taxes of the central government are estimated to take roughly 18.5 per cent of the national income,[8] or, for that matter, with the United States

[6] See pp. 54-5.
[7] See Appendix C.
[8] London *Economist*, April 5, 1924, p. 726.

where the total taxes—national, state, and local—
absorbed in 1923 about 11.5 per cent of the national
income.[9] And if one bears in mind that the national
income in the United States is about $605 per capita,
in Great Britain $395 per capita, and in France only
about $195 per capita, it will be evident that the tax
burden in France is indeed a heavy one. The absence of any considerable number of very large fortunes in France on which very high rates can be
levied makes the burden on the average man the
more onerous.

When a tax burden rises as high as 20 per cent of
the national income it becomes difficult to collect
additional taxes without incurring excessive administration costs. At the same time, the mere levying
of higher taxes may produce unfortunate economic
consequences. The following statement from the
1924 annual report of a French banking house, the
Société Générale, is certainly not without some
truth.[10]

. May we be permitted to remark that the tax charges to which
our country today finds itself subjected have attained a scale such
that the fiscal mechanism must of necessity be handled with in-
finite caution and a profound knowledge of its repercussions, if we
are not to see the taxable material shrink, and therefore the prospect of equilibrium vanish anew?

While a 40 per cent increase of taxes, such as
would be required to balance the budget by that
means, cannot possibly be expected, is it not still

[9] *Tax Burdens and Public Expenditures*, Publication of National
Industrial Conference Board, 1925, p. 12.
[10] The *Statist*, April 11, 1925, p. 593.

true that the tax revenues can be materially increased? Are there not wholesale evasions that could readily be checked? Can not the farmers be forced to contribute more? Will not the devastated areas when reconstructed yield much larger revenues?

With reference to the first question, it is of course not to be denied that evasion is all too common an evil in France, as in other countries where the burden is heavy: high taxes stimulate evasion. But the figures of actual collections in France constitute the best proof that the evasion evil has been very greatly magnified in public discussions. Let is be repeated that the actual *collections* equal 20 per cent of the national income. The inevitable conclusion is that although in the course of time the fiscal machinery can no doubt be improved and evasions lessened, no early improvement of the budget situation is to be found in this direction.

Nor is there any denying that the agricultural class in France, as in other countries, constitutes a potential source of increased tax revenues. But devising economical means of collecting such income is a difficult problem. Levying heavier taxes on the agricultural class is no new thought to French Ministers of Finance. Ways and means of accomplishing the desired end have been discussed repeatedly, and indeed for the last two or three years almost continuously. Gradually and eventually something may be accomplished; but this and next year's budget difficulties are not thus to be solved.

The reconstruction of the devastated areas has long been looked to as a source of an eventual increase in tax revenues. And indeed the tax returns from those departments have shown a gratifying increase since the war. In 1923, the 10 devastated departments produced roughly 20 per cent of the total taxes, while in 1913, the same departments produced only 16 per cent of the total. There is no ground for believing that the revenues of these departments will increase much, if any, during the next two or three years. As the enormous activity and large business profits resulting from the great construction boom disappear, to be followed perhaps by a period of depression, the revenues may for a time be less than they were in 1923.[11]

Similarly, higher indirect tax levies afford no avenue of escape from present fiscal difficulties. Such taxes are customarily shifted to the ultimate consumers of the goods on which the duties are levied —and the consumers are already near the point of revolt over the rising cost of living. Moreover, the pyramiding of prices following the increase of taxes in the spring of 1924 helped to bring on the banking and currency crisis that developed before the end of that year.

The most that can reasonably be expected in the near future from increases of present tax rates and

[11] At the time of writing the figures for 1924 are not available. For 1923 figures, see *Documents Parlêmentaires, Chambre*, 1924, p. 364. For 1913 data, see *Bulletin de Statistique et de Législation Comparée*, February, 1914, pp. 326-33; May, 1914, pp. 636-9; June, 1914, pp. 740-5.

improved collections is perhaps 2 billions of francs, leaving a deficit of 10 billion francs to be eliminated by other means. Additional tax revenues may, however, be derived from a new form of direct tax, to be discussed after we have described the general fiscal plan which it is believed offers the best chance of procuring a balanced budget. In the meantime, we must turn to a consideration of the problem of reducing expenditures.

Expenditures can be reduced but little by means of the economies that are ordinarily suggested. Total expenditures in 1924 amounted to about 45.5 billion francs. In the table given at the top of page 196 these outlays are classified into five broad groups without reference to their division into ordinary, recoverable, and extra-budgetary expenditures.[12]

[12] The interest item apparently includes about a billion and a half francs of amortization charges. The military charges are computed from *Journal officiel* (*lois et décrets*), April 9, 1925, pp. 3647-8. The total credits granted under the ordinary budget to the Minister of War were 5,247 millions; to the Minister of Marine, 1,673 millions. In a special treasury account for Troops of Occupation is an item of 661 millions, and in the recoverable budget an item of 31 millions under the administration of the Minister of War. These items together total 7,639 million francs. In this figure no allowance is made for some millions of credits opened for military expenses in the colonies and for military pensions.

The figure of eight billions for physical reconstruction is explained on page 190 of the text. The outlays for civil expenditures represent the remainder of the 45.5 billions. They include besides the regular outlays for the Civil departments the net deficits from operation of State enterprises and various miscellaneous recoverable and extraordinary expenditures.

	Billions of Francs
Interest on the public debt........	16.5
Pensions	3.6
Military charges.................	7.6
Civil expenditures...............	9.8
Physical reconstruction...........	8.0
Total	45.5

It will be apparent from a moment's reflection that such suggestions as that the government should sell its present buildings and move into cheaper quarters, if carried out, would have scarcely a perceptible effect upon the budget. Similarly, the elimination of loans to Poland and other buffer states would be of a little more importance, for the effects of such loans upon the budget have thus far been of negligible importance. The total of such loans from 1919 to the end of 1924 aggregated about 4 billion francs.[13] The great bulk, however, represented not money outlays at all; but the sale of excess second-hand war supplies which would otherwise have been practically a net loss. The charges so frequently heard that France has been able to find huge sums with which to finance her post-war political allies but none with which to pay her debts, are of a piece with many of the charges previously made against Germany. While in the future such loans might conceivably impose a considerable burden upon the budget, up to the present time they have been of quite negligible importance from the fiscal point of view.

[13] See Appendix A, p. 364.

The expenditures for Civil Services can be reduced but little if at all. The government payrolls in France are not greatly padded, and the salaries paid are all too inadequate. Indeed, the expenditures of the Civil Services—allowing for the change in the level of prices—are only a little larger now than in 1913, despite the greatly increased scope of government activities.

The sale of state enterprises—posts, telegraphs, and telephones, and the railroads—to private interests is frequently urged as an important means of eliminating the budget deficits. In this connection, two pertinent questions at once present themselves. First, how much would thus be saved, and second, can the transfer of these properties to private hands be accomplished in the near future?

The deficits incurred on account of the posts, telegraphs, and telephones, is negligible, amounting in 1923 to only a little more than three million francs; [14] they may therefore be dismissed from consideration. The deficits in connection with the state railways amounted to 1,115 millions in 1923, and thanks to the great volume of business activity, the provisional figures for 1924 show a deficit of only 458 millions.[15] The saving effected by a complete elimination of the deficit would thus not go far toward balancing the state budget.

[14] M. Clémentel, *Inventaire*, p. 101.
[15] The railway deficits for a period of years have been as follows (figures in millions of francs):

1913	79	1919	1,212	1921	2,027
1918	480	1920	2,794	1922	1,147

The second question, whether any private parties can be found willing to undergo the risk of operating the railways at a loss can not, of course, be definitely answered. The railways of France are in part privately and in part publicly owned and operated. This mixed system is the outgrowth of a long, history of co-operation between the government and private enterprise in the development of railway transportation, dating as far back as 1842. The situation is thus a very complex one, and the equities involved as between the public, the government, and the private railways would be extremely difficult to adjust in any thoroughgoing reorganization of the whole transportation system. Moreover, the roads that are operated by the government are in direct competition with private lines and they do not appear to offer an attractive opportunity to private enterprise. Not until there is some reason to believe that they could be made to yield profits will the government be able to get rid of them. The simple expedient of raising rates will not do, for the repercussions elsewhere in the economic and financial system might more than counterbalance the fiscal gains from the reduction of operating deficits. All that can be hoped for is a gradual elimination of the remaining railway deficits.[16]

[16] In this connection the recent Italian experiment is interesting. Although the Italian dictator gave to the railroad administration *carte blanche* in instituting extensive reductions in personnel and in suppressing all unprofitable services, quite regardless of the interests of particular groups or political constituencies, more than

Could not pensions be abolished or greatly reduced? The answer here must be an unqualified negative. The pension system in France is by no means over-generous; and for political and social reasons a reduction of rates is out of the question. Only gradually, as present pensioners pass away and are not replaced by new ones, can the pension bill—which now amounts to about 3.8 billion francs —be reduced.

The reduction of military expenditures has of course often been suggested as the one outstanding remedy for the budget situation. How much are the military outlays, in fact? According to the computation above (see footnote page 195), the total military expenditures in 1924 amounted to about 7.6 billion francs, including an important item for police service. It is clear, therefore, that if the military expenditures could be completely eliminated and the soldiery transferred to productive operations, budgetary difficulties would be on the highroad to solution.

While no one seriously believes that France could think of completely disarming, unless other nations did so simultaneously, many contend that she could and should greatly reduce her military establishment. It is undoubtedly true that France has since the war been more disposed to seek the maintenance and improvement of her general position through

two years will have been necessary to wipe out the railway deficit. For a full discussion of this experiment the reader must be referred to a forthcoming publication of the Institute of Economics on the Italian financial problem.

the show of military strength than have most other countries; but it does not follow that any considerable reduction of military outlays can now suddenly be effected. A 20 per cent curtailment of military expenses within the next few years is all that can reasonably be hoped for—in the absence of a security pact and an international agreement for a reduction of armaments. Incidentally, it may be noted that the outlays in 1924, making allowances for the depreciation of the currency, were no greater than in 1913. A 20 per cent reduction would save approximately 1.5 billion francs.

All told it is difficult to see how expenditures could be reduced by more than 2 billion francs. After these miscellaneous fiscal reforms are effected, therefore, the budget deficit would still remain at roughly 8 billion francs. In these estimates it is assumed that no larger reparation instalments than 'those now being received will be forthcoming and that no interest on the foreign political debt is to be paid.[17] We do not allow for larger reparation receipts simply because Germany has as yet demonstrated no capacity to develop an export surplus,[18] and because the interest on the $200,000,000 reconstruction loan has a definitely established priority to

[17] See Chapter XII for a discussion of these debts.

[18] The trade deficit was 2,770,000,000 gold marks in 1924. During the first three months of 1925 it was 1,479 million gold marks. The excess has been covered by the return of liquid funds sent abroad at the time of the depreciation of the mark, and by the huge foreign loans procured since the inauguration of the Dawes plan.

whatever export surplus may be developed. In practice, also, the interest on the large foreign loans recently procured by German private interests is likely to come ahead of reparation payments. Accordingly, we do not believe that the Finance Minister should count on reparation receipts as an important source of revenue.

No series of minor reforms will effect a solution of France's financial problem; a major operation is required. Only by means of a drastic reduction in the interest account can the budget be brought into balance. In the absence of a heavy reduction of the debt charges the following things will undoubtedly occur: (1) The budget will remain heavily unbalanced. (2) Additional borrowing from the Bank of France will be necessary. (3) Currency will further depreciate and exchange will decline. (4) In due course existing government bonds will become practically worthless. (5) In the process, private bond investments and mortgages will also be destroyed.

The involuntary obliteration of domestic debts both public and private by the processes of inflation is the line of least resistance. But it is also the line of maximum cost and sacrifice.

Several means of reducing the interest charge on the public debt have been suggested. The two most commonly favored are, first, ordinary refunding of the debt at lower rates of interest, and second, a capital levy, the proceeds of which would be de-

voted to a reduction of interest charges. The possibilities of each must be briefly considered.

B. REFUNDING NOT A REMEDY

Refunding at lower rates of interest is the usual
and approved means of reducing interest charges.
The process involves issuing new bonds—usually
long-term bonds—bearing a lower rate of interest
and using the proceeds to pay off outstanding obligations—mainly the floating debt—bearing a high
rate of interest. Great Britain and the United
States, for example, have effected large savings in
interest since the war by such refunding operations.

The possibility of refunding at lower rates has
been given much consideration by French finan-
ciers, and it has been hoped that in due course refunding operations on a large scale might be put
through. This was particularly the case in the
summer of 1924, when the franc had been temporarily stabilized and business conditions appeared so
generally favorable. But the resulting commercial
expansion, which absorbed the supply of liquid capital, dried up the bond market, and raised interest
rates, has rendered any such operations—for the
time being—quite out of the question.

This method of reducing interest charges is, however, still looked to by many people as a genuine
solution of the budget problem. It may well be
asked whether in the event of a business reaction
which would release funds from commercial operations, reduce interest rates and once more enliven

the bond market, it would not be possible to put out a large consolidation loan at a rate of interest substantially below rates now prevailing. It is urged that if a large part of this loan were floated abroad a twofold purpose would be accomplished. It would not only reduce the interest burden of the government, but it would also enable the French banking institutions, which now hold so large a volume of government obligations, to liquidate some of their holdings, thus improving the general banking and currency situation.

The domestic debt, it may be recalled, consists of three classes (exclusive of the pension debt); the perpetual or long-term, the short-term, and the floating debt. For convenience, the figures previously presented (for November 30, 1924) are reproduced at this place.

	Millions of Francs
Perpetual debt	153,716.9
Short-term	39,845.0
Floating debt	90,688.4
Total	284,250.3 [a]

[a] For a detailed classification of this debt, see Appendix D.

Of the perpetual debt, 22.6 billion francs bear a rate of 3 per cent; 29.7 billions, a rate of 4 per cent; 34.6 billions, a rate of 5 per cent; 17.3 billions, a rate of 5.5 per cent; and 27.4 billions, a rate of 6 per cent. The rest of the perpetual debt represents the value of annuities capitalized at rates varying from 5 to 7 per cent. The interest on the short-term debt

averages close to 6 per cent, and the same is true of
the floating debt, with the exception of the loans
from the Bank of France, which were procured during the war period at the nominal rate of 1 per
cent. Taking the domestic debt as a whole the interest averages somewhere near 5 per cent.[19]

To effect a reduction of 8 billion francs in the interest charge would require a refunding of the entire
public debt at rates much lower than those now prevailing. It is apparent from the figure given above
that the bulk of the long-term debt could not be refunded by ordinary refunding processes at rates any
lower than those which now exist. Nor is there the
slightest possibility that the rest of the debt—even
under the conditions that would prevail after the
preliminary part of the program that has been suggested above is in operation—could be voluntarily
refunded at rates much below 5 per cent. In this
connection it should be noted that there is a vital
contrast between the French situation and that
existing in Great Britain and the United States.
The difference lies precisely in the fact that since the
war the latter countries have had their budgets in
balance and have therefore not continuously flooded
the markets with new issues of securities.

The price at which government bonds can be marketed depends in part upon the abundance of liquid

[19] The reader will bear in mind in this connection that this is
merely the nominal rate on the face value of the securities. The
real cost of borrowing to the government, as shown in Chapter V,
has recently been as high as 8.62 per cent.

funds available, and in part upon the degree of risk
of non-payment involved. From neither standpoint
is there any reason to believe that the French fiscal
problem can be solved by ordinary refunding
operations.

C. A CAPITAL LEVY NOT A REMEDY

A second method of reducing the interest charge
is by means of a capital levy. A levy on capital in
the strict sense of the term means collecting a tax
on a certain percentage of the *capital* of an individual or corporation rather than a certain percentage of the *income*. It is understood that such a
levy is for the emergency only, and therefore is not
to recur.

Some part of the proceeds of a capital levy would
have to be used to wipe out the deficit for the
year 1926, which would amount, as we have seen, to
roughly 8 billion francs after all possible tax
increases and reductions of expenditures had been
effected. The amount available for liquidating outstanding bond and bill obligations of the government would, therefore, be represented by the
amount that could be raised in excess of 8 billions. The total domestic debt in November, 1924,
was 284 billion francs, and by the end of 1925 it will
amount to approximately 300 billion francs. To cut
the interest charge in two it would, therefore, be
necessary to raise well over 150 billion francs, a sum
greater than the entire national income of 145
billions.

Since great sections of the population would be automatically excluded by necessary exemption provisions from the operation of the capital levy, the burden on the corporations and individuals on which it would fall would be a crushing one. It would have to rise as high as 40 or 50 per cent of the capital. A tax of even 10 per cent on the capital of business enterprises, levied at a time when the supply of liquid funds is all too inadequate for commercial requirements, would inevitably produce grave business consequences. Vast sums can not suddenly be collected from one section of the community and transferred to another without seriously dislocating the economic life of the country. Permitting industrial bonds or property to be turned over to the government in lieu of cash would by no means eliminate the economic dislocations involved in the scheme.

From an administrative point of view a capital levy of large proportions is also practically impossible. A large increase in treasury personnel would be required, and the costs of collection would be enormous. At the same time, liquid funds would be converted into foreign currency for deposit abroad and wholesale evasions would be inevitable. An indication of what would occur if a genuine levy on capital were instituted was furnished by the popular reaction to the so-called capital levy advanced by the Herriot régime. Although the proposal was in reality only a forced loan, as those contributing were to receive interest at 3 per cent, capi-

tal began to flow from the country "by automobile
and aeroplane" as well as by more normal processes
of depositing the proceeds of exports in foreign
banks.

D. A POSSIBLE BUDGET REMEDY

There is a third method which from an economic
point of view offers a real possibility of balancing
the budget. It embodies two features: (1) an arbitrary reduction of the interest payable on the entire
internal debt to a flat rate of 2 per cent, and (2) the
levying of a special surtax on high incomes. Each
part of the plan requires explanation as well as
justification.

A rough computation shows that if interest were
paid at only 2 per cent on the par value of all outstanding government securities,—long-term, short-
term, and floating,—the annual interest charges
would be reduced by approximately 7.5 billion
francs. This reduction would not, of course, apply
to the bulk of the loans from the Bank of France,
which were procured at a rate of 1 per cent, nor
would it affect the annuities.

Since the outstanding issues bear nominal rates of
interest varying from 3 to 6 per cent, it is obvious
that under this method the rates will be reduced
more on some issues than on others. While no
method of reducing the interest charge would be
free from inequities as among the holders of different issues, this third plan works in the direction of
equity in that the holders of the earlier low-rate is-

sues have already sustained heavy sacrifices as a result of the depreciation of the franc.[20]

This plan simply recognizes that the people's corporation known as the French government is unable to meet its obligations is full and that accordingly the people must for the time being accept smaller dividends, so to speak. The heavy sacrifices of hard-earned savings involved in this plan will naturally lead to strenuous objections; but such objections reflect dislike of the disease, rather than of the remedy. The preceding analysis has shown that a major operation is required; and it must be taken without an anesthetic. The alternative is financial gangrene.

In the course of a few years conditions may possibly be sufficiently improved to warrant a restoration of higher rates. Accordingly, the plan should be viewed as an emergency measure, one that may be subsequently modified. It would be well to provide, however, that the reduction of interest rates should remain in effect for a five-year period, at the end of which time the whole situation would be reconsidered.

It is useful to recall in this connection that once before in French history—late in September, 1797—heroic measures were required to restore financial stability. At that time French paper currency had fallen in value practically to zero, and all roads to

[20] An alternative method sometimes suggested is to compute current interest rates on the market, rather than on the face, value of the different issues. For the purpose here in hand the method is open to the prime objection that it would not reduce the total interest charges sufficiently.

reform were blocked by the large internal debt of the country. The remedy resorted to at that time was virtual cancellation of two-thirds of the debt, that is to say, the government paid the bondholders, in worthless assignats, for two-thirds of their holdings.[21] This method accomplished the same result as the one here discussed for the present emergency; but it is a method not so easily administered, and one that practically closes the door to a subsequent revision.

It remains to inquire whether a reduction of interest payments to the extent of 7.5 billion francs would not proportionately reduce the taxes that could be collected. That is to say, if the French people received 7.5 billions less in the form of interest, would not their capacity to pay taxes be reduced by an equal amount? While it is impossible to calculate the net effects upon the reduction of taxes, it is safe to assume that the collections will not be reduced by more than 1 billion francs at the outside. The farmers would undoubtedly pay quite as large taxes as now. It is also undoubtedly true that the banks can stand heavier taxes than they are now paying. In fact, the reduction of the interest rate is at bottom merely a device for collecting more taxes from these groups than they are now paying.

When it comes to the middle classes, however, the taxes might be reduced somewhat—to the extent

[21] The law covering this transaction was dated 9th Vendémiaire, year VI. Allix, Edgar, *Traité élémentaire de science des finances*, 1921, p. 535.

that the loss of interest reduces consumption and the indirect taxes levied thereon. In this connection it should be borne in mind, however, that a comparatively small percentage of the bondholders live entirely on interest from government securities; the great majority have some other means of support. In the light of these considerations it is apparent that the elimination of 7.5 billions of interest will not very greatly reduce the total tax revenues. If it reduced them by as much as 1 billion francs the net budget saving would be 6.5 billion francs, leaving a deficit of 1.5 billions still to be covered.

With what justice would a reduction of interest on government bonds work out as among the various classes in society? Would it not be putting the whole burden upon the bond-holding class as such? In other words, would not those who have patriotically furnished the funds with which to carry the government along in its hours of adversity now be made to hold the bag while other members of •society escaped? There can be no denying the fact that the sacrifice would fall somewhat more heavily upon certain classes than upon others, and it is for this reason that a special surtax on large incomes is suggested as a supplementary and corrective measure. But first let us appraise, as well as may be, the way in which the different classes in France would be affected by a reduction in the interest rate.

As everyone is aware, the ownership of government securities is more widely distributed in France than in any other country. Consequently, the great majority of people would sustain some sacrifice. The important bond-holding groups are (1) the farmers, (2) the banks, and (3) the middle classes, including savings banks and co-operative associa-tions. The farmers have long invested the bulk of their savings in government *rentes*, and the middle classes have done the same. Since the war, as we have seen in Chapter VI, the banks have purchased enormous quantities of government securities and now hold no small percentage of the total. These are the classes, therefore, which would be hardest hit.

Since the farmers have not borne as heavy a tax burden as other classes in France, it is only fair that they should now contribute to the common cause by sustaining a loss on their government securities. It is likewise equitable that the banks should take a sacrifice in this way. Owing to the enormous vol-ume of financial operations in France during the last few years, including transactions in govern-ment securities, the banks have earned unusually high profits. They are therefore in a relatively strong position to make this sacrifice. The only antidote to the pain involved for farmers and bank-ers in writing off 60 or 70 per cent of the nominal value of these securities, is the reflection that the alternative is a gradual writing off, as a result of inflation, of 100 per cent of the value of both gov-ernment and private securities.

With the middle classes and the savings and co-operative institutions, however, a reduction of interest on government bonds is a very serious matter. The multitude of small shopkeepers, the salaried man, the widow and orphan, the young lady with her *dot*—all will be hard hit. The high indirect taxes have borne heavily upon these classes, who have likewise suffered reductions in income because of the shrinkage in the purchasing power of the franc. The savings banks, co-operative societies, and kindred institutions will also be seriously affected if the interest on government bonds is thus reduced.

While the plan will impose a heavy and perhaps unjustifiable burden upon these classes, the other alternative—complete obliteration of the value of all securities through inflation—is worse. There is moreover a partial offsetting gain to this class. A 30 per cent fall in prices incident to the program of business and financial stabilization discussed below, would to some degree compensate these groups for the loss of interest. Each franc received would purchase substantially more than has been the case during the past year, at least.

A special surtax on high incomes is necessary to equalize the financial burden sustained by different groups. Under this third plan industrial and commercial establishments and individuals with very high incomes would not be bearing their proportionate share of the burdens involved. The members of this group are typically not large holders of securities, and it is for this reason that we suggest the levying of a special surtax on large corporate and individual incomes. The existing direct taxes should be retained, with the surtax levied with a view to imposing a substantially heavier burden upon those who would not be seriously affected by the reduction of the interest rate. If effectively administered, such a tax would, it is believed, yield close to 2 billion francs. The administrative details of the plan need not be discussed, for we are here concerned only with the general principles involved.

This surtax is necessary simply because it is clear that any plan of financial reorganization, to be acceptable, must require all the major groups of society to make a substantial sacrifice for the common good. It is believed that the plan outlined comes as near to attaining this goal as any that can be devised, although a detailed study of the incidence of present taxes and the distribution of the public debt would, perhaps, suggest certain refinements of the plan that would be calculated to distribute even more equitably the burdens involved.

The administration of the plan would be neither difficult nor costly. Unlike a capital levy, the reduction of interest, once authorized, is easily administered. There is no possibility of evading the reduction of interest; the dividend declared is simply 2 per cent and there is no recourse. It would be necessary, however, to compel the refunding of all bonds maturing during the life of the plan, since to pay them off would require the sale of new bonds at higher market rates of interest.

Nothing would be gained by sending bonds out of the country. Everyone, in short, would have to take his full goblet of medicine, just as is the case when a private corporation can not pay dividends in full. At the same time it is apparent that the cost of administration would be practically zero.

The administration of the surtax on incomes is, of course, another matter. It would be necessary to collect this revenue, and evasions would no doubt be attempted. But if the real gravity of the present financial situation, together with the alternatives, were made clear to the public, and a well-rounded constructive plan giving genuine promise of placing France once more upon a sound financial basis were presented, it is believed that the administration of a surtax would be reasonably successful. Until a comprehensive plan, conceived on broad lines and with a view to distributing the burden with some approach to equity among all classes in society, is presented, one can hardly expect much financial patriotism to be manifested.

The means of balancing the budget under this plan may now be summarized. Starting with a probable deficit of 12 billion francs, after eliminating outlays for physical reconstruction, the deficit would be met in the following ways:

Increase in existing taxes...................	2.0	billions
Special surtax on large corporate and individual incomes	1.5	"
Reduction of ordinary expenditures.........	2.0	"
Reduction of interest on domestic debt......	6.5	"
Total	12.0	"

No one recognizes more clearly than the authors the uncertain character of some of the estimates made. In the very nature of the case estimates of increased revenues and decreased expenditures, except in the case of the reduction of the interest item, can be but tentative—dependent as they are upon economic, social, and political considerations which are incapable of precise appraisal. It is reasonably certain, nevertheless, that *there is a way out* for France along the lines here indicated. Whether the French government and the French people are willing to take it is another question upon which some light may be shed by the political and social appraisal of the French point of view, which is the subject of the following chapter.

III. THE STABILIZATION OF THE FRANC

The finances of France will not have finally been placed upon a satisfactory basis until foreign exchange has been stabilized and the gold standard has been restored. Fortunately, these parts of the program of financial rehabilitation are not very difficult of solution once the fiscal reforms discussed in the preceding sections of this chapter have been successfully carried out.

The stabilization of foreign exchange depends upon two primary conditions: (1) a balanced state of international trade and financial relations, and (2) a balanced domestic budget and the cessation of internal borrowing. So long as the balance of accounts is adverse—and can not be met by gold shipments—and so long as the government continues to cover large operating deficits by borrowing either at home or abroad, foreign exchange rates are certain to fall. With either the budget or international trade unbalanced, pegging operations through the medium of credit can only temporarily arrest a decline. These are elementary principles of finance.

At the present time France fortunately possesses a favorable balance in her international trade and financial accounts. Accordingly, if the fiscal reforms outlined above are instituted and prove successful, the problem of exchange stability will automatically be solved. While some temporary difficulties might be encountered, they can readily be encompassed by means presently to be discussed. For the moment, it is sufficient to recognize that a balanced international trade and financial situation and a balanced domestic budget constitute the two fundamental requisites for a stable franc in the foreign exchange markets.[22]

There still remains for consideration the rate at which the exchange should be stabilized. Should the value of the paper franc be fixed at three, five, or seven cents? Should it not be raised to the old pre-war parity with the dollar at 19.3 cents? To answer this question it is necessary to appraise a number of very important commercial, banking, and fiscal considerations which are involved.

[22] The relation of the foreign debt to the problem in hand will be discussed in Chapter XI.

A return to the pre-war parity of exchange—if possible of accomplishment—would mean economic suicide for France. It would involve a reduction of commodity prices almost to pre-war levels, attended by intense business depression. If the return were made by gradual stages, as is usually suggested should be the case, it would only protract the commercial and industrial agony involved. The reduction in prices would necessarily be accompanied by a decline in wages, salaries, and profits (as measured in money terms); and the tax receipts would in consequence be cut almost to one-fourth their present totals without any coresponding decline in interest charges. In other words, the burden of the public debt would be very greatly increased for the reason that a large part of it was contracted when the franc was worth from five to nine cents. All this is, of course, merely equivalent to saying that a return to the pre-war par of exchange is, in fact, an economic impossibility.

Financial stabilization will best be promoted if the value of the franc is fixed at about one-third the pre-war exchange parity, or at 6.43 cents. The raising of the franc to 6.43 cents would not only more evenly distribute the losses and sacrifices involved in the balancing of the budget, but it would be accompanied by developments that would greatly strengthen the general financial and business situation. Although the problems involved have already been touched upon in connection with the analysis of the budget, they require elaboration and emphasis here.

In the first place, the great rise in prices during the past year has, as we have seen, led to a note issue crisis at the Bank of France, a shortage of liquid funds, and high interest rates. A reduction of prices of approximately 30 per cent, which would be involved in stabilizing the franc at 6.43 cents, would lead to a great improvement in the financial situation. A period of deflation would strengthen the condition of the banks, relieve the present currency shortage, lower the rates on commercial loans, enlarge the capacity of the bond market, and provide a basis for sound financial development. This, it may be recalled, is precisely what happened in 1920-1921, not only in France but in the United States and other countries as well. It is what must occur now if the French banking and currency situation is again to be placed on a solid foundation.

The business depression attending a price deflation of 30 per cent would doubtless be somewhat less severe and less protracted than that of 1920-1922, when wholesale prices fell from 588 in April, 1920, to 306 in January, 1922. A period of liquidation is the price which must be paid, if the French banking, currency, and bond market crisis is to be relieved and a sound financial condition restored.

In the second place, a reduction in prices of roughly 30 per cent would greatly mitigate the serious cost of living crisis at the present time and thus help to make the acceptance of a reduction in the

rate of interest on government securities palatable
to the middle classes.   It has already been shown,
moreover, that a substantial reduction in prices is
necessary for anything approaching an equitable
distribution of the financial sacrifices involved in restoring sound financial conditions.

*The restoration of the gold standard is the final
step in the program of financial rehabilitation.*
Once the budget, as well as international trade and
finance, is in a condition of stable equilibrium, a
return to the gold standard would present no in-
superable obstacle.   The paper franc would not, of
course, be made exchangeable for gold—franc for
franc—but only at the rate of three francs paper to
one franc of gold.   The question then is, Does the
Bank of France possess a sufficient supply of gold
to make such a redemption possible?

The total outstanding note issue of the Bank of
France at the present time is approximately 43
billion francs, while the total specie reserve is about
four billion francs.   With the paper exchangeable
at a value of 6.43 instead of 19.3 cents to the
gold franc, this reserve is equivalent to nearly 30
per cent.   While this is a relatively low reserve as
compared with what the Bank of France maintained
before the war, it is higher than the banks of the
United States maintained before the establishment
of the Federal Reserve System; it is higher than the
reserve of the new Reichsbank; and it is as high as
was the reserve of the Bank of England when the
gold standard was recently re-established.   It is

quite high enough to enable France to return to the gold standard,—provided the period of transition can be safely traversed.

Provision must, however, also be made for a resumption of the free international movement of gold. That is to say, France can not maintain the gold standard unless foreign bills of exchange, as well as domestic paper francs, are payable in gold upon demand. It is impossible to enter upon a discussion of the technical phases of this problem; and it must suffice to state that until gold is allowed to flow out of the country whenever there are adverse balances to be met, the gold standard will not have been fully restored.

As a safeguard against possible heavy withdrawals of gold, either for hoarding at home, or for export abroad, France would perhaps have to be granted some foreign credits during the transition period. There is not the slightest doubt that such credits would be readily forthcoming—and on reasonable terms—if thoroughgoing fiscal and financial reforms of the kind discussed in this chapter are instituted. Otherwise, they will be neither deserved nor forthcoming.

CHAPTER X

THE FRENCH POINT OF VIEW *

THE preceding chapters have endeavored to present the story of French finance in all its essential aspects. They portray the changes which have taken place in the economic situation of France as producer and trader, investor and borrower, and reveal the close interrelations between international finance, government budget, currency and exchange, and the condition of French trade and industry. In the light of this analysis, a plan was outlined which from an economic point of view seems to offer a way out of the present difficulties.

Whether such a plan can be accepted in France depends upon conditions which to a large extent are not financial in character. This has been clearly shown in the last few months during which the French people have been considering their economic and financial difficulties most earnestly. Every financial proposal which has been advanced in the course of this discussion has been entangled with political ideas and has been affected by fears and hopes which spring not so much from financial as from general economic, political, and social condi-

* This chapter has been written by Dr. Louis Levine.

221

tions. The present chapter seeks to link the French financial problem to French life as a whole by setting forth these conditions which go to make what may be called the "French point of view."

The fact of primary importance is that there is not one but several points of view in France. This is evidenced by the very multiplicity of financial programs. Only to a limited degree is such multiplicity the result of the usual and inevitable disagreement among individuals on matters of economic principle and policy. To a much larger extent, it is due to the divergence of ideas and interests among the various elements of the French people. That is, the various groups of the population look at the realities of finance through the prism of ideas and interests which have become bound up with their economic and social existence. The study of the French point of view thus resolves itself into a study of the way in which the social problems and the mental attitudes of the separate groups of the population affect the current proposals for the "financial purification" of France.

I. ECONOMIC AND SOCIAL GROUPS AND PROBLEMS

One may distinguish five more or less well-recognized economic and social groups in France. (1) There is the peasantry, which is generally held to include the small landowners, the small farmers who lease the land of the large landowners on a cash or sharing basis, and a considerable number of agricultural laborers who own a small plot of ground.

(2) There is the *petite bourgeoisie,* the lower middle class, which includes the small employers of labor, small merchants and shop-keepers, the bulk of the civil servants, the artisans, and a large though ill-defined group of small *rentiers* or investors. (3) There is the middle bourgeoisie which includes the higher ranks of the liberal professions, the higher government officials, the teachers in the higher educational institutions and the well-to-do business men and *rentiers.* (4) There is the *grande,* or upper, *bourgeoisie,* which includes the large industrialists and merchants, the banking and financial community, and the large landowners. (5) Finally, there are the workers, that is the industrial wage earners and the landless agricultural laborers.

The relative numerical strength of the five groups can be measured only approximately. It is safe to say that about 40 per cent of the French population consist of the small peasantry, about 20 per cent of the small bourgeoisie, about 35 per cent are composed of the industrial and agricultural workers, and the remaining 5 per cent are made up by the middle and upper bourgeoisie.

A. THE PEASANTRY

Of the five groups, the peasantry has perhaps been most profoundly affected by changes in its problems of life and land. Before the war, the lot of the small peasant was hard. Still worse was the condition of the agricultural laborer and of the farm servant. Their working hours were long and painfully laborious, their lodgings primitive, and their food coarse and monotonous.[1]

The economic disadvantages of the system of small land holdings were thought to be more than offset by larger economic and social results The system presumably supplied a happy combination of labor and property and of possession with the ideal of extending it, and was thus supposed to provide the incentive for the industriousness and the steadfastness of the peasantry on which the country relied. It made of the peasants "dreamers who lived on hope and resignation rather than bookkeepers interested in their profit and loss accounts." [2] And though this also made the peasants "eager for gain, economical to the point of avarice, cunning, distrustful to the point of stupidity, conservative to the point of routine, egotistic and envious," these doubtful traits were accepted as the "virtues" of a "tyrannical passion."

For a decade before the war there were signs of dissatisfaction among the French peasantry. But only since the war has it assumed the character of a wide and deep movement. Those who have been most profoundly affected are the agricultural laborers and servants. Large numbers of them, at the end of the war and upon return to their homes, found themselves in a "tragic" condition. The price

[1] See Augé-Laribé, Michel, *Le paysan français*, Paris, 1923; Risler, George, *Le travailleur agricole français*, Paris, 1923; and Regnier, Pierre, *L'ouvrier agricole*, Paris, 1924.

[2] Augé-Laribé, *ibid.*, p. 17.

of land had gone up and the chance of becoming a landowner had become correspondingly attenuated. Rather than face the old conditions of work and life, they turned towards the city where new opportunities of work and play were beckoning. This was true not only of the formerly landless laborers, but also of those who had a little land of their own, and of some of the very small peasants as well.

On the other hand, large numbers of the tenant farmers and of the small peasantry profited by the war and the post-war prosperity of 1918-1920 to acquire land and to increase their holdings. High prices, government war allowances, and depreciating money enabled them to pay off their mortgages and to round out their possessions. Laborers who went to the city, war widows and old parents of men killed in the war, and so-called *rentiers du sol*, that is, people who held land as an investment, sold out to the peasants who for the first time in many decades had money enough to gratify their "passion" for the land. In general, the tendency, has been for properties of 15 to 50 acres to gain at the expense of the very small and of the very large holdings.[3]

The economic position of the small and middle peasantry has thus been considerably strengthened. But the reverse side of the medal has not been so bright. There is the "anguish" of the labor shortage due to the rural exodus. Also since 1921, the old cry against the middleman has become more insistent. The peasants complain that not they but the

[3] André Bouton, *Journal des economistes*, Nov. 15, 1924.

millers, the packing companies, and other middlemen profit by the high prices of agricultural products.[4] They complain that freight rates are too high. They complain about the lack of nitrogenous fertilizers and the lack of grain elevators. They feel that not enough is done to improve the general condition of agriculture and to extend credit facilities to those who need them.

The economic discontent is accompanied by a general restlessness. A general desire for more intense living and for higher standards of comfort and pleasure has affected the mass of the peasantry. They want better food, better housing, better roads, more opportunities for association, and more of the diversions of the city population. The charm of the traditional life of the village centering around the *place* and the *café* seems to be no longer sufficient for those who have to live it daily. It induces ennui, a sure sign to the Frenchman that the village has been caught in the throes of a "moral revolution." [5]

As a result of these conditions the peasantry make three demands on the State. First, they demand that the government assure them an adequate labor supply,—by organizing the importation and distribution of foreign agricultural labor. Second, they demand that the government improve the conditions of agricultural production and market-

[4] See *Journal officiel, Débats, Chambre,* Feb. 6, 1925.
[5] See Maurice Lair, *Le socialisme et l'agriculture française,* Paris, 1922, pp. 52, 90-1; also Laurin, M. T., *"La revolution agraire en france,"* in *L'information sociale,* Jan. 22, 1925.

ing,—by increasing the number of agricultural schools, by providing cheap fertilizers, by extending credit for the reclamation of waste and abandoned lands, by decreasing freight rates on agricultural machinery, and by aiding the co-operative and mutual societies which the peasants have organized for these various purposes. Third, they demand that the government improve the material and moral conditions of life in the country—by extending credit for the purchase of land, the building of homes, and particularly for the electrification of the French countryside. Eloquent speeches in the Chamber and Senate proclaim that the development of electrical power will alleviate the consequences of the labor shortage in the villages, supply motor force to rural craft, banish darkness from the peasants' homes, and in every way make life in the villages and on the farms more alluring.[6] In a word, electricity means *toute une renaissance* of the village which will put an end to its present *malaise*.

Like all other groups of the French population, the peasantry tries to give organized expression to its ideas through special economic organizations. True, the vast majority of these organizations are small and local in character. But there has been an increase in the number of those which unite the

[6] Some even claim that electric light would give the rural youth a better *chance d'amour* than exists in the unlighted darkness of the present-day village. See *Journal officiel, Débats, Sénat,* April 8, 1925.

peasantry of a department or of a larger region.[7]
The general interests of the peasantry are represented by several national organizations. The most
important is the Central Union of the Agricultural Syndicates of France, which was organized as
far back as 1886 and which now claims 28 regional
unions, 4,000 syndicates, and about a million members. Its avowed purpose is to "defend the general
interests of agriculture and to present the grievances
of the peasantry to the government." Its leadership has been in close contact with the Catholic
movement and with the conservative political parties. Another is the League of Peasants, which is
not influenced by religious considerations and is primarily interested in the defense of property interests. The General Confederation of Agriculture is
attempting to bring about a greater unity among
the agricultural producers on problems of production
and marketing.

B. THE *PETITE BOURGEOISIE*

The *petite bourgeoisie* is the most heterogeneous
group in France, but its component elements have
in common the fact that they, more than any other

[7] Such are for instance, the Agricultural Syndicat of Loir-et-
Cher with 23,000 members, the agricultural syndicat of Manche
with 15,000 members, the Southwest Union with 735 syndicates in
10 departments, the Federation of agricultural syndicates of the
East with 100,000 members, the Federation of the syndicates of
the Center. There are also national syndicates of specialized
branches of agriculture such as the Federation of Wine-growers of
the South, the General Federation of Wheat-growers, the General
Federation of Milk-producers, and others.

group of the population, depend on fixed salaries and on incomes from small investments. Together with the peasantry, the *petite bourgeoisie* was regarded as the social bulwark of pre-war France. A large proportion lived in the small provincial towns in close contact with the peasantry. But whether in small town or metropolitan center, this group exemplified to the world the French preference for a static and peaceful life "without hurry and bustle." It was from this group of the population that France for many years recruited its so-called small *rentiers*, that is, persons who retired at a comparatively early age from active life and spent the remainder of their days on the modest returns of their moderate investments or on a small pension or on both. This group also, together with the peasantry, was supposed to exemplify the "equal and democratic distribution" of property in France.[8]

The *petite bourgeoisie* has been most adversely affected by the war and post-war developments. It has suffered from the loss of some of its investments, from the depreciation of the purchasing power of the rest, and from the high cost of living. It may be an exaggeration to say, as some have said, that the war "has ruined the *petite bourgeoisie*."[9] But it is certain that the life of this group of the population has become immeasurably harder than before the war.

The *petite bourgeoisie* calls for State aid in a va-

[8] See Michaud, Edgar, *La marche au socialisme*, Paris, 1920.
[9] *Journal officiel, Débats, Sénat*, March 31, 1925.

riety of ways. It is interested in laws for the extension of State credit to building associations. It asks for State subsidies to the "popular banks" which have been organized since 1917 to provide cheaper credit to the small and middling employers and merchants. It wants state grants for its various co-operative enterprises. It is also enthusiastically interested in the plans for the "electrification" of France. By far the most serious effect on the budget has, however, been the demand of the civil servants for increases in salaries and for larger pensions on retirement. It is well known that the civil servants of France are poorly paid. The need for granting them higher salaries was recognized by law in 1921 and in 1923. The budget of 1925 appropriated over a billion francs for this purpose, though the minimum basic salary of 6,000 francs a year (about $300) which the civil servants asked for was not granted.

The heterogeneity of the *petite bourgeoisie* is shown by its lack of a common organization. Thus, the small merchants and employers are organized in syndicates and associations of their own. They are also connected with the Chambers of Commerce and with some of the larger employers' associations in which the middle and larger bourgeoisie play the leading part.

On the other hand, the business employees and the civil servants tend to hitch up with the wage-earners. The former are but little organized, but the civil servants are well represented by two kinds of organizations. One is the so-called friendly or general association, the other is the syndicate or trade-union. Among the most important of the latter are the National Union of Teachers, with over 75,000 members, the Federation of Postal Workers, the National Syndicate of the Post, Telegraph, and Telephone Agents, which are united in the Federation of Functionaries. ·

Even more pronounced are the dispersive tendencies among the intellectualist elements of the lower and middle bourgeoisie. The growth of organization among these elements is almost entirely a post-war development. But the importance of intellectual leadership and the French "cult of intellect" have made all groups of the population and all schools of thought anxious to "capturè" as much of this organizational movement as possible. Thus to offset the General Confederation of Intellectual Workers,[10] the monarchists and reactionaries organized the Confederation of French Intelligence and Production, while the Catholics organized the Professional Confederation of Catholic Intellectuals. Similarly, there is the Syndical Union of French Engineers and alongside of it the Social Union of Catholic Engineers. These organizations supply the competing intellectual leadership of the country.

[10] This includes the General Association of Physicians, with 10,000 members, the Association of Republican Journalists, The Middle Class of Railroad Employees, and others. It claims a total membership of 150,000. See report of Conseil Supérieur du Travail, *La participation aux bénéfices*, Paris, 1924, p. 17; also Sageret, Jules, *Le syndicalisme intellectuel*, Paris, 1922.

C. THE *MIDDLE BOURGEOISIE*

The middle bourgeoisie occupies a position midway between the *petite* and *grande bourgeoisie*. Insofar as some of its component elements are dependent on salaries and on investments with fixed returns, it shares the fate and the viewpoint of the lower middle class. Insofar, however, as it consists also of fairly well-to-do business men and of professional men with high earning capacity, it shades off into the *grande bourgeoisie*. Because of this position, the middle bourgeoisie is frequently able to play a mediatory and conciliatory part in economic and political life. From its midst are recruited many of the leading writers and publicists who play• an influential part in shaping public opinion.

D. THE *GRANDE BOURGEOISIE*

Quite different from the post-war story of the lower middle class, is the story of the upper, or *grande bourgeoisie*. Its economic position has been greatly strengthened. Aided by the credit policies described in other chapters, the industries of France generally have expanded in size and output and have increased their permanent productive capacity by improvements in technique and organization. Just as striking has been the growth of the large banking and financial institutions, which have shared in the prosperity of France and in the benefits of the "credit boom" since 1922. It is this industrial and financial development, stimulated by the expansive psychology of a "credit boom," that has given France that new air which so forcibly strikes the outside observer. It is responsible for that new atmosphere of push and hustle, of promotion and scheming which has changed the old peaceful and secure rhythm of France. It has displaced old solid bourgeois families by *nouveaux riches*, leisurely gaiety by restless excitement, a static outlook by the psychology of alternating "booms" and "crises."

The demand of the *grande bourgeoisie* is not so much for immediate financial aid as for definite general policies. It claims that it has reasons to be apprehensive about its "precarious" situation. It points out that French industry is hampered by the poverty of the country in many important raw materials and in fuel resources. It complains that transportation is slow, inefficient, and expensive. It is irritated by the growing demands of organized labor, especially by the insistence on the observance of the eight-hour law. It wants a larger and more flexible labor-supply. Above all, it is worried by the prospects of international competition. It claims that the rapid industrialization of France has been out of proportion to the development of the home market and that foreign markets are therefore a necessity. It complains that French tariff rates are not high enough, that Germany is again invading the world markets, that French costs of production are too high because of high taxes, and that for these and other reasons the French position in the international markets is not secure. It calls for a "policy of raw materials," for a "fuel policy," for a "policy of markets," and for a "tariff policy." It is this group which more than any other emphasizes the need and possibilities of developing the colonial empire of France and which would subordinate all other problems to those of productive growth and of market-expansion.

The *grande bourgeoisie* has a strong net-work of organizations for the promotion of its ideas. It is the influential element in the 150 Chambers of Commerce which are organized in all the larger towns of France. It is well represented by the national industrial federations, some of which were organized many years ago, but a large number of which have sprung up since 1914.[11]

Even more remarkable, however, is the consolidated front which the upper bourgeoisie presents in regard to what it considers its general interests. This is shown by the growth of large and compact organizations of national scope for the promotion of wider economic and social ends. Such is the National Association for Economic Expansion organized in 1916, the Federation of Employers of Labor organized with the aid of Clémentel in 1919, the Federation of French Industrialists and Merchants, and the Confederation of French Commercial and Industrial Groups. But above all are the two organizations which crown the entire edifice:

[11] Such are the Comité des Forges organized in 1864, the Union of Metallurgical and Mining Industries, the Central Committee of Coal Mines of France, the General Syndicat of the French Cotton Industry, the Federation of the Silk Industry, and many others.

the General Confederation of French Production organized in 1920, and the Union of Economic Interests, which though older has grown strikingly since 1919 and now includes over 75 of the largest Chambers of Commerce, industrial federations, alliances, and national associations. Both these organizations are combative in their attitude towards organized labor, and exercise an enormous influence in the Chamber of Deputies and in the Senate through committees and through representatives of various parliamentary groups.[12]

E. THE WAGE-EARNERS

The industrialization of France has in many ways improved the condition of the wage-earners. The French workers themselves regard the eight-hour law as their most important gain since the war. The law was passed in 1919 and has been gradually extended to various industries. The workers also emphasize the improvements which have been made in protective labor legislation. They lay special stress on the increased recognition which they have obtained in the national life. It was largely owing to their pressure that the government organized the Supreme Economic Council which is composed of representatives of all groups of the people and whose function it is to examine and to recommend large economic policies. As to wages and earnings, the workers claim that though earnings have been

[12] See Villey, Etienne, *L'Organisation professionnelle des employeurs dans l'industrie française*, Paris, 1924.

improved because of steadier employment, it has been a hard race against rising prices and that in this race the less organized and weaker sections of the working population have been falling behind.[13]

The post-war developments have profoundly affected the mental attitude of the French workers. Before the war, the French labor movement was noted for its advocacy of revolutionary and syndicalist aims and for its highly explosive and violent methods. In recent years, its interest has shifted to the problems of wages, hours, conditions, and control of employment, and it has shown a willingness to make compromises in order to obtain immediate results.

Accordingly, the French workers have been more insistent than ever before for State aid in achieving their present aims. They call for government measures against the high cost of living. They demand that the government enforce the eight-hour law more strictly and extend it to the merchant marine and other industries where it has not yet been introduced. They want the government to do something about the housing shortage and to appropriate more money for "cheap" houses. The most elaborate demand of the French workers is for a comprehensive system of social insurance.

In general, since the end of the war, a considerable expansion of labor organizations has taken

[13] See Welden, Ellwood A., *Labor, Wages and Unemployment in France*, Report of United States Department of Commerce, Washington, August, 1924.

place in France. The local unions have grown in size and in number and have been more closely brought together in their respective departmental and national unions. In the most important industries large national unions have come into being with hundreds of thousands of members and with a command over funds which would have seemed "fabulous" to the workers in 1914.[14]

The power of the organized workers has been sapped, however, by internal divisions and struggles. Since January, 1922, the entire French labor movement has been split between two central organizations, the General Confederation of Labor and the General Unitary Confederation of Labor.[15] The former under the leadership of Jouhaux, sometimes referred to as the French Gompers, is recognized as the "bona fide" organization and exercises considerable influence in political and governmental circles. Its "ultimate" ideal is a socialist society, but its chief interest is centered on pushing its so-called "program minimum" which consists of a series of

[14] Such are the National Union of Mine Workers with over 30,000 members, the National Union of Metal Workers with 110,000 members, the Union of Railway Workers with 150,000 workers, the national unions in the building trades, chemical and leather industries. The total number of workers' syndicates on January 1, 1923, was 6,540, with 1,809,000 members.

[15] The headquarters of the former are in Rue Lafayette and those of the latter in Rue La Grange. The adherents of the former are, therefore, referred to as Lafayettistes and those of the latter as Unitaires. The General Confederation of Labor Rue Lafayette claims from 500,000 to 700,000. The Unitaires claim about 500,000 members. But in either case no statistics of membership are published.

demands for the eight-hour day, for cheap housing, for social insurance, for the nationalization of the large monopolistic industries, for workers' control, for free trade, and for a pacific foreign policy. The Unitary Confederation is led by the communists and is the industrial tail to the communist political kite. There are two other central labor organizations which are of some influence in the general labor movement. Of these the more significant is the French Confederation of Christian Workers with about 125,000 members under Catholic leadership.[16]

II. POLITICAL PARTIES AND FINANCIAL PROGRAMS

The relation of group problems and group organizations to State finances is evident enough. The demands of the various groups mean budget appropriations and the need of larger revenues, The "grievances" of the groups include complaints

[16] In addition to the group organizations described, there are a number of influential associations which cut across several groups and which are the product of the war. Such is the National Union of Associations of Reserve Officers which is trying to bring together the 120,000 reserve officers of France for political and social purposes. Such are the National Federation of French Associations of War Wounded, Reformed and War Widows; the National Federation of Former War Prisoners; the Republican Association of Soldiers of the World War; the Association of Sufferers from Lung-Wounds. These are the so-called "grand associations" which exercise a strong pressure on the government in the matter of pensions and of special legislation for their members. Some of these associations are under conservative, others under more radical leadership, while the communists have separate organizations of "war wounded workers and peasants."

of high taxes. The position of the various groups as holders of government securities leads to a duality in their attitude as claimants for a share of the interest payments on the public debt and as contributors of the taxes out of which this interest is paid.

Each group tries to impress its point of view on the government by bombarding Parliament with resolutions, by sending delegates to interview ministers, by lobbying, by bringing pressure to bear on deputies through its economic organization, and by stirring up public sympathy in the country for its demands and grievances. This interpenetration of economics and politics is tightened through the interrelations between the social groups and the political parties which carry on the government of the country.

It is thus inevitable that the divisions in the economic and social life of France should be at the basis of the various financial policies now before the French people. Such policies are not the mere formulation of the specific demands and views of one or another group. On the contrary, each program is an attempt to reconcile in one way or another the views and interests of several groups and to bridge over group divisions by means of general principles and political formulas. But in each program the views of one or another group predominate.

One may distinguish six more or less clearly defined financial programs. They correspond to the general divisions of political and social thought which are the result not only of the economic divi-

FRENCH POLITICAL PARTIES *

Designation	Representative organizations and parties	Parliamentary groups in Chamber of Deputies with number of deputies belonging to each group	Parliamentary groups in the Senate with number of senators belonging to each
A. Reactionary or "Extreme Right"	A. { Ligue des Patriotes, Ligue de l'Action Française	A. { None. Some members are among "deputies belonging to no group."	A. La Droite 10
B. Conservative or "Right" and "Right Center"	B. { Action Liberale Populaire, Ligue Républicaine Nationale, Fédération Républicaine, Parti Républicain, Démocratique et Social	B. { Union Républicaine Démocratique ......104; Gauche Républicaine Démocratique ... 44; Groupe des Démocrates ...... 14; Républicains de Gauche ...... } 36	B. { Union Républicaine ...... 88; Gauche Républicaine 30
C. Moderate "Left Center"	C. { Parti Républicain, Démocratique et Social	C. { Républicains de Gauche ......; Gauche Radicale. 41	C. { Union Démocratique et Radicale 23

D. Progressivist	D. {	Parti Radical et Radical Socialiste Républicains Socialistes	D. {	Groupe Radical et Radical - Socialiste ......140 Groupe des Républicains Socialistes 43	D. and E. {	Groupe de la Gauche Démocratique, Radicale et Radicale-Socialiste 157
E. Socialist	E.	Parti Socialiste	E. {	Groupe du parti Socialiste 104		
F. Revolutionary	F. {	Parti Communiste Français	F. {	Groupe Communiste 26		

* The above classification of political parties and of parliamentary groups, as well as of economic groupings, is tentative. From another point of view and for other purposes, political and economic groups might be arranged in different order. The somewhat indefinite character of some of the political groups is shown by the fact that they appear under two subdivisions. The membership of the groups in the Chamber is taken from the *Journal officiel* for Jan. 20, 1925; for the Senate from the *Journal officiel* for Nov. 14, 1924.

sions but of the intellectual and political history of France. Accordingly, these programs may be designated as (1) reactionary, (2) conservative, (3) moderate, (4) progressivist, (5) socialist, and (6) revolutionary or communist. In outlining the financial policies of these various groups, the intent is not to pass judgment upon any of them. The sole purpose is to portray as clearly as possible the extent to which the point of view and the programs of the numerous political parties are at variance.

The standard-bearers of these programs are the larger political combinations which may be designated by the same names. Despite the multiplicity of political parties in France, the looseness of political affiliations, and the "perplexing self-labeling of most of the parties with the wrong labels," the various political organizations and parliamentary groups may be classified under the headings adopted here, as is shown by the table on the opposite page. In general, in accordance with our economic analysis, the reactionary elements may be said to represent the less modernized sections of the rural population and of the intellectuals, the conservative elements are dominated by the *grande bourgeoisie*, the progressivists are essentially the representatives of the *petite bourgeoisie*, while the socialists and communists draw their main support and inspiration from the wage-earning classes.

A. THE REACTIONARIES

In the present financial crisis, the royalists, who are the mainstay of the reactionaries, can not be said to offer a definite peaceful program. From their point of view, the present predicament of France must be regarded as a logical culmination of the "false" and "destructive" ideas which were let loose by the French Revolution and which were further developed during the "stupid" nineteenth century. Their recipe for France is to return at once to an absolute hereditary monarchy based on a somewhat modernized system of "corporate estates." They are convinced that the "reactionary wave . . . is destined to carry everything before it and within a very short time." [17] In the words of Leon Daudet, "France will be monarchist within ten years or even within five years, or she will cease to be." [18] According to the royalists the disillusionment of the youth about democracy makes France even more receptive to the ideas of "reaction" than Italy was when it turned to fascism, which the French royalists, by the way, consider a mere "imitation of the Camelots du Roi." [19]

The royalists are avowedly willing to take advantage of any opportunity to force a change on France, if necessary by means of a *coup d'état.* While preparing for such emergency, by organizing

---

[17] Daudet, Léon, *Moloch et Minerve,* 1924, p. 8.
[18] Daudet, Léon, *Le stupide XIX siecle,* 1919, p. 305.
[19] Daudet, Léon, *Moloch et Minerve,* p. 167.

244 THE FRENCH DEBT PROBLEM

their followers into *centurions*, they carry on a continuous fire against the government in the press, in public meetings, and in Parliament. They denounce the *bloc de gauche* as a *bloc de Boche*, they spit fire at the "absurd and anti-physical" Treaty of Versailles, they attack the leaders of the Left for having made France a "vassal" of England and of the United States, and they pour out invective upon the "plutocratic democracy" which is dominated by "men of gold" and which has failed to carry on a "vigorous and nationalistic" policy, the "true" policy of "traditional and national" France.

In the financial sphere this "reactionary" spirit is expressed in a negative attitude towards all efforts to find a way out of the present difficulty. "Necessity," writes Leon Daudet, "has not brought forward a single remarkable financier. . . . The country has held on to the old expedients of loans, of Treasury notes, of innumerable transfers and counter-transfers. No plan for the comprehensive liquidation of an onerous situation was ever attempted." [20] Of course, in their opinion no solution is possible without a return to monarchy. But while awaiting the "coming king," they condemn every proposal that is being made such as the capital levy, increase of the inheritance taxes, or the income tax, which they denounce as "detestable." At the same time, they claim credit for having warned against "systematic and gradual" inflation. Insofar

---

[20] Daudet, Léon, *Moloch et Minerve*, p. 242. See also Valois, Georges, *La monnaie saine tuera la vie chère*, Paris, 1920.

as the external debt is concerned, they would use
French claims on Germany and on Russia to offset
the French debt to England and the United States.[21]
The roots of the royalist party are rural and aris-
tocratic and its flowery blossoms are in the upper
military ranks and in certain literary circles. Its
influence depends upon the more imponderable elements of French life. Though small in numbers,
this group is fairly compact, and is supported by a
considerable proportion of impulsive and vociferous
college men who can be easily marshalled for parades
and demonstrations. In general, its influence is to
accentuate the political and social instability of
French life, and to confuse the public mind with
reference to the financial problems.

Similar in influence are several intermediate
groups which stand between the reactionaries and
conservatives. Such is the group of Bonapartists
which maintains the Napoleonic tradition in France.
The most significant and influential of these intermediate groups is the Action Libérale Populaire.
In previous years it maintained a separate parliamentary group in the Chamber, but in the present
Chamber its members are affiliated with the various
conservative groups. It maintains, however, a distinct party organization outside the Chamber and
claims several hundred thousand members throughout the country who are organized into local committees and into district federations.

The Action Libérale Populaire is a Catholic party
[21] *Journal officiel, Débats, Sénat,* April 2, 1925.

whose main purpose is to reorganize social life on the basis of Catholic doctrine and to defend the interests of the Catholic Church. It has "rallied" to the republican form of government in France in order that this political issue may not hinder its major purpose. The political reforms which it advocates, such as the freedom of religious association and the right to maintain sectarian schools, are intended to strengthen the Catholic element of the country. The party has attached to itself some of the youth of France through such subsidiary organizations as the Jeunesse Catholique and the Jeunesse Libérale. It also has a following among the women workers and business and commercial employees who have been organized into special Catholic unions and for whom the party demands protective and social legislation.[22]

Insofar as financial policies are concerned, the Action Libérale Populaire may be said to work with the conservative groups. But insofar as it subordinates national financial interests to its other interests and activities, it can not but have the effect of complicating and confusing the financial issues. This was clearly shown by the fate of the Herriot government, whose announced intention was not only to break off diplomatic relations with the Vatican but also to reorganize Alsace on the basis of the "secular" system which exists in the rest of France. The "school strike" which followed in Alsace, and the

[22] See Moon, Thomas Parker, *The Labor Problem and the Social Catholic Movement in France*, New York, 1921.

"Cardinals' Manifesto" which was soon afterwards issued by the general assembly of the cardinals and archbishops of France, were warnings of the serious political and religious complications which were inherent in the situation. The "Cardinals' Manifesto" declared that the laws were unjust and "contrary to the formal rights of God," that it was not necessary to obey them, and that demonstrations and mass action were desirable in order to bring pressure on the government to change its policy.

Herriot's speech in the Chamber on March 10, 1925, in which he accused the Catholics of waging a campaign "against secularism and against the spirit of modern societies" and in which he contrasted the "young, pure and unsophisticated Christianity of the Catacombs" with the "Christianity of the bankers" resulted in one of the stormiest sessions of the Chamber and hastened the fall of his government. The present government has made peace with the militant Catholic elements by conceding their demands in relation to the Vatican and to Alsace-Lorraine, but the religious issue can not be said to have been eliminated as a potential factor in the general political as well as in the special financial situation.

B. THE CONSERVATIVES

The conservative element is represented in the Chamber most distinctively by the Union Républicaine Démocratique, the Groupe des Democrates and the Groupe la Gauche Républicaine Démocratique. These three groups in the Chamber are generally referred to as the Right. The corresponding leading group in the Senate is the Union Républicaine. The leading conservative politicians are found in these groups. Thus, among the members of the Union Républicaine Démocratique are Louis Dubois, Henri Auriol, Louis Marin, George Bonnefous. The Gauche Républicaine Démocratique includes among its members Maurice Bokanowski, and Yves Le Trocquer. In the Senate, the conservative element is led by Henry Chéron, Aléxandre Millerand, François-Marsal and Raymond Poincaré.

Outside the Chamber and the Senate, the conservative element is represented by a number of major and minor political organizations. There is the Ligue Républicaine Nationale organized a short time ago by Millerand. With the Ligue Républicaine Nationale are affiliated a number of minor political groups which have been springing up throughout the country recently. Much more important than these, however, is the comparatively small but well organized and well financed Republican Federation. This is a regular political party with local committees throughout the country which unites the wealthy members of the community. And more numerous than all the others is the Parti Républicain Démocratique et Social which includes many of the influential members of the Parliamentary groups mentioned above.

The members of the various conservative organizations differ somewhat on a number of political and social questions. The Fédération Républicaine, for instance, is strongly opposed to labor and social legislation and stresses the doctrine of *laissez-faire*. The other parties favor "social legislation which would give to citizens the guarantees which are indispensable against the risks of life," that is, old-age pensions, compensation laws and the like. Some of the conservative elements are less tolerant in the matter of religion than others. But in the present situation these differences are of little importance as compared with the ideas and beliefs they hold in common. In general, the conservatives are militantly interested in maintaining the status quo and in defending private enterprise under the leadership of the large property owners.

In the present financial situation the conservatives have been displaying a curious mixture of alarmism and optimism. They show alarm when they think and speak of what their political opponents have been doing since May 11, 1924. They not only blame the Radical Cartel for having failed in every promise it made to the country, namely, to improve the exchange, to decrease taxes and to reduce the cost of living; they also accuse it of trying to subvert the entire social structure of France. The budget bill of 1925, which originally carried proposals favorable to small employers and workers, has been denounced by them as an "assault upon property and the family" [23] and as a "defiance of the prin-

[23] Lafarge, Réne, *La révue de Paris*, April, 1925.

ciples of French civilization which is based on the Rights of Man and of the citizen." [24] At a mass meeting organized by the Ligue Républicaine Nationale, Senator François-Marshal summed up this view of the conservative parties in the following words: "For the first time the budget is presented not as a means of assuring the needs of the country, on the basis of a balance between receipts and expenditures, but for an entirely different purpose; namely, the overthrow of the social and moral order of the country." [25]

On the other hand, the conservatives are optimistic that France could easily solve its financial problem, if the political situation were different. Said Henry Chéron in the Senate: "Let us say quite loudly that not only are our finances not in a desperate state, but that the solution of the problem is entirely clear, if we know how to do our duty." [26] In brief, it is argued that the "objective" condition of France has steadily improved, as shown by the trade balance of 1924, by the decrease in railroad deficits, by the increase of revenues, and by the general economic situation. The improvement, it is claimed, was due to the policy of the National Bloc which "practically" balanced the budget of 1924. The real trouble supposedly began only when the French people realized that the Herriot government was a "prisoner" of the socialists who were driving the country

[24] Le Temps, April 4, 1925.
[25] Le Figaro, March 23, 1925.
[26] Journal officiel, Débats, Sénat, April 1, 1925.

to ruin. The financial crisis is thus entirely due to psychologic causes; it is a "crisis of confidence."

In general terms, the program of financial reconstruction of the conservative parties may perhaps be stated best in the words of François-Marsal as follows: ". . . We base our economic policy on liberty to work, to produce and to earn; our fiscal policy on liberty to hold, save, and bequeath; our financial policy on consolidation, debt amortization, and on the scrupulous respect of engagements which is at the root of confidence and credit; our currency policy on the slow and gradual restoration of the value of the franc, which is the only means of ensuring cheap money and of saving thousands of good Frenchmen from grievous and undeserved suffering." [27]

Concretely, the conservative groups demand "ferocious economy" and reductions in State expenditures. The Confédération Générale de la Production Française, for instance, has protested against the increases of salaries and pensions to the civil servants.[28] Most of the representatives of these groups in the Chamber and in the Senate, however, have asked for larger appropriations to help agriculture and industry and to strengthen the navy and army. For, though these groups "want peace," they claim that they "will have it only insofar as they will be strong."

The conservatives are opposed to any new taxes

[27] *Economic Review,* Feb. 13, 1925.
[28] *Information sociale,* April 16, 1925.

unless they are proved to be absolutely necessary,
and they demand the discontinuance of "vexatious
policies" and of "fiscal tyranny." They maintain
that there is an easy way of increasing the State
revenues by turning over the State monopolies in
tobacco, matches, telephones and telegraphs to private enterprise and control. They claim that the
abolition of the eight-hour law in industry would increase output and thus result in greater returns to
the State from industry and commerce.

As to the internal debt, the conservative groups
are especially optimistic. Given "confidence" in
the government, the floating debt can be renewed for
some time, until it is converted. The conversion
and amortization of the entire internal debt is regarded as equally possible. The amortization of the
internal debt can be "easily" secured by providing
a sinking fund for a period of 60 to 80 years. By
adding "only" 600 to 700 million francs to the present annual payments of interest, it is possible to
create annuities which in some 60 years would wipe
out a debt of 200 billion francs.[29]

As to the external debt, the conservative groups
maintain the "French thesis" that it must be re-
examined in the light of what France suffered and
of Germany's failure to carry out the provisions
of the Peace Treaty. According to this thesis,
"pounds sterling and dollars furnished during the
war by the allies was but one form of their con-
tribution towards a struggle which was carried on

[29] *Journal officiel, Débats, Sénat,* April 1, 1925.

in common." Also the "debt of France to her allies is most indissolubly bound up" with French claims on Germany.

Confidence, increased output and conservative financing would also solve the problem of the franc. For some time the conservatives talked about the "restoration of the franc," but more recently they have shifted their emphasis to the necessity of keeping the franc at its present level. This has given rise to the accusation that they, especially the large industrial and commercial elements, are in favor of further currency inflation. The conservative groups, however, vehemently deny this charge.[30]

C. THE MODERATES

There are sections among the business men of France and especially among the middle bourgeoisie which feel that the conservative program is inadequate. These sections of the middle bourgeoisie are represented by the moderate groups in the Chamber which are usually referred to as the Left Center. They include some of the Republicains de Gauche who are under the leadership of Adrian Dariac, François Pietri, and Georges Leygues, and most of the members of the Gauche Radicale whose most outstanding members are Loucheur, Failleres, Paul Morel, and Victor Boret.

These moderate groups feel that the "time for easy solutions has passed" and that France must show "financial courage" and make a "real effort."

[30] See, for example, *"Information sociale,* April 16, 1925.

They can not see how the French people can avoid
paying high taxes for some time to come, but they
demand a better distribution of the tax burden.
They claim that at present certain "categories of
citizens are crushed" under this burden. On the
other hand, they want to reduce the charge of the
internal debt on the budget. Their chief proposals,
made by Loucheur, are concerned with the conversion and amortization of this debt. For this they
have recommended two distinct measures. One is
a "forced conversion" of the internal debt at 3.5
per cent interest. The second is what they call
a "super-tax" of 10 per cent levied on "the income
of capital" as long as it is necessary. This super-
tax should be paid entirely into a sinking fund and
should be used exclusively for the amortization of
the internal debt.

D. THE PROGRESSIVISTS

More elaborate are the programs of those elements which we have termed progressivist. They
are represented by the Groupe Radical et Radical-
Socialiste and by the Groupe Republicain-Social-
iste in the Chamber, and by the corresponding
Groupe de la Gauche Democratique, Radicale, et
Radicale-Socialiste in the Senate. Of the two groups
in the Chamber, the Groupe Radical et Radical-
Socialiste is by far the most important and is the
parliamentary counterpart of the large and influential political party known by the same name.

The progressivists are essentially the party of the

petite bourgeoisie. As such, they are opposed to the "egotistical conception of the school of *laissez-faire*" and advocate economic and social reforms of a moderately collectivist nature. Without accepting socialism in the large sense of the term, they stand for the extension of the functions and powers of the State for the purpose of regulating and controlling industry and for the State ownership of natural and economic monopolies. It is the party which carried out the separation of Church and State in 1905 and is decidedly anti-clerical in spirit. It is led by Edouard Herriot, Franklin-Bouillon, and Jammy Schmidt in the Chamber of Deputies, and by Bienvenu-Martin and René Renoult in the Senate. Among its outstanding members are Caillaux and Malvy.

The Groupe Republicaine-Socialiste is less definite in character and composition. Its origin and continued existence are largely the result of the centrifugal tendencies of French politics. It was organized some fifteen years ago by socialists who could not work with the socialist party. It stands now midway between the radical and socialist parties, but some of its members are neither socialists nor radicals. They are "political personages" who for one reason or another do not fit in elsewhere and who can play a big part in politics by occupying an intermediate position between "right" and "left." Among the members of this group are Aristide Briand, Maurice Viollette, and the present premier, Paul Painlevé.

In contrast to the conservatives, the progressivists have been frankly and increasingly worried about the condition of French State finance. They have for some time now been stressing the idea that the "time for easy solutions" has passed and that France has not a moment to lose in finding a way out. They have no hesitation in expressing anxiety about the growth of the tax burden and about the difficulties of the debt situation. "A terrible problem confronts us," said Maurice Viollette, in reporting the budget of 1925 to the Chamber. "It is terrible to think that our country has to carry such a heavy load on her shoulders."[31]

The progressivists throw upon the conservatives all the blame for the present state of French finance. They accuse the various governments of the Bloc National, and especially that of Poincaré for having consciously refused to face the facts of the situation and for having pursued a "policy of illusions" which resulted in a distorted budget and in a swollen public debt. They also lay the blame for the recent embarrassment of the Treasury at the door of the conservatives. Former Finance Minister Clémentel said in the Chamber that these recent difficulties were due to a campaign of whispers *"de bouche à oreille"* conducted by the conservative elements of the country against the government and "the public credit of France." [32]

On the other hand, the progressivists claim credit

[31] *Journal officiel, Débats, Chambre,* Feb. 14, 1925.
[31] *Ibid.,* Feb. 14, 1925.

for opening up a new chapter in the handling of the budget. Their merit, in their opinion, is threefold. They revealed the true state of affairs to the people and thus dispelled the clouds of illusion which were obscuring the financial horizon. They gave the people for the first time a "unified" budget in which all expenditures and revenues were treated together, thus doing away with the former practices of confusing the situation. And finally, they "balanced" the budget and thus started France on the road towards financial reconstruction.

Whatever basis there may be for these claims, the progressivists have been telling the French people that no ordinary measures would suffice for the solution of the present financial problem. In presenting the budget of 1925 to the Chamber, they pointed out that very few, if any, further reductions in expenditures were possible. On the other hand, France, in their opinion, was making the maximum effort in the way of tax-paying which could be expected of the country. But without the possibility of either reducing expenditures or of increasing revenues in any considerable degree, the problem of "making a budget" was a hopeless task because the fixed annual interest charges on the public debt were more than France could bear.

The crux of the financial problem, according to the progressivists, is this annual charge of interest on the public debt. There is no chance for "financial reconstruction" except by reducing in one way or another this charge. The progressivists are not so much concerned about the foreign debt. In general, their views on the foreign debt do not differ from those of the conservatives. It was by a vote of almost the entire Chamber of Deputies that the speech on the subject of the conservative deputy Louis Marin was placarded all over the country at public expense. The flurry caused by this speech made the progressivists, as the government party, a little more cautious on this "delicate and sad" subject. In the words of deputy Viollette, though one could think a lot about the inter-allied debts, one should say little about them. It was best to leave them to the processes of diplomacy.[33]

It is in regard to the problem of the internal debt that the progressivists have been at loggerheads with the conservatives. The progressivists have denounced all "easy solutions" of this problem as "lazy ideas." They have refused to consider not only the possibility of "inflation" but also that of the "devaluation of the franc." Inflation would mean the "death of the country," while stabilization of the franc at its present value would mean "semi-bankruptcy" and the "worst expropriation of capital." Even more vehemently than the conservatives, the progressivists have been talking about the necessity of "restoring the franc." "It is necessary," declared Herriot when still premier, "to pursue a policy of revalorization of the franc. . . . It is necessary that all Frenchmen should know that the

[33] *Journal officiel, Débats, Chambre,* Feb. 14, 1925.

franc is a national value which they must defend with all means at their command."

As opposed to "lazy ideas," the progressivists have been calling for a *politique d'effort*, for a *politique de grandeur*. It was in this spirit of "grandeur" that Herriot at first broached the plan of a capital levy and then the plan of a "forced loan" which took the form of De Monzie's bill. Since the overthrow of the Herriot government, the radical and radical-socialist group has not advanced any other definite plan in the expectation of a solution to be found by the new minister of finance Caillaux. The general idea of the group, however, is that some effort will have to be made for the conversion of the floating debt and for the creation of an amortization fund.

E. THE SOCIALISTS

The French Socialist Party has been an important factor in French politics since 1900. It was partly responsible for the success of the radical party in carrying out its anti-clerical policies between 1900 and 1906. During and immediately after the World War, the Socialist party lost seriously in membership and in its representation in Parliament. It was further weakened in 1920 by the splitting off of the communist wing. But in the elections of 1924, it showed that it had more than regained its losses and came back to the Chamber as the second largest political group.

As at present constituted, the Socialist party has

a membership of over 75,000. Its supporters are among the industrial population and among some sections of the lower middle class. Since 1919, the Socialist Party has been guided by ideas which are far removed from the old time Marxian formulas. Though the party stands for the "socialist commonwealth," it regards its coming as a matter of a gradual evolution. Meanwhile, the party demands betterments for the workers and salaried people and general political and social reforms. It also demands reforms in land tenure which are intended to improve the position of the small property-holder and to give land to the laborers. In foreign policy the party is more or less pacifistic and is affiliated with the new Socialist International which was formed in Hamburg in 1923 and which considers itself the heir of the former so-called Second International. The leaders of the Socialist group in the Chamber and of the party in general are Vincent Auriol, Léon Blum, Paul Boncour, Compère-Morel, Pierre Renaudel, and Jean Longuet.

The financial program of the socialists hinges on three ideas. One is to decrease expenditures by decreasing military outlays, especially by reducing the period of military service to one year. The socialists, however, demand salary increases for civil servants and a comprehensive scheme of social insurance which would add considerably to State expenditures. The second idea is to increase revenues by a more rigorous fiscal policy, especially by taxing the "big landlords" on the same basis as the large industrialists and merchants. The third and most important idea of the Socialists, which they advanced as far back as 1921, is that of a thoroughgoing capital levy as the only way of pulling the country out of its financial difficulties.

F. THE COMMUNISTS

The Communist Party in France, as in other countries, is a post-war development and has fluctuated in strength with the ups and downs of the general international situation. It is affiliated with the Third International and shares the program of the latter, which contemplates a "world revolution" as inevitable. The French communists have tried to adapt somewhat their general revolutionary program to French conditions so as to make an appeal to the small landowners and even to the *petite bourgeoisie* in the cities. The leading members of the communist party and of its group in the Chamber of Deputies are Marcel Cachin, Renaud Jean, Loriot, Paul Vaillant-Courturier, and Albert Treint.

In accordance with their general theory of revolution, the communists poke fun at the efforts of the other parties to solve the financial problem of France. "No general principle," declared Cachin in the Chamber, "guides the empiricism of our financial policy. Are we on our way to inflation, to deflation, or to stabilization? . . . Deflation? I merely have to point out that in the country where it has been applied, it means unemployment. . . . Stabilization? . . . That means the ruin of the pre-war *rentiers.* . . . Inflation? That would evidently mean a more or less gradual death of the franc and all the social troubles which must follow." [34]

The communists take pleasure in pointing out that such "financial empiricism" is an inevitable result of the conflict of class interests in France. They denounce everything and everybody from this point of view. The Senate in their opinion, is "merely a branch of the banks and of the powerful corporations." François-Marsal is the servant of the banks in the Senate. François Poncet is the "lackey of the Comité des Forges in the Chamber." Clémentel as finance minister worked "for capitalism." Caillaux is the "friend of the bankers," who are the "masters of the nation." The budget of 1925 prepared by the progressivists and socialists is one of the "most conservative of the entire régime"; it is a "class budget easy for the rich and heavy on the poor people."

For some time the communists were content with such criticism and with desultory general outbursts of a "semi-practical" character. Such was their "demand" in the Chamber to jail the "speculators" on the Paris Exchange. Such was Cachin's "proposal" in the Chamber to make the banks pay back the commissions they made in placing French money in Russian securities before the war. Such also was their call to "strike at the banks in general."

As the financial discussion became more serious, however, the communists came out with a "definite"

[34] *Journal officiel, Débats, Chambre,* Feb. 18, 1925.

financial program. One of the demands in this program is to abolish the Senate. Another is to "lay hands" on the banks, insurance companies, and "large fortunes" in general and with the money thus obtained to "stabilize" the franc and to carry out such other reforms as a guarantee of the eight-hour day; tax exemption and rural credit for the small peasants; the reduction of military service; the expulsion of the royalist army officers; and the payment of one franc a day to all soldiers of the army. Besides, the communists would furnish free fertilizers to the farmers, would electrify the villages, and would give the workers "favorable social legislation." [35]

III. GROUP CONFLICT AND NATIONAL POLICY

A comparison of the main financial programs described above shows that they contain certain general ideas in common. They all voice a desire to avoid inflation, a recognition of the necessity of consolidating the public debt, and of providing for its amortization. They differ in the methods which they propose for carrying out these policies and for dealing with the currency problem and in the way in which they would throw the burden of "financial purification" on one or the other groups of the population. These differences in programs are accentuated by the fact that they are entangled in the conflicts of the political groups and parties.

Since the discussion of the financial situation be-

[35] *L'Humanité*, April 21, 1925.

gan in earnest, various political leaders have called
for a sort of "union sacrée" in finance. Said Clémentel in the Senate when still minister of finance:
"The finances of a party or of the government are
words devoid of meaning. We know only the finances of France." [36] Henry Chéron, the leader of
the conservatives in the Senate, declared: "For my
part, I have always suffered and I still suffer every
time I hear how the various parties accuse one another *à propos* of our finances." [37] Similar statements are being made all the time in the Chamber
of Deputies, in the press, and in public meetings.

To a large extent, however, such speeches are regarded as mere political voices in the financial wil-
derness. In other words, there is a widespread feeling that politics and finance in France can not be
divorced for a long time to come. If there was
any doubt about it, it was put to rest by the Senate
itself when it passed the resolution which overthrew
the Herriot government and which read as follows:
". . . The Senate is convinced that the financial
problem is intimately bound up with general politics,
and is resolved to grant confidence only to a government which will re-establish internal peace and national harmony by a union of all republicans."

At the same time, however, each economic and
social group forms but a minority of the population and no single political group or party can obtain a majority in the Chamber and in the Senate to

[36] *Journal officiel, Débats, Sénat,* April 3, 1925.
[37] *Ibid.,* April 1, 1925.

hold political power. Government in France must continue to be carried on by one or another combination of groups. This in a way was the situation in France before the war and was the cause of the formation of the earlier "political blocs." The war only aggravated this condition as was shown by the formation of the "National Republican Bloc" which governed France from November 1919 to May 1924, when it was succeeded by the present Cartel des Gauches which is composed in the Chamber of the Gauche Radicale, the Groupe Radical et Radical-Socialiste, the Socialistes-Républicains and the Socialist Party.

In the face of the present financial crisis both conservatives and progressivists recognize the necessity for a greater concentration of opposing forces. Senator Anton Ratier, in addressing the recent conference of the Parti Republicain Démocratique et Social, made the following declaration on this point: "What we want is the concentration of all the forces of democracy against the forces of revolution in order to form a national government capable of assuring order, discipline, respect for law, and of gratifying the generous aspirations of democracy and its ardent desire for social justice." [38] Under the forces of revolution the conservatives include all the groups of the Cartel des Gauches. In the words of deputy Paul Reynaud, "communism means revolution by express train . . . socialism means revolution by fast train, and the radicalism of the Cartel

[38] *Le Temps*, April 4, 1925.

des Gauches means revolution by slow train.[39]   The
"political question of today," said he, is whether
"in face of such socialistic demagogy" there will be
formed a sort of French Unionist party similar to the
British party which will unite "all the sane forces
of the country which accept the republican constitu-
tion." [40]   On the other hand, Caillaux on his reap-
pearance upon the political stage declared that the
"hour of economic and financial penitence" had arrived and called for a "Union des Gauches" as a
necessary political prerequisite for going through
with such penitence.[41]

The fall of the Herriot government was inter-
preted as a failure of the progressivist-socialist combination to carry out an aggressive financial policy.
Herriot and his associates had clearly expressed the
idea of an opposition between their progressivism

[39] *Le Temps,* April 4, 1925.

[40] *Ibid.*

[41] The point of view of the "left" was stated in an interesting
way in the manifesto of the Federation of the Syndicats of Civil
Servants during the recent municipal elections. This manifesto
contrasts the "bloc of the people" to the "bloc of the privileged"
and makes the following summary of the situation: "The elections
have become a real social struggle. On one side are the small
peasants, the artisans, the small shop-keepers, the workers, the
civil servants, those in retirement and on pensions, the small rentiers, who have but modest means for themselves and their families. On the other side are the privileged people of wealth, the
large economic and financial organizations, the war-profiteers, the
profiteers of the liberated regions, the large merchants, who ruled
the country from 1919 to 1924 in their own interests and who refuse
to make the necessary sacrifices." From *L'information sociale,*
May 7, 1925.

and the conservatism of their opponents. "We oppose our idea of a democratic solution," said Viollette in reporting the budget to the Chamber, "to the idea of financial feudalism." "We shall never accept" the plans of the conservatives, he continued, in order that the large industrialists "may pursue more freely the conquest of world markets." In his parting speech at Fontainebleau, a few days before his resignation, Herriot had said: "I have no intention of submitting to the summons of the privileged, to the demands of the most insolent luxury which France has known since the Directoire, to the reactions of fear, to the menaces of defrauders, or of those who send their capital out of the country." The claim of the progressivist-socialist combination was that "France would be saved again by the workers and peasants" whom they presumably represented. When Herriot bowed before the adverse vote of the Senate, it was taken to mean that the conservative elements of the latter had asserted themselves once more as the final judges of public opinion and as the keepers of the "equilibrium between the financial and the social order" of the country.

It was this fact that made the conservative groups jubilant and in their turn aggressive. They were sure that the Cartel des Gauches, the "paradox and scandal of French politics," had been completely beaten. They began calling for new parliamentary elections on the assumption that the time had again come for them to assume power. Deputy Bouteille expressed this general feeling of his group at a meeting of the National Republican League when he said: "What we want is a dissolution (of the Chamber), that is, a fight for the government, for all the power of government." [42]

The recent municipal elections came as a damper on this political enthusiasm and belligerent zeal. The results of these elections proved that the conservative forces had little to hope for from new elections at the present time. Evidently, the changes in the economic and social life of France, described above, have made a dent in its political configuration. The shift of the population to the cities has weakened the villages politically. The growth of the industrial population has added strength to the socialistic element. The change from the position of a creditor to that of a debtor nation has made the small *rentier* less dependent on the leadership of "high finance." At the same time the fear of the middle classes that the *grande bourgeoisie* is favorable to further currency inflation and is unsympathetic to its needs is destroying the old-time prestige which the upper bourgeoisie had in French political life.

These facts have given rise to the idea that some sort of a compromise between the conservative and progressivist forces might be arranged. The industrialist and financial groups of France are seemingly ready to make concessions, if the solution of the financial problem can be made relatively painless

[42] *Le Matin*, April 20, 1925.

to them. On the other hand, a large element among the representatives of the middle and small bourgeoisie seem willing to forego an aggressive policy, if they can be assured of some security in their financial status.

The concrete proposals for such a compromise center around six main points. First, to obtain as favorable a settlement of the foreign debt as possible. Second, to obtain a foreign loan. Third, to increase both indirect and direct taxes, the latter to be obtained largely by making the present tax system more effective and by imposing larger but not immoderate burdens on the agricultural population and on the wealthier classes. Fourth, to "stabilize the franc" at or about its present value. Fifth, to conduct a policy of conciliation among the various groups in relation to internal questions such as the position of the Church, and the parochial schools. Sixth, to continue French foreign policy along established lines with "security" and French continental predominance as the central ideas.

The Painlevé government has been hailed as the first step towards such a compromise. It is generally admitted that this government can not last long. On the one hand, the socialists, who must keep their ear to the wage-earners' ground and meet the fire of the communists, can not maintain their alliance with the progressivists on the basis of ideas which would reconcile the conservatives. On the other hand, the conservative political leaders are not ready to support indefinitely a government

in which they have no share. In the words of
Maginot, the "national republican minority" while
not opposing the Painlevé government indiscrimi-
nately, does not intend to "become a permanent
element of the ministerial majority" because this
would mean "to abdicate and to discourage the very
hopes to which it has given birth."[43]

In other words, the effort to carry out the compromise outlined above would result in some rearrangement of groups and parties. The expectation
is that the majority of the conservatives, the groups
of the middle bourgeoisie, or the Center, and some
of the progressivists would combine to carry through
the policy of "financial conciliation." As these elements are heterogeneous, some strong men are
looked for to hold them together. This is the source
of the fervent faith in "great personalities" which
has again seized the French imagination. Such personalities, however, must belong to the intermediate
groups in order to be able to appeal to left and
right. That is why the greatest possibilities seem to
open up for the leaders of the Gauche Radicale and
of the Republicains Socialistes, such as Loucheur,
Briand, and others. The faith in Caillaux is an
expression of the same trend. Caillaux is being
compared to Necker, and well-known journalists are
drawing comparisons between his facial features and
those of Napoleon.

Opposed to this shift towards the Center and
Right is the possible reorganization of the govern-

[43] *Le Figaro*, May 26, 1925.

ment so as to strengthen the present Cartel des Gauches. This is the basis of the talk of a new government in which Herriot would again be the leading figure. The tightening of the Left Alliance depends, however, on the ability of such a "left" government to carry out drastic financial reforms and also to satisfy the demands of its socialistic element. The weaknesses and contradictions of the progressivist-socialist alliance are inevitably brought to the surface whenever a critical situation arises.

These contradictions and causes of conflict feed the hopes and agitation of the extreme elements. The royalists on the right continue to fire away at everything connected with democracy. The Catholics are developing a wider propaganda through the Federation of Catholics and their other organizations. On the other hand, the communists on the extreme left are drilling their organizations for a "fight against the fascists." For the moment, the communists feel somewhat depressed as a result of the municipal elections in which the progressivists and socialists made headway at their expense. They have therefore ceased calling for a "government of workers and peasants" which is equivalent to a call for an immediate revolution. All they demand now is a "true radical government" similar to that of Herriot which preceded the Painlevé government. The Moroccan campaign and M. Caillaux's repudiation of the capital levy have given them ammunition which they are using to drive the socialists to a position still further to the left.

To sum up: because of divergent group interests and conflicting points of view, French finance is caught in the currents and cross-currents of French politics. As a result, group partisanship and political passion, combined with a natural disinclination to face hardships, have prevented the French people from realizing fully the seriousness of their financial problem and from considering measures drastic enough to meet the exigencies of the situation.

The question in France now is whether the French people can rise above the level of their particularistic preconceptions and preoccupations and face financial realities with a new determination for bold and united action. There are signs that the acrimonious and bitter discussions of the last few months have done some good in this respect, but there is still a long way to go. It is for this reason that one can not but agree with those Frenchmen who feel that France is passing through one of the most dramatic and fateful moments in her entire history.

CHAPTER XI

THE FOREIGN DEBT PROBLEM

In discussing the debt problem of France in its relation to financial stability, we have thus far been concerned chiefly with the domestic debt. We must now consider the bearing of foreign obligations upon the problem of restoring sound financial conditions. While the war debt of the French government has all along been in the background of the picture—a sort of impending cloud looming from the West—it is only recently that it has been moved into the forefront of discussion and become a concrete, definite, problem with which the government of France must reckon.

In relating the foreign debt to the general financial problem of France, it will be the purposes of this chapter: (1) to set forth the controlling factors in the problem of meeting foreign debts—that is, the guiding principles for any plan of settlement designed to promote international financial stability; (2) to show what is the present capacity of France to pay, and the factors that will govern her capacity in the near future; and (3) to indicate the economic results to be expected from various plans of settlement that have been proposed.

I. CONTROLLING PRINCIPLES

No extended statement of the controlling factors in the payment of international debts is here necessary. They have been set forth with some fullness in previous studies of the Institute; [1] moreover, the discussion in preceding chapters of this volume, particularly VII, VIII, IX, and X, in which the interrelations between fiscal operations, banking, exchange, and trade have been revealed, goes far toward elucidating the general principles and problems involved. The following brief statement with reference to foreign debt payments, therefore, grows naturally out of the preceding discussion.

First, the government's budget surplus must equal the sums to be paid abroad. The government must collect from the people the funds required both for domestic expenses and for external payments. The indispensable minimum of domestic expenditures required to maintain the government and its services, constitutes a first charge on the revenues from taxation. For, if foreign debt payments were attempted when there was no excess of revenues over necessary domestic expenditures, budgetary disorganization, currency inflation, and business, social, and political instability would shortly ensue.

Second, the nation's net international income from trade and service operations must equal the payments to be made. To transfer the budget surplus,

---

[1] See Moulton and McGuire, *Germany's Capacity to Pay;* and Moulton, *The Reparation Plan.*

collected in domestic currency, into acceptable foreign money requires the purchase of bills of exchange derived from selling goods and rendering services to foreigners. If the government should buy up all the foreign bills in the market, importers would be unable to procure foreign money with which to pay for necessary imports of foodstuffs, raw materials, etc. With a highly complex international economic organization, the bulk of the proceeds of exports and services must always be currently made available for the purchase of necessary imports, if the economic system of the country is to continue to function; hence the government can afford to take out of the exchange market only the *surplus* of exchange—that is, such quantity of exchange as is not indispensably necessary for the conduct of private operations.

This is only another way of saying that the actual payments that a nation makes abroad consist of of goods and services. If the nation does not send more goods and render more services to foreigners than it receives from foreigners, it can not pay any debts abroad. The necessary bills of exchange are merely the results of the transactions in goods and services.

It is, however, possible for a nation to acquire foreign currency—for a time—when there is no excess of bills in the market, namely, by selling domestic currency abroad for foreign money. This method would work provided the amounts involved were small and if the process did not need to be continued long. It leads, however, to a depreciation of the value of the domestic exchange and, if the operations are extensive, it results in a general disorganization of the whole currency, budget, and business situation.[2]

Budget, banking, exchange, and trade considerations act and react upon each other. If the budget becomes unbalanced as a result of the burden of foreign obligations, the internal banking, currency, and exchange situation will be disorganized, with resulting repercussions upon the budget. If payments are required in excess of the capacity as measured by the favorable balance of payments, and domestic currency is sold abroad for foreign money, the exchanges will be disorganized and internal currency

[2] Economists who hold to the doctrine that this method should be followed, contend that the depreciation of the exchange will stimulate exports and therefore automatically provide in a short time the precise surplus of bills of exchange that is necessary. It is undoubtedly true that a depreciation of the exchange *temporarily* stimulates exports, but the extent to which the trade balance may thus be expanded depends upon a complex of factors, varying at different times and in different countries. There is no assurance whatever that in any given case the increase in exports would be quantitatively sufficient for the purposes in hand. In the period from 1920 to 1923, for example, the sale of German currency depreciated the mark, it is true; but instead of automatically producing a surplus of exports it contributed in a very important way to the disorganization of the entire financial and economic system of the country. Space does not here permit a full analysis of the issues involved in this problem. It must suffice to state that those who hold that the export surplus will take care of itself ignore, or greatly underestimate, the effects of the interrelated and interacting forces discussed in Chapters VII and VIII as well as in the present chapter.

and business instability will ensue—and the budget will in turn be adversely affected.

These principles, or controlling factors, in the settlement of international debts, were not commonly understood or appreciated when post-war international problems first began to be discussed. But they have now come to be pretty generally recognized and they have been definitely accepted as guides to the practical administration of the reparation plans for both Hungary and Germany. On one phase of the problem, however, much confusion of mind still exists, and further elaboration is therefore required.

Payments must in the long run be made out of net income and not out of loans. Temporarily some payments may be effected without a balanced budget and without any net income from international trade and service operations—by means of domestic and foreign loans. But they can not be continued over a long period of years unless net income is available for the purpose. As the first committee of reparation experts stated: "Loan operations may disguise the position, or postpone its practical result, but they can not alter it." It is evident that the borrowed funds themselves give rise to new interest obligations and thus increase rather than diminish the subsequent instalments to be met.

It should be borne in mind in this connection that either one or the other of two types of borrowing operations may be involved: (1) When the budget is unbalanced domestic loans may be floated for the purpose of giving the government the means of buying available bills of exchange; (2) When there is a dearth of foreign bills in consequence of an unfavorable balance of payments, the government may float foreign loans and thus procure the foreign currency required. The results of recent French experience in covering budget deficits afford convincing evidence of the soundness of the contention that loan operations not only disguise the real financial situation and postpone the day of reckoning, but they make the final settlement an even more painful one.

The proposition that loans are but a makeshift is equally true in connection with the external or transfer problem. It may be possible for a time to borrow from John to pay Samuel; it might even be possible to borrow from Samuel the means with which to pay Samuel. Is it not a matter of everyday business experience that a banker actually prefers to renew loans to his customers and even to loan them more rather than to have the account liquidated? Is it not also true that in pre-war days debtor nations borrowed ever increasing amounts from their creditors instead of liquidating their obligations? Is it not therefore absurd to assume that debts really have to be liquidated?

The answer is that the debtor must at least be able to meet current interest charges. A banker will indeed renew loans and grant additional credits to a customer; but only when the customer has demonstrated his capacity to repay the principal, if repayment should be demanded, and has actually been paying the interest. If a borrowing corporation has no net income and is insolvent, the bank will not loan it the money with which to pay the interest due the bank. The same is true in the field of international loans. If any government has a demonstrated incapacity to pay interest because of a persistently unfavorable trade situation, it will not long be granted new loans with which to meet its interest obligations.[3]

Akin to loan operations is the suggestion that payments can be made by delivering to the creditor the bonds of private corporations. Such a method merely substitutes in the place of the Government as debtor certain private institutions within the country, and it in no way increases the nation's capacity to pay. In either case interest and sinking fund operations on the bond can be met only if bills of exchange are available for the purpose. The industrial and railway securities put up under the Dawes Plan are no whit better than the bonds of the Government—so far at least as the transfer side of the problem is concerned. Indeed, the security of these bonds is supposed to be strengthened

[3] International loans have, however, sometimes been continued for a considerable period where the debtor's capacity to pay the interest without new borrowing was far from established. In other words, because of inadequate credit analyses, or especially because of the political considerations involved, the day of settlement is sometimes postponed for a number of years, as, for example, in the case of the Russian debt before the Great War. See Pasvolsky and Moulton, *Russian Debts and Russian Reconstruction*, 1924.

by the fact that they are made the obligation of the government.

In short, while loan operations of various kinds may tide a nation over an emergency, they can not obviate the necessity of both a budget and a trade surplus if the interest is to be met continuously and the debt ultimately liquidated.

In summary, then, the guiding principles are as follows: (1) Viewed from the internal or budget angle of the problem, the amount that can be paid will be governed by the excess of real revenues that can be raised over and above the indispensable minimum of domestic expenditures; (2) on the external or transfer side, the amount that can be paid will depend upon the net international income from ordinary trade and service operations. To exact payments when either the budget or the international trade situation is unbalanced will promote financial instability; and thus in the long run reduce the amounts that can be paid.

II. ECONOMIC POSSIBILITIES OF DEBT SETTLEMENT PLANS

In the light of the foregoing principles it becomes a relatively simple matter to appraise the economic possibilities of the principal plans of debt settlement that have been suggested. No detailed analysis of the various problems is required; it is necessary merely to present the salient features of each plan.

The principal of the debt, together with accrued interest, is as follows:

FRENCH FOREIGN DEBT, NOVEMBER 30, 1924 *
(In millions of francs at par)

Creditor Country	Principal	Accrued Interest [a]	Total
Great Britain	11,423	4,393	15,816
United States	15,194	4,193	19,387
Total	26,617	8,586	35,203

* *Journal officiel, Sénat, Annexe*, Jan. 27, 1925, p. 526.

[a] The interest on the debt to Great Britain has been regularly capitalized at a rate of interest equal to the discount rate of the Bank of England; and the interest on the debt to the United States is computed at a simple rate of interest of 5 per cent.

Translated into paper francs at the rate of exchange for November 30, 1924, the principal of the debt is 110.4 billion francs and the total, including accrued interest, 125.7 billion francs. The annual payments required will, of course, differ with different plans of settlement.

A. A MELLON-BALDWIN PLAN FOR FRANCE

A debt settlement for France worked out along the lines of the Mellon-Baldwin Agreement of 1923 with reference to the British debt would require payments to be begun at once at the rate of 3 per cent interest, plus amortization charges, for the first ten years; and 3½ per cent interest, plus amortization charges, for the next fifty-two years. With such a plan the annual payments on the entire debt of 35.2 billion gold francs (including accumulated interest) would during the first ten years be approximately 1.25 billion gold francs and for the next fifty-two years 1.5 billions. If, as a part of the settlement, the accumulated interest were cancelled, with only the principal of the debt involved, the annual payments required would be about 1.08 billion gold francs during the first ten years, and approximately 1.25 billions thereafter for the following fifty-two years. Since the transfer problem is less difficult in the case of France than the internal budget problem, we shall give it first consideration.

So far as the external transfer problem is concerned France could in 1924 have paid in full. In that year, as we have seen, France possessed a net international income available for meeting foreign debt charges amounting to approximately 6.6 billion paper francs,[4] equivalent to about 1.85 billion gold francs. While some of the trade and financial operations going to make up this favorable balance may not have given rise to bills of exchange that could be mobilized for debt payments, there is little doubt that if the government could have procured the domestic funds with which to buy the foreign exchange bills that were available, France could have transferred in 1924 the full amount required under the plan here being considered.[5] It will be recalled, however, that the trade surplus was considerably augmented in 1924 as a result of the inflation boom. If the plan of financial reorganization suggested in the

---

[4] See Appendix A, p. 370.

[5] It may be recalled in this connection that approximately 5 billion francs of the exchange available were, in fact, used in the re-purchase of francs held by foreigners.

preceding chapter is instituted, the favorable balance of payments, as we have seen, is likely to be considerably reduced.

The budget situation was such as to render the making of any payments economically disastrous. Instead of a budget surplus with which to meet interest on the foreign debt, France now has an annual budget deficit, and if a plan of thoroughgoing financial reorganization is effected along the lines suggested in Chapter IX, the best that can reasonably be hoped for during the course of the next few years is a budget balance, not a surplus. It may be recalled that in the budget estimates in Chapter IX no allowance whatever was made for payments on account of the foreign political debt.

The inescapable conclusion, therefore, is that a settlement along the lines of the Mellon-Baldwin Agreement, requiring large payments to be made in the years 1926 and 1927, would result in further disorganization of the French financial system. By borrowing operations, currency inflation, and the sacrifice of capital assets, some payments might actually be made; but the result would be disastrous.

But it may be objected that when Great Britain began to make payments no such financial disorganization resulted, and there is no more reason to think that such would be the case if France were asked to begin payments immediately. The vital difference between the British and French situation lies in the fact that at the time the British debt settlement was made Great Britain possessed both a balanced budget and a balanced international trade and financial position. Great Britain was able to pay without financial disorganization precisely because she had *net income* available for the purpose.

B. A REINVESTMENT PLAN

A plan for settling the French debt to the United States has been set forth by a member of the World War Foreign Debt Commission. Though of an unofficial character, the plan has received so much attention that it requires a brief consideration at this place.

The plan, in brief, proposes that "not less than one-half of the amounts collected annually from the French government be retained in France under the control, and invested for the account, of the United States, in first mortgage sinking fund 5 per cent gold bonds of French enterprises, such as railroads, public utilities, etc., owned, controlled, and operated by private interests, one-half of such investments to be used for industrial development only. The sinking fund requirements of these bonds should provide for their redemption in cash at the end of twenty-five or thirty years." The plan also provides for a moratorium of five years during which no internal collections or transfers should be required.

It will be seen that the plan is based on the assumption that the primary difficulty lies with the transfer rather than with the internal collection problem. It is assumed that at the end of a five-year moratorium period the French government would have no difficulty in balancing the budget and in addition collecting the funds required for external debt payment. The only difficulty is supposed to lie on the transfer side. The analysis of the present volume shows, however, that in the case of France, unlike Germany, the internal collection problem presents much greater difficulty than the transfer problem.

The constructive part of the plan—directed at the assumed transfer difficulty—is the provision that a substantial part of the payments due during the first twenty-five years should be reinvested in French railroads, public utilities and industries. It is naïvely believed by the author of the plan that this means of settling a debt will actually make France richer rather than poorer, for he says that: "By one and the same act, debt will be liquidated, and industry will be developed." It is pointed out that France is in great need of capital with which to develop her water-power, her public utilities, her railroads, and her industry, and it is implied that the plan proposed will actually furnish France this necessary capital.

In order to substantiate the contention, it would be necessary for the author to show how the collection of money from French taxpayers for investment in French bonds, the interest on which is to be paid to the United States, would actually increase the capital of France. The truth, of course, is that since all the funds for investment would have to come from the French people themselves, the plan would not increase capital for industrial expansion in France; but on the contrary would reduce it by the extent of the annual interest payments. The most that can be said for the plan is that it would lessen the amount of the annual transfers required in the first twenty-five years, and increase them thereafter.

C. A DAWES PLAN FOR FRANCE

There has been an interesting reluctance both in Great Britain and the United States to consider the application of the principles underlying the Dawes Plan to the problem of the French debt. The principles laid down and the administrative machinery devised for dealing with the German reparation problem have been quite properly extolled as genuinely constructive in character,—calculated to substitute economic reality for political chimera. The question therefore very naturally arises: Why should not a Dawes Plan be regarded as an equally constructive means of dealing with the French debt problem? In any event, it will be useful to inquire what volume of payments might be expected during the next few years if such a plan were in operation.

It may be recalled that on the internal or collection side, the Dawes Plan has two features: first, the industries and the railroads are to contribute a part of the annual collections, in the form of interest on bonds specifically pledged with the Agent for Reparation Payments; second, certain taxation receipts (called controlled revenues) are to be paid directly into the reparation account. Let us see what would be the result of this part of the plan as applied to the present French situation.

The French railroads are now conducted at a loss, with the government making up the deficit. Accordingly, if the railroads were required to pay interest to the government amounting to, say, one billion francs a year, the government's budget deficit on railroad account would merely be increased by that amount. In effect, what was received by the government from the railroads would have first to be paid by the government to the railroads. In the case of the industries the situation is, however, somewhat different. They are conducted at a profit, and some additional revenues might therefore possibly be raised from this source. But in view of the onerous burden of taxes that will have to rest upon the industries if the budget is to be brought merely into balance, in accordance with the plan suggested in Chapter IX, the prospect for still further revenues from this source is not good, to say the least.

The second requirement, that certain revenues are to be earmarked for the meeting of foreign obligations and paid directly into the reparation account, would in no sense solve the French budget problem. The Dawes Plan recognizes that the indispensable minimum of government expenditures must take precedence over everything else. The Dawes Committee stated that if the reparation obligation together with the irreducible minimum of domestic expenditures "make up in a given year a sum beyond the nation's taxable capacity, then budget instability at once ensues and currency instability is also probably involved. . . . The amount that can safely be fixed for reparation purposes tends, therefore, to be the difference between the maximum revenue and minimum expenditure for Germany's own needs."

Applying this principle to the French situation would require that no revenues—controlled or otherwise—should be utilized for foreign debt payments, until the indispensable minimum of domestic expenditures had first been provided for. In other words, if France can get a real surplus of revenues over expenditures she can set aside funds for foreign payments, without disorganizing her financial system; otherwise she can not.

On the external, or transfer, side the Dawes Plan stipulates that the sums to be transferred shall be determined by the amount of the foreign bills of exchange that are available for the purpose. For a time, and to a limited extent, the sums collected may be invested in German corporate securities; but in the long run the total payments to be made are to be gauged by the actual export surplus available. It is perhaps necessary to point out that the interest on the domestic securities that may be purchased can also be paid only with the proceeds of bills of exchange; hence, this feature of the plan in no wise obviates the necessity of an export surplus.

If a Dawes Plan had been in operation for France in 1924, the full amount of the debt instalments could have been transferred; but none could have been collected internally. In 1925 and 1926, the amount that could be transferred will undoubtedly be less, for reasons discussed in previous chapters. As in 1924 no budget surplus—even if the fiscal reforms outlined in Chapter IX were put into operation—will be available for making foreign debt payments.

In this appraisal of the results of a Dawes Plan for France, no allowance has been made for reparation receipts from Germany, or for interest on the Russian debt. To the extent that France receives reparation from Germany and interest from Russia her own paying capacity will, of course be modified. But since the payments forthcoming from Germany are, under the Dawes Plan, contingent upon the development of both a budget and an export surplus in Germany, no definite figures can be set down for revenues from this source. If a Dawes Plan were instituted for France, it would, therefore, be necessary to put a question mark after the heading "Revenues Derived from Reparation Payments," and the same is true as regards interest on the Russian debt.[6]

It has sometimes been proposed that French payments to the Allies should be governed solely by the sums received from Germany. In other words, instead of utilizing reparation receipts for her own purposes, let France transfer the funds received to

[6] For an analysis of the Russian debt problem see Pasvolsky and Moulton, *Russian Debts and Russian Reconstruction*.

the Allies in settlement of her war debts. The reparation receipts would thus constitute a *special revenue account*, similar to the controlled revenues from taxation and from the railroads and industries provided under the Dawes Plan. Such a method of making payments would, however, not be sound in principle—that is to say, it would not safeguard French financial stability. Suppose, for example, the French budget lacked five billion paper francs of being balanced and the reparation receipts from Germany equalled five billion paper francs. The transfer of these funds to the Allies would leave the French budget unbalanced and result in financial disorganization. The principle enunciated above, that the indispensable minimum of domestic expenditures constitutes a prior charge against all revenues, applies to reparation receipts quite as much as to any other form of revenue.

We may conclude this discussion by a quotation from an address by Mr. Roland Boyden, formerly unofficial adviser of the United States on the Reparation Commission, in which he asks: Why should not the United States apply the Dawes Plan to the French debt?

Beyond a certain limit, whatever that limit may be, any demand for the making of such payments and their transformation into dollars would have in a much smaller way the effect which the demands upon Germany had upon her. It would demoralize French exchange and the French budget; it would lead to inflation of French currency and destroy the whole domestic economy of France. Besides all that, it would put an end to further payments. This is the principle back of the Dawes Plan. If you go beyond a certain point you are not only trying to get something you cannot get, but your futile attempt to get this something destroys the possibility of getting what you might otherwise get.[7]

We do not here urge the adoption of a Dawes Plan for France. Any plan proposed must take into account delicate political issues, and we are concerned only with the economic aspects of the problem. We express no opinion on the ethical aspects of the cancellation issue; we are not concerned with suggesting a total sum at which the debt should be funded; we do not discuss whether the creditors should supervise French financial administration; and we take no position on the question whether the present time is a propitious one for bringing about a wise and enduring settlement of the debt problem. We are concerned only with the economic capacity of France to meet her external debts and the economic results that will follow from the application of plans which are not based upon the lessons of experience and administered in accordance with the economic realities of the situation.

[7] Address delivered before the American Academy of Political and Social Science, Philadelphia, May 14, 1925.

CHAPTER XII

WHAT OF THE FUTURE?

THE analysis which we have been making of French financial and economic conditions relates only to the present and the immediate future. While an economic analysis properly closes at this point, it is not usually thus terminated in popular discussions. Admitting that French finances are in a very bad way at the present and that a "breathing spell" is necessary before payments on foreign debts can begin, it is nevertheless commonly argued that within a few years the situation will be very different. Present policies with reference to international debt settlements are, moreover, being suggested on the assumption that economic developments of great significance, resulting in a rapid increase of wealth, are quite certain to occur in the very near future. Accordingly, this final chapter must give some consideration to these prophesies about the future.

The roseate prognostications about the economic future of Europe are commonly supported by the observation that wealth increased with enormous rapidity before the war and by the reflection that the march of economic progress is always onward. It is, accordingly, urged that the European debts of

292

the present will look no more formidable 20 or 30 years hence than those of 1880 or 1890 appear to us at the present time. It is specifically contended that, since the world's international commerce doubles every 15 or 20 years, the difficulty of bearing the foreign debt burden, which now looms so large, will shortly appear insignificant. If these statements about the lessons of the past and the expectations of the future are really applicable to France, the debt problem in the long run will indeed be easy of solution. The evidence, unfortunately, shows that such statements about the growth of national income and international trade in the past are gross exaggerations, particularly as applied to a country like France.

The national income of France increased at the rate of about 1 per cent a year in the two decades prior to the Great War. The figures of wealth production commonly cited in connection with discussions of the European debts are for the world as a whole,—the new and developing regions as well as the older and more nearly static countries—and they make no allowance for the great rise in prices which occurred in the latter years before the war. In consequence, they are valueless for the purpose in hand. The two decades from 1893 to 1913 were those of most rapid economic improvement in modern French history; but, as the figures on page 56 indicate, the national income in real, as distinguished from money, terms increased by only about 20 per cent, or at the rate of 1 per cent a year. Eliminating the rise in prices, the annual national income of France increased during these two decades by only about six billion francs. From the fiscal point of view it is, moreover, important to note that the entire increase in national income can by no means be taken by the government in taxes. The government would be fortunate indeed if it could appropriate as much as 25 per cent of the increase.

On the foreign trade side one finds that the aggregate value of imports and exports, as measured in terms of money, increased by approximately 118 per cent in the 20 years between 1893 and 1913. In terms of real values, however, the increase was not more than 75 per cent. Between 1880 and 1913 the increase in real values was only 87 per cent. This is a very different matter than doubling every 15 or 20 years. It is, moreover, important to recognize that the growth in the *total quantity* of foreign trade is not, as commonly assumed, the true measure of the increase in debt-paying capacity. It is the export surplus that is important from the point of view of debts.

If the total foreign trade doubles in a given period, the export surplus will not necessarily increase one-hundred fold; on the contrary, it *may* not increase at all. For example, imports increased faster than exports during the 33 years prior to the Great War, the *import* surplus standing at 1,511 million francs in 1880 and at 1,460 million francs in 1913. The explanation of this is in part that as standards of living increased the proceeds of exports were used in buying imports for consumption. More largely, however, the explanation is to be found in the fact that as the wealth and productive capacity of the country expanded, larger imports of raw materials and partly manufactured goods were required by the industries which produce for export. For example, if more textiles were to be exported, more cotton and wool had to be imported; if the exports of iron and steel products were to increase, more imports of coal and coke were a prerequisite. We are not here interested in attempting to measure the extent to which exports might be increased relatively to imports. We are concerned only with stressing the point so commonly ignored in popular discussion, that it is the difference between imports and exports and not the aggregate volume of trade that is important.

The comforting reflection that rapid economic progress is the order of the day also needs to be sprinkled with the salt of reality. If one takes no account of limiting factors, it is easy to conjure up a most enchanting picture of the economic future of France. But if one faces certain stern realities, the prospect does not appear quite so alluring. The principal factors to be considered in any appraisal of the economic future of France are, (1) agricultural resources, (2) industrial resources, (3) international competition, (4) population and (5) financial resources.

No vast expansion of French agricultural produc-

tion is possible. The land area is limited, and the great bulk of it is already under cultivation. The possibility of increasing output therefore depends almost entirely upon the possibility of making each acre yield more; and this in turn depends principally upon the utilization of more fertilizers, though to some extent an adequate labor supply is also involved. Fortunately, the possibility of gradually increasing the yield by means of better fertilization is reasonably good.

With the acquisition of Alsace, France came into possession of very rich deposits of potash, the exploitation of which would mean a great deal to French agriculture. As respects nitrogenous fertilizers, however, the situation is not so favorable. Nitrogen may be produced either as a by-product of the coking industry or it may be extracted from the air by the utilization of electrical energy. France does not possess either the quantity or quality of coking coal required for large production of nitrogen. There is more possibility from the second method, but there are many competing uses for electrical energy. It is, however, perhaps not too much to expect that French agricultural production might be substantially increased in the course of the next two or three decades, thereby lessening the import requirements.

There are important obstacles in the way of a rapid expansion of the iron and steel industry. It is commonly argued that the acquisition by France of Lorraine, with its great reserves of iron ore and extensive equipment for the manufacture of crude iron and steel, provides the necessary basis for the rapid development of a highly integrated iron and steel industry similar to that in Germany and Great Britain. The problem of procuring an adequate supply of fuel, both coal and coke, is, however, an important factor in the situation.

France is now short of coal because of inadequate domestic production and she is particularly short of coke, because neither the French nor Sarre coal is well adapted to the manufacture of coke. Now if France is to achieve a great expansion and elaboration of the iron and steel industry, producing finished as well as crude products, and if she is to expand other lines of production, she must have a very great increase in her fuel supply. The question of the fuel problem in relation to the future of the French iron and steel industry is discussed at considerable length in another publication of the Institute.[1] Here it must suffice to observe that while a gradual expansion of French industry in general, and the iron and steel industry in particular, may be expected, no phenomenal growth may be counted upon.

While the development of water power is looked to by many to provide the basis of a great industrial expansion, the truth is that the potential water-power resources of France are equal to only about one-half the already developed resources of the

[1] Greer, Guy, *The Ruhr-Lorraine Industrial Problem,* Chs. VIII and IX.

United States.[2] Over one-third of the potential resources are already being utilized.[3]

*International competition for markets presents a
serious obstacle to French industrial expansion.*
The domestic market of France is not adequate
to absorb a great increase of goods, restricted as it
must be by high taxes. Accordingly, if French industry is to be greatly expanded, foreign markets
must be found. This is important not merely from
the standpoint of obtaining an export surplus; it is
equally important as a means of increasing wealth
and making possible a balanced budget.

In certain lines of production France has a distinct advantage over her competitors—as a result of
a long established prestige of French goods—but in
other lines, and particularly in the lines where it is
supposed that the great expansion is to come, the
competition is certain to prove very keen. The
table on the following page shows the value of the
principal groups of French exports in 1924.

It will be observed from this table that the French
export trade is very broad in character, with no single group of commodities predominant. It will be
observed also that the importance of the finer arts

[2] *Bulletin de la Statistique Générale de la France,* Jan., 1924,
p. 183.

[3] According to the *Journée Industrielle,* Feb. 24, 1925, p. 3, the
estimated output in 1925 is about 3 million horse power, while the
theoretical maximum output is approximately 9 million horse
power. The amount that can actually be utilized will doubtless
prove to be considerably less than this. For an indication of the
variety of ways in which water power is expected to alleviate
economic and social conditions in France, see p. 227 of this book.

in French trade is not quite so great as has commonly been assumed. The first group, the heavy industries, furnish nearly 16 per cent of the total; and

PRINCIPAL FRENCH EXPORTS, 1924

Commodities	In Millions of Francs	As a Percentage of Total
Ores, pig iron, iron, and steel..........	2,075.4	5.0
Tools and machines...................	2,239.5	5.4
Automobiles	1,512.8	3.6
Coal	323.6	.8
Wood	367.5	.9
Textiles, including yarns..............	9,862.6	23.8
Clothing	3,254.7	7.9
Wool and woolen waste..............	1,347.0	3.2
Raw silk	305.0	.7
Cotton and cotton waste..............	207.7	.5
Hides, skins, and leather goods........	1,598.2	3.9
Rubber goods	815.0	2.0
Chemicals	1,072.1	2.6
Vegetable oils	471.1	1.1
Perfumery, soap, and medicinal compounds	728.7	1.8
Wines, brandies, liqueurs, mineral waters, etc.	1,324.4	3.2
Fruits and fresh vegetables...........	615.0	1.5
Pottery, porcelain, glass, and crystal....	380.0	.9
Pearls and precious stones.............	2,685.5	6.5
Books, magazines, pictures, cinema films, etc.	514.3	1.2
All others	9,754.0	23.5
Total	41,454.1	100.0

coarse textile products are also important. The "all others" class includes a great variety of commodities, including raw materials and farm products, as well as manufactured goods.

In gauging the possibilities of a great expansion of French foreign trade, it is important to note that in iron and steel, machinery and tools, automobiles, textiles and clothing, leather and rubber, and chemicals—comprising nearly 55 per cent of the total exports in 1924—international competition is certain to be extremely keen in the future. Germany is hoping to meet her foreign obligations chiefly by expanding exports in these very lines. Great Britain is hoping to re-establish her industrial prosperity by an expansion of exports principally in these lines. Numerous other countries of Europe have enlarged producing capacity in some of these lines—notably Italy in textiles—and are hoping to penetrate foreign markets with their products. Even the United States, as a result of extending foreign loans, is counting upon not only maintaining but expanding her exports of these commodities.

Owing to the free use of credit resources and the low value of the franc, France has recently been enjoying great prosperity in these lines. If the credit policies which have brought France to the borderland of collapse are abandoned and a program of stabilization is successfully carried out, these temporary trade advantages will disappear. Whether she will then be able to hold her own in iron and steel, tools and machinery, automobiles, textiles, leather goods, rubber, and chemicals, in competition with such highly developed industrial countries as Germany, Great Britain, and the United States, is a question which we can here make

no attempt to answer. We merely observe that
those who contend that a vast expansion of French
foreign trade is assured have given no adequate consideration to the problems of international competition in the years ahead.

*The French colonies are looked to by many as the
great future outlet for French exports.* International competition can there be restrained, and
whatever disadvantages France might have elsewhere, she may be expected to have an inside track
in her own colonial markets. The present importance
of the colonial trade is indicated by the following
table showing the distribution by countries of
French exports in 1924:

THE EXPORT MARKETS OF FRANCE, 1924

Country of Destination	In Millions of Francs	As Percentage of Total
Foreign countries:	36,154	87.2
Great Britain	7,818	18.8
Belgium and Luxemburg	7,114	17.2
Germany	3,773	9.1
United States	3,144	7.6
Switzerland	2,613	6.3
Italy	1,479	3.6
The Sarre	1,371	3.3
Netherlands	1,161	2.8
Spain	1,158	2.8
Other foreign countries	6,523	15.7
Colonies and protectorates:	5,300	12.8
Algeria	2,504	6.0
Morocco	688	1.7
French Indo-China	571	1.4
Other colonies and protectorates	1,537	3.7
Total	41,454	100.0

It will be noted that the exports to Great Britain, notwithstanding the depression there, were 50 per cent greater in 1924 than the total to all her colonies and protectorates, while Belgium and Luxemburg bought nearly three times as many French goods as Algeria. The continent of Europe has always been the great market for French goods. In the course of time, a substantial improvement in standards of living and in the ability to purchase French goods will perhaps occur among French colonial peoples. But in the light of the economic, political, and racial considerations that are involved, there would seem to be little assurance that in the next two or three decades the colonies will become rich markets for French goods.

A stationary population presents obstacles to rapid economic expansion. The negligible growth of French population during the past 50 years has been a subject of perennial discussion, and it has occasioned much concern in France, from the economic and social as well as from the military point of view. The table on the opposite page shows the population figures for each census year since the Franco-Prussian War.

It is unnecessary to enter into any discussion of the economic and social factors responsible for this practically stationary population. It will suffice to recall that the birth-control movement was well under way in France even before Malthus was writing in England his gloomy predictions about overpopulation, and that there is no evidence that the

POPULATION OF FRANCE FOR EACH CENSUS YEAR, 1872-1921

Year	Total (in millions)	Urban		Rural	
		In Millions	As Percentage of Total	In Millions	As Percentage of Total
1872 (87 departments)	36.1	11.2	*31.1*	24.9	*68.9*
1876 "	36.9	12.0	*32.5*	24.9	*67.5*
1881 "	37.7	13.1	*34.8*	24.6	*65.2*
1886 "	38.2	13.8	*35.9*	24.4	*64.1*
1891 "	38.3	14.3	*37.4*	24.0	*62.6*
1896 "	38.5	15.0	*39.1*	23.5	*60.9*
1901 "	39.0	16.0	*40.9*	23.0	*59.1*
1906 "	39.3	16.5	*42.1*	22.8	*57.9*
1911 "	39.6	17.5	*44.2*	22.1	*55.8*
1921 "	37.5	17.4	*46.2*	20.1	*53.7*
1921 [a] (90 departments)	39.2	18.2	*46.4*	21.0	*53.6*

[a] The 1921 census showed that 5 per cent of the population consisted of aliens as against 10 per cent 70 years earlier. Between 1872 and 1921 the decline in total population in some departments was as great as 25,30 and 37 per cent—this being partly attributable, of course, to shifts of population within the country. See "La population de la France en 1921," *Annales de géographie* XXXI (1922), pp. 37-51.

causes responsible for the situation are ceasing to operate. Immediately after the war, there was some increase in the annual average of births over deaths, but the birth rate has gradually fallen again to practically the pre-war figures. The rate of population increase in France is less than one-third that of Germany, England, Australia, Hungary, Belgium, Spain, and Switzerland; less than one-fifth that of Italy and Norway; and only about one-seventh that of Holland.

We would not wish to over-estimate the importance of a growing native population for purposes of industrial expansion. The development of larger-scale production and the utilization of labor-saving devices in industry and in agriculture make it possible for a nation with a stationary population gradually to increase its wealth and income, as was the case in France before the war. With a static population, however, there is a tendency for the whole social and economic system to become relatively static and for the cake of custom to clog the wheels of progress.

Immigration may also lessen the importance of an increasing native population. Immigration, however, gives rise to political and social difficulties; and it may be noted that an immigrant exclusion movement has already developed in France, as a result of the influx of considerable numbers of alien laborers within the last few years. It may also be questioned whether immigrant labor is as efficient as native French labor, particularly in the more highly skilled occupations; if not, the possibilities of effective competition in international markets would be reduced. All in all, there would seem to be little doubt that a stationary native population constitutes an impediment to an era of great economic development. Even though plausible theoretical arguments may be advanced to show that an increasing native population is of little importance, it is interesting to reflect in this connection that no country has had a period of rapid economic expansion when the native birth rate was stationary.

Inadequate financial resources may prove an im-

pediment to French trade development. Economic history clearly indicates that industrial expansion is accelerated when the supply of liquid capital is abundant and retarded when it is scarce. If the volume of business is to expand rapidly in the future a rapid increase in the supply of funds will therefore be necessary. Steadily falling prices, it is true, would make the existing supply of funds go further; but a long period of falling prices would not promote industrial expansion. The business system appears to work best when prices are gradually rising. Accordingly, the supply of money, or liquid funds, is a matter of the first importance.

Unfortunately, the French banking situation, as shown in preceding chapters, is anything but favorable. The credit debauch of recent years has all but cut the foundations from beneath the French financial structure. Even with a devaluation of the paper franc in terms of gold as suggested in Chapter IX, the gold reserve of the Bank of France would be only about 30 per cent, as compared with more than 80 per cent in the latter years before the war. At the same time the private banking establishments are burdened with vast holdings of government securities which are difficult if not impossible to liquidate.

This shortage of liquid funds with which to finance an era of industrial expansion may be gradually overcome, it is true, by means of new foreign loans. But such additional loans would have to be contracted at high interest rates, and they would complicate the French financial problem in other ways. Obtaining an adequate supply of liquid capital with which to finance a continued era of expansion is clearly a problem which can not be ignored in estimating the future growth of French trade. The demands for subsidies and more abundant liquid resources by the various economic groups in France, as revealed in Chapter X, are not without significance in this connection.

Such limiting factors as those here briefly outlined can not be overlooked by one who would appraise the economic future of France. Moreover, as a preliminary to everything else, and underlying all other problems, is the difficult task of uniting the divergent social and political groups in France sufficiently to make possible the carrying through of a constructive program of financial stabilization. Unless this can be done any discussion of future growth and development is idle. Whether it can be done is the essence of the French problem today.

APPENDICES

INTRODUCTION

THE analyses and conclusions of this book have been largely based upon quantitative data. We are fully aware of the shortcomings of statistical data, particularly those bearing upon international trade and financial operations. The official data are in some respects open to serious criticism; while on numerous phases of the problem no official statistics are compiled and such unofficial figures as are available leave much to be desired.

The economist who would attempt an appraisal of the general financial position of a country is, therefore, faced with something of a dilemma. Either he must make a purely theoretical analysis, or he must use statistical evidence which he knows to be somewhat faulty. Since the first alternative leads to barren results, one must resort to the second, endeavoring by a careful appraisal and sifting of data to minimize the deficiencies. While a considerable margin of error will necessarily remain, the results obtained are infinitely better than those based on guess work or theoretical hypotheses unsupported by factual data.

As it was impossible to include in the text a critical appraisal of the French statistical data set forth in the various tables and charts, without obscuring the story by a mass of technical discussion, this material has all been gathered in the following appendices. It is hoped that these will be of value to the student, and that they will contribute something toward an appreciation of the necessity for more adequate economic statistics, and stimulate governments to co-operate in the fullest measure with the various international organizations which are now endeavoring to standardize and improve such statistics.

APPENDIX A

INTERNATIONAL TRADE AND FINANCIAL ACCOUNTS

THE international trade and financial data comprise first, the official figures of foreign trade and of international shipments of specie; and second, the unofficial estimates of interest on foreign investments and the returns from the various service accounts.

No systematic data with reference to interest on foreign investments, tourist expenditures, shipping, banking, and other services have ever been compiled. The French government has never undertaken a complete study of these items, and the only figures available are those presented by independent investigators who have been concerned with particular items of international income and expenditures. For some of the items no estimates are available and it has therefore been necessary to make independent estimates for these—by methods explained below.

Section I of this appendix is devoted to a discussion of the official trade figures. The following sections are given over to a critical study of the service accounts of France—for the pre-war, war, and post-war periods.

I. TRADE AND SPECIE STATISTICS [1]

An intelligent use of the trade figures of a country requires an understanding of what these figures include,

[1] The information presented in this section is based on various documents and discussions, as follows: (1) *Tableau général du*

the method of valuing the trade, how the quantity figures are compiled, and how the country of source or destination is recorded. The discussion in this section summarizes French practice on these points.

A. WHAT THE FIGURES INCLUDE

In theory the foreign trade statistics of France, like those of other countries, include all the merchandise which passes over the country's boundaries. In practice there are some goods that escape official enumeration, such as contraband goods, personal effects of travellers and goods smuggled in by travellers, goods which the custom house officials overlook, etc. Two sets of trade figures are compiled by the government, showing: (1) the *general commerce*, and (2) the *special commerce* of France.

General commerce includes among imports *all* of the foreign merchandise brought in from other countries, from the colonies, and from deep-sea fisheries; by land or by sea; whether declared for consumption, for transit trade, for storage in bonded warehouses, for transshipment in French ports, for re-export, or for temporary admission into the country. Among exports, general commerce includes *all* of the merchandise actually sent from France, both of foreign and domestic origin, whether it is merchandise which leaves the country as part of the transit trade, goods transshipped in French ports to some foreign destination, goods taken from bonded ware-

commerce et de la navigation, 1917, Part I; (2) *Rapports presentées à la XVe Session de l'Institut International de Statistique à Bruxelles,* October, 1923; (3) Olivier, Maurice, "Le Commerce Extérieur," *Revue d'économie politique,* March-April, 1924, p. 233; and (4) an unpublished report to the United States Department of Commerce by Commercial Attaché Huntington.

houses for re-export, or goods which are re-exported after having been temporarily admitted to the country for repairs or for some manufacturing process. Thus, general commerce includes certain imports that are not for French consumption, and certain exports that are in no way the products of French industry.

The special trade figures represent fairly closely the actual trade of France. By definition the *special trade* includes among imports only the merchandise brought into the country for consumption. Prior to 1860, when all foreign goods brought into the country for consumption were subject to duty, it was to the interest of foreign traders to distinguish between goods intended for transit or for storage in warehouses and goods brought in for consumption in France. At that time, therefore, the special trade figures agreed pretty well with the theoretical definition of special trade. After the treaties of 1860, some classes of goods intended for consumption in France were admitted free of duty, and the custom house formalities in the case of these goods were less troublesome than for similar goods intended for transit trade or storage. The result has been that foreign traders followed the easier course, and have uniformly declared for home consumption all duty-free goods brought into the country as well as dutiable goods actually brought in for French consumption. This makes for a slight overstatement of imports in the special trade figures.

Among exports the special trade includes all domestic merchandise sent out of the country and all foreign goods brought into the country, resold in the French markets and shipped out of the country again.

Foreign goods brought into the country for further manufacture and re-export are shown in the trade sta-

tistics as *temporary admissions* and *re-exports*. These
imports and exports are not included in the special trade.
It should be pointed out that sugar is an exception to
this rule. Since 1864, sugar brought in for re-export
has been included in the special import figures. All
sugar refined in France and shipped out—whether the
raw sugar was imported or grown in France—is included
in the special exports.

*The trade figures for bullion and specie are less
accurate than those for goods.* In this connection it
should be noted that the trade figures represent only the
declared imports and exports of gold and silver. As in
the case of other commodities, they do not include the
quantities which travellers bring in or carry away with
them. Léon Say, in his study of the French indemnity
of 1871, commented on "the inaccuracy in the customs
statistics concerning gold," saying that "this had been
discovered in various investigations with regard to banks
and money." [2] For the years 1871, 1872, and 1873, he
himself checked the official import and export figures for
gold and silver, using special information which he obtained from large banking houses in Paris. His conclusions were that the official data gave a figure for net exports that was too low, particularly for gold. A somewhat similar check of the official figures for the years
1914-1919 shows that the net exports of gold and silver
were again under-valued.

It was therefore necessary in using the bullion and
specie data in the tables on pages 24 and 25 to take notice
of the fact that figures compiled from official sources are
open to criticism. As a rule the errors in the figures are
relatively unimportant, but during exceptional years a

[2] *Rapport sur le paiement de l'indemnité de guerre*, 1874, p. 62.

considerable error may be introduced into the balance of accounts if these figures are used without correction.

It is scarcely necessary to say that we have used the special, rather than the general, trade figures, since the special trade is more nearly an accurate measure of essentially French trade. A correction in these figures is necessary, however, if they are to show the net French income or outgo on account of foreign trade, because of the fact that "temporary admissions and re-exports" are not included in them. This correction has been made in tables on pages 16, 25, and 30 of the text and corresponding tables of this appendix. Correction of other minor inaccuracies that have been pointed out would be required to make the figures altogether exact, but such corrections are practically impossible.

B. METHOD OF VALUING THE TRADE

There are two methods of determining the value of imports and exports: the method of official values and the method of declared values. Until recently, France was one of the countries that employed the method of official valuation. But in 1922, as we shall presently note, the method of declared values was adopted for imports although no change was made in the method of valuing exports.

Present practice with regard to valuing the trade is the result of long evolution. In early times—and the French government was one of the first to compile foreign trade figures—the French customs houses kept account of the quantities of goods passing over the frontiers, but made no record of the value of the goods. The value figures reported for these early years were based on price information which the government gathered informally from business and manufacturing concerns. This method, as one writer put it, was "absurd and arbitrary and permitted abuses when there was a temptation to show a favorable balance of trade."

In 1826, therefore, a special price inquiry was made, on the basis of which a "permanent schedule" of values was worked out. From 1827 until 1847, this schedule was used for evaluating the commerce of France. This was unsatisfactory because it did not take account of fluctuations in the prices of particular goods or changes in the general price level.

Accordingly, in 1847, a "Permanent Customs Evaluation Commission" was established whose function was to make up each year a schedule of the average price of the principal commodities of commerce, this schedule to be used in valuing the year's trade. This change was put into force with some difficulty. It was argued that such a change would make the trade figures useless as a basis for comparisons between the past and future foreign trade of the country. To meet this objection the Customs Administration, from 1848 to 1861, compiled two sets of value figures, putting them in parallel columns in its publications. One set was based on the old schedule of "permanent" values, the other on the schedule of "revised" values. After 1861, they discontinued the figures based on the "permanent" schedule of values, and published only those compiled by the new method.

In 1861, the Customs Administration began publishing a monthly trade bulletin, a step which has indirectly worked in favor of a change from the method of official values to that of declared values. Until then only annual statistics had been compiled for the foreign trade: no monthly figures were published. It was decided that the monthly value figures published in this bulletin should be considered as *provisional* and should be based on the schedule fixed for the preceding year. At the end of each year, when the schedule of values for the year had been worked out, the provisional figures were revised on the basis of the new schedule.

During the pre-war period the provisional figures in the monthly bulletin were accurate enough for all practical purposes, because price changes from year to year were relatively unimportant. A French customs report for 1913 states that "as a whole 1913 prices as compared with those for 1912, have shown only the slight change of a decrease of 1.02 per cent for imports and 0.07 per cent for exports." After the outbreak of the war, however, price fluctuations became so great that very considerable errors in the monthly provisional figures resulted from the use of the price schedule of the preceding year. The government accordingly set the Permanent Commission the task of working out coefficients of price changes from month to month, by means of which the value schedule for the preceding year was to be brought more nearly into line with actual prices. When this was found impracticable, a change from the method of official values to the method of declared values was decided upon.

A decree was issued October 25, 1916, making obligatory the declaration of values both for imports and for exports. This decree, however, carried no penalties for failure to furnish true and accurate information. The values reported were accordingly so inaccurate that the system was given up and the Customs Administration returned to the old method of official values, which continued in vogue until 1921.

When the Customs Administration was ready to publish the export and import figures for the first six months of 1921, they had before them the schedule of official values for the year 1920 which normally would have been used as a basis for the provisional figures during 1921. Prices had fallen to such an extent, however, that the use of the 1920 schedule in valuing the 1921 trade would have exaggerated the figures enormously, making them perhaps as much as 27 per cent greater than they should have been. After a study of price index numbers, the Customs Administration decided to use the 1919 schedule of values as a basis for the provisional monthly figures for 1921. Because of this situation the question of "official" versus "declared" values was again raised for consideration.

In 1922 the method of declared values was adopted for imports but not for exports. Beginning with January 1 of that year, the value of imports has been based exclusively on declarations made out by the importers and checked by the Customs officials. Export statistics, on the other hand, have continued to be based on the table of official values made up by the Permanent Commission, a system of coefficients being used for the provisional monthly figures to adjust the official rates to current conditions.[3]

The explanation of the present system is that foreign trade figures are by-products of fiscal administration. Certain changes in connection with the tariff and certain provisions in the business turnover tax law made it easy to adopt a new method of valuing the imports, but prac-

[3] For further discussion see Olivier, Maurice, "Le Commerce extérieur," *Revue d'économie politique,* March-April, 1924, pp. 233-6.

tical reasons of this sort did not arise in connection with exports. ·

The French customs tariff is a tariff of specific duties. In years of relatively stable prices such duties are, of course, equivalent to a fairly constant ad valorem rate; but in a period of rising prices they represent a decreasing ad valorem rate. After the outbreak of the war, France continued to use her pre-war tariff rates, attempting at first to adjust them to the new level of prices by the use of ad valorem surtaxes. Since the middle of 1919 the adjustment has been made by means of a coefficient system—the basic rate of the tariff was left unchanged, but in practice this rate was multiplied by a changing coefficient of 2, 3, 5, or what not. By this method the customs duties are adjusted to changes in the price level in such a way as practically to maintain an unchanging level of protection to domestic industries; and to minimize the effect of the depreciation of the franc on government customs receipts.

As a basis for these tariff coefficients, it was necessary that the government should have declarations from importers with regard to the actual prices they were paying for their goods. The business turnover tax, which applies to importers (law of June 25, 1920), makes importers' declarations necessary, and specifically calls for them. For these reasons declared values of imports were easily available by the end of 1921, and their publication was a matter of mere routine.

In the case of exports, however, there were not the same compelling fiscal reasons in favor of declared values. French exports, with the exception of hats, dresses, cloaks, laces, and feathers, are specifically exempted from the business turnover tax. Thus the tax argument could not be invoked in favor of exporters' declarations. French businessmen are solidly against any more government interference in business than appears to be clearly necessary, and would stubbornly resist if exporters' declarations were required merely for statistical purposes.

The practice of evaluating imports by one method and exports by another makes the French trade balance an uncertain quantity. It is generally believed that by adopting the system of declared values for her imports, France has made a step in the right direction. Nevertheless, the fact that the system of official values is retained in the case of exports raises some questions with regard to the reliability of the yearly trade balance shown by the French trade reports since 1922. It is contended by some, however, that the evaluation of exports by the Permanent Customs Evaluation Commission is so carefully made that the yearly figures very closely approximate those that would be obtained by export declarations. The monthly figures are admittedly much less accurate.

The Evaluation Commission, which is now placed under the Ministry of Commerce, is composed of 106 members, divided into five sections. The first section, which has charge of the direction and centralization of the Commission's work, is made up of high government officials, among whom are the Director General of Customs, the Director of Political and Commercial Affairs of the Ministry of Foreign Affairs, and the Director of the Bureau of Commercial and Industrial Affairs of the Ministry of Commerce. The other four sections are formed of distinguished merchants and manufacturers, serving without pay, who are chosen for their special knowledge of certain commodity groups.

At the beginning of the calendar year the directing section of the Commission draws up a set of questionnaires which are sent to the 106 members. These questionnaires are made explicit and definite so as to save the time of the business members of the Commission and to restrict each of them closely to his particular field. As a rule, the investigation is practically finished by the month of June, when the members of the five sections are called together in Paris to consider the estimates which have been submitted. There is usually no difficulty in fixing the schedule of values at these meetings, but in case there is a wide difference of opinion as to particular values, a member may be asked to make a further investigation. In October another meeting of the Commission is held, at which further reports are rendered with regard to economic and business conditions during the year in question. The report of the Commission is finally brought together and published in December.

A former commercial attaché of the United States at Paris, C. E. Huntington, reports that the Commission's work is evidently conscientious and thorough, though the method is cumbersome. He concludes that "there is no ground for some of the suspicions which have been expressed that the system now in use unduly exaggerates exports as compared with imports, thus giving a distorted picture of the real trade balance."

There is, nevertheless, some ground for holding that the difference of method does tend to exaggerate exports relatively to imports. With a view to lowering customs duties, the importers naturally declare their imports at as low figures as they think may possibly be accepted. And though the customs officials will raise these values as much as they think they can without creating serious opposition, the probability is that the import figures finally accepted represent under- rather than over-valuations. On the other hand, with export values determined by a commission which is not concerned with customs or tax problems, the tendency would be for full export values to be registered. Indeed, in view of the universal desire to have exports bulk large in the national economy, the Commission would probably unconsciously exaggerate the export figures, for it would be an easy matter in drawing up the schedule of prices to accept the larger of two possible figures.

C. THE QUANTITY STATISTICS

The figures showing the volume of the *special commerce*, both imports and exports, are compiled from traders' declarations made in conformity with customs house instructions. According to these instructions the more highly taxed imports are declared in net weight terms, while all others are declared in gross weight terms. In order to make the figures comparable in the published reports, the gross weight figures are officially converted to net weight terms.

D. COUNTRY OF SOURCE OR DESTINATION

The official trade statisticians of France call attention to the fact that theoretically the geographical classification of the trade should show the actual origin of imports and the ultimate destination of exports. But they show that in practice this would be a difficult rule to apply in all cases. They, therefore, record the actual source or destination of the goods where that is known;

otherwise they simply record the country to which the goods are shipped or from which they come. In many cases the best that can be done with regard to goods shipped by rail is to credit them to the country shown in the railway bill of lading; while goods shipped by river or canal are usually credited to the contiguous country.

It is easy to see that the French trade figures—like those of other countries—do not furnish an absolutely accurate record of the source and destination of French trade. Nevertheless, they give a reasonably good picture of the trade relations of France with other countries.

II. PRE-WAR FOREIGN INVESTMENTS

There is no source to which one may turn for complete statistical data concerning French investments abroad. In the words of Paul Leroy-Beaulieu, "no one, absolutely no one, can know, except in an approximate way, concerning the foreign investments belonging to France."[4] Our estimates are offered, therefore, without any pretense at absolute accuracy, and with a ready admission that they may be either somewhat too large or somewhat too small. It is contended, however, that these estimates are very much better than unsupported guesses.

A. CAPITAL VALUE AND GROWTH OF PRE-WAR INVESTMENTS

Turning first to the question of the capital value and growth of pre-war investments, the investigator finds that a number of methods or combinations of methods are open to him. (1) He may undertake a census of the holdings of foreign securities. (2) He may seek to ascer-

[4] *L'Economiste Français*, Oct. 4, 1902, p. 450.

tain the increase of foreign investments from year to year by a study of stock exchange transactions in foreign securities. (3) He may estimate the sums available for new investments from year to year from a study of international receipts and expenditures. Each of these methods, however, has its disadvantages.

Only a government can conduct a comprehensive census, and governments have seldom been interested in making such a census. A study of the securities markets can at best indicate only the annual increase, while it is very difficult to ascertain the volume of sales of foreign securities in a given year with any high degree of accuracy. To do so, one would have to know the volume both of French purchases and sales of foreign securities during the year, and also the capital value of the securities that have matured and been paid off. These are figures that it is difficult to determine because the same securities are traded in on many international markets and are in constant movement from country to country. The third method, like the second, can reveal only the growth of investments, and the accuracy of the results depends upon the adequacy of the data with reference to the items entering into the balance of payments. Probably the method most commonly used has been the second one described above, that of basing an estimate on an analysis of the movement of securities.

In the table which follows are gathered together the estimates that have been made—by whatever method—for pre-war years. This will be followed by a computation of our own made upon the basis of the French trade and service operations, which will then be compared with the other estimates.

ESTIMATES OF PRE-WAR FOREIGN INVESTMENTS
(In billions of francs)

Year	Estimate	Authority	Year	Estimate	Authority
1850 [a]	2.5	E. Théry [1]	1904 [a]	27 to 30	Alfred Neymarck [2]
1869 [a]	10.	A. Neymarck [2]	1906 [a]	30 to 32	Alfred Neymarck [2]
1870	12 to 14	Léon Say [3]	1907	37.15	Edmond Théry [12]
1880	12 to 15	Paul Leroy-Beaulieu [4]	1908	At least 30	Alfred Neymarck [13]
			1908 [a]	32 to 35	Alfred Neymarck [2]
1880 [a]	15.	A. Neymarck [2]	1908 [a]	38.	Edmond Théry [6]
1888	20.	A. Neymarck [5]	1909	40.	Edgar Crammond [14]
1890 [a]	20.	A. Neymarck [2]	1910 [a]	38 to 40	Alfred Neymarck [2]
1892 [a]	21.	E. Théry [6]	1910	40.	Walter Zollinger [15]
1897	26.	R. G. Levy [7]	1912	40 to 42	Alfred Neymarck [2]
	26.2	E. Théry [8]	1912	40.	Yves Guyot [16]
1899 [a]	27.	E. Théry [9]	1914	50.	Germain Martin [17]
	20.3	A. Neymarck [10]	Pre-War	65.	F. S. Schmidt [18]
1902 [a]	25 to 27	A. Neymarck [2]	"	45.	C. K. Hobson [19]
1902	30.	Official investigation [11]	"	55 to 60	Hans Jürgen von Kleist [20]

[a] The writer states that the estimate is for December 31.
[1] Cited by Théry, André, *Les grands établissements de crédit français*, pp. 80-1.
[2] *Bulletin de l'Institut International de Statistique*, 1913, Vol. XX, Part II, p. 1406. Neymarck's figures are for total French investments abroad, no allowance being made for investments of foreigners in France. He gives other data, however, from which his estimates may be reduced to net figures. He estimates that foreigners' investments in France on the average, have amounted to about 10 per cent of existing French securities, and also gives a table of French security issues (*ibid.*, p. 1406). The following computation of net French investments abroad have been compiled from these data. The figures are in billions of francs.

Year	French Investments Abroad	Foreigners' Investments in France	Net French Investments Abroad	Year	French Investments Abroad	Foreigners' Investments in France	Net French Investments Abroad
1869	10	2.3	7.7	1906	30–32	6.7	23.3–25.3
1880	15	4.1	10.9	1908	32–35	7.0	25.0–28.0
1890	20	5.4	14.6	1910	38–40	7.0	31.0–33.0
1904	27–30	6.3	20.7–23.7	1912	40–42	7.0	33.1–35.1

[3] Say, Léon, *Rapport sur la paiement de l'indemnité de guerre*, 1874, pp. 70-71. Say estimated the income of France from foreign investments at 600 to 700 million francs at the outbreak of the Franco-Prussian war. He estimated the sale of securities during the war at 2 billion francs, and the consequent loss of income at 100 million francs a year. On this basis the capitalized value of pre-war income was 12 to 14 billion francs. Deducting about 2 billions for investments of foreigners in France leaves a net figure of 10 to 12 billions.
[4] *Économiste française*, Oct. 23, 1880, p. 499.
[5] *Journal de la Société de Statistique de Paris*, 1888, p. 222.
[6] Théry, Edmond, *Fortune publique de la France*, 1911, p. 197.
[7] *Revue des deux mondes*, March 15, 1897, p. 440.
[8] Théry, Edmond, *Les valeurs mobilières en France*, 1897, p. 185.
[9] Théry, Edmond, *Conséquences économiques de la guerre pour la France*, p. 336.
[10] *Bulletin de l'Institut International de Statistique*, 1899, Vol. XI, p. 11.

Practically all of the figures in the table above represent estimates of the total or gross foreign holdings of France. For some purposes, however, it is more important to know the net amount of French foreign holdings—the difference between French investments abroad and foreign investments in France—than to know the total of investments abroad. The footnotes appended to the table make it possible to reduce some of these estimates to net figures. By selecting from the table, at approximately 10-year intervals, the estimates which appear on the surface to be most reliable and by reducing these estimates to net figures (in billions of francs) we arrive at the following table:

1870....................	10 to 12	Léon Say
1880....................	10	Neymarck
1890....................	15	"
1902....................	19 to 21	"
1913....................	35 to 43	Various writers

[11] Under the direction of the Minister of Foreign Affairs, questionnaires were sent to French diplomatic agents and consuls abroad concerning French investments in their territories. The results of the inquiry were published in the *Journal officiel* for Sept. 25, 1902, and in the *Bulletin de statistique et de législation comparée*, October, 1902, p. 450. A good résumé was published in the *Journal of the Royal Statistical Society*, December, 1903, p. 729; and a critical analysis of it, by P. Leroy-Beaulieu, was published in *l'Économiste Français*, Oct. 4, 1902, pp. 449-51.

[12] Théry, Edmond, *Le progrès économique de la France*, 1908, p. 307.

[13] Neymarck, Alfred, *French Savings and Their Influence on the Bank of France* (published by the United States Monetary Commission), p. 176. A rearrangement of Neymarck's table is given on pages 333-4 of this appendix.

[14] *Journal of the Royal Statistical Society*, September, 1909, p. 483.

[15] Zollinger, Walter, *Die Bilanz der internationalen Wertübertragungen*, pp. 111-2. Zollinger's figure is for securities only.

[16] *Annals of the American Academy*, November, 1916, pp. 41-3.

[17] Martin, Germain, *La situation financière de la France*, 1914-24, pp. 100 and 106. On pp. 30-1 he sets the figure at 50 to 60 billions, but in the later discussion he uses only the lower figure.

[18] Schmidt, F. S., *Internationaler Zahlungsverkehr und Wechselkurse*, pp. 20 and 33. Schmidt puts the total of French investments abroad before the war at 65 billion francs. From this he subtracts 5 billions on account of foreign capital invested in France. This leaves a net investment abroad of 60 billions. For an explanation of this very high estimate, see footnote 7, p. 328.

[19] *Annals of the American Academy*, November, 1916, p. 32.

[20] Von Kleist, Hans Jürgen, *Die Ausländische Kapitalbeteiligung in Deutschland*, 1921, p. 27. For an explanation of this estimate, see footnote 7, p. 328.

A study of French international trade and service operations furnishes an independent check upon these figures. Foreign investments, it must be borne in mind can be derived only from net international income. An estimate of the net amount of French investments abroad in 1870—based upon Say's report—may be used as a starting point. Then by calculating the total invisible income of the country from services (including interest, shipping, tourist trade, etc.), year after year, and subtracting from this amount the deficit in the commodity and specie accounts, a balance will be found which represents the net annual sums which were available for new investment abroad. (The final column in the income statement given on page 326 has been worked out according to this plan.) These amounts added to —or subtracted from—the original 10 to 12 billions will show year by year the net total of the French investments abroad.

A detailed explanation of the particular items shown in the table on page 326 is given in Section III of this appendix, pages 340-5. For the present it is sufficient to say that the interest item has been computed at a constant rate of 5 per cent, and that other estimates have taken into account whatever relevant data are available. The interest rate of 5 per cent may appear too low if one considers only the high effective rate fixed by the French for many of their loans to foreign governments. On the other hand, it may appear much too high if one considers only the great losses which frequently have to be met—because of default in interest payments; because of forced conversions, sometimes resulting in as much as a 50 per cent reduction in the principal of a debt; and because of an occasional

INTERNATIONAL INCOME AND EXPENDITURES, 1871-1913

(Average amounts for years specified, in millions of francs.)

Period	Net Income from Services					Net Outgo for Commodities and Specie [a]	Net Income (Available for New Foreign Investment)
	Interest	Shipping	Tourists	Commissions, etc.	Total		
1871-75..	485 to 585	185	200	70	940 to 1,040	181	759 to 859
1876-80..	500 to 600	175	320	75	1,070 to 1,170	1,120	−50 to 50 [b]
1881-85..	480 to 580	170	370	80	1,100 to 1,200	1,202	−102 to −2
1886-90..	515 to 615	155	430	75	1,175 to 1,275	742	433 to 533
1891-96..	640 to 740	125	475	75	1,315 to 1,415	796	519 to 619
1897-02..	915 to 1,015	138	525	85	1,663 to 1,763	506	1,157 to 1,257
1903-08..	1,315 to 1,415	160	585	100	2,160 to 2,260	801	1,359 to 1,459
1909-13..	1,705 to 1,805	215	625	150	2,695 to 2,795	1,456	1,239 to 1,339 [c]

[a] Including temporary admissions and re-exports.

[b] The minus sign denotes an unfavorable balance.

[c] M. René Pupin has estimated the net international income of France for the years 1912 and 1913 in his book, *Richesse privée et finances françaises*, 1919, pp. 25-6. In a study for the Paris Statistical Society (*Journal de la Société de Statistique de Paris*, 1916, pp. 394-8) he included a second and different set of estimates for the year 1912. His figures for the total income from services are very close to ours, and his interest figures are practically identical with ours. On the other hand, his figures for the tourist item are considerably larger than ours. His high estimates for this item are, however, substantially offset by certain omissions, as follows: (1) He fails to include an estimate for commissions. (2) He makes no adjustment for the re-export trade. (3) He fails to include any shipping figure in the studies published in his book; and in his study for the Statistical Society he has even set down a net outlay of 350 million francs for shipping. Such an estimate for shipping overlooks the fact that expenditures for shipping are included as a part of the valuation of imports (see our discussion, pp. 342-5.

outright repudiation of debt. On the whole, 5 per cent has seemed a fairly generous rate to assume.[5]

From this table it appears that during the years 1871-1875 France had an average net income of 759 to 859 million francs a year, or a total for the five years of 3,795 to 4,295 millions. It must be remembered, however, that from June 1, 1871 to September 5, 1873, France paid to Germany a war indemnity amounting in all to about 5.3 billion francs. A part of these payments have a direct bearing on the balance of accounts and the foreign holdings of France.

About 2 billion francs of the indemnity of 1871 was met by the proceeds from the sale of French holdings of foreign securities. Another 2.3 billions were procured through the sale to foreigners of French government bonds. The payment of the indemnity thus resulted in reducing the net foreign holdings of France by about 4.3 billion francs. The remaining one billion of the indemnity was met by the surrender of certain railroad rights in Alsace-Lorraine, by the use of German money brought into France by the German army, and by the transfer of French gold and silver—items which either do not affect the balance of payments or have already been taken into account in the balance given.[6]

---

[5] See discussion of this general question in Moulton and McGuire, *Germany's Capacity to Pay*, p. 258. For a discussion of the doubtful character of some of the foreign loans floated in the French market, see Lysis, *Contre l'oligarchie financière en France*.

[6] For a full exposition of the way the indemnity was met see Appendix F. According to Léon Say a large share of the gold sent out of France during the years 1871-73 was not recorded in the bullion and specie statistics. (Say, *Rapport sur la paiement de l'indemnité de guerre*, pp. 66-9.) This unrecorded sum offsets the amount of gold and silver that was transferred to Germany, so

The aggregate net income of only 3.8 to 4.3 billion francs for the five years 1871-75 was thus scarcely sufficient to offset the reduction in foreign investments that resulted from the indemnity. Therefore, the net foreign holdings of the country remained practically the same at the end of the period as at the beginning.

For the years from 1876 to 1913 no extraordinary items of income or outgo are to be accounted for. The growth of French foreign investments during these years is therefore roughly indicated by the international income statement, the figures in the final column of which show the average annual balance available for new investments during each period.[7] From this it appears that that no adjustment in the balance of payments is required for either of these items.

[7] The following estimates of the rate of increase of French foreign investments are of interest. In 1905, M. Henri Germain, now deceased—president and founder—of the Crédit Lyonnais, stated that 1.5 billions of French capital was annually invested in foreign securities. (Cited by Théry, André, *Les grands éstablissements de crédit français*, pp. 82-83.) Edmond Théry estimated that the export of capital between 1892 and 1908 amounted to 17 billions, or an annual rate of about 1.1 billion francs (*Conséquences économiques de la guerre pour la France*, 1922, p. 336), and that in the 11 years preceding the war France had acquired about 20 billions of new foreign securities, which would amount to an annual increase of about 1.8 billion francs (*ibid.*, p. 45). In 1880 Paul Leroy-Beaulieu estimated French savings at from 2.5 to 3 billions a year, of which he said about one-third was invested abroad (*l'Économist français*, Oct. 23, 1880, p. 498). In 1910 he estimated the amount annually invested abroad, exclusive of investments in the colonies, at 1.5 billions (*ibid.*, May 21, 1910, p. 755).

These estimates are clearly much too high in view of the available data on the balance out of which investments must come. They are also very high as compared with the estimates given above of the net foreign investments at various periods. It was on the basis of these estimates of rapid growth that Schmidt and

the aggregate amount available for new investments
abroad during each period was as follows:

Period	Millions of Francs
1871-1875 (5 years)...............	—500 to 0
1876-1880 (5 years)...............	—250 to 250
1881-1885 (5 years)...............	—510 to —10
1886-1890 (5 years)...............	2,150 to 2,650
1891-1896 (6 years)...............	3,125 to 3,725
1897-1902 (6 years)...............	6,950 to 7,550
1903-1908 (6 years)...............	8,155 to 8,755
1909-1913 (5 years)...............	6,200 to 6,700

The results of this method of calculating the net
amount of French investments abroad may now be set
down for comparison with the table on page 324. The
figures are for December 31 of the respective years, and
are shown in billions of francs.

Year	Estimates Based on International Trade and Service Operations	Other Estimates
1870................	10 to 12	10 to 12
1875................	9.75 to 11.75	
1880................	9.75 to 11.75	10
1885................	9.5 to 11.5	
1890................	12 to 14	15
1896................	15.5 to 17.5	
1902................	22.5 to 24.5	19 to 21
1908................	31 to 33	
1913................	37.5 to 39.5	35 to 43

von Kleist (see table p. 323) estimated that the total by 1914 must
have been around 60 billions. The explanation of these over-
estimates apparently is that the writers had in mind only gross
figures. Alfred Neymarck, in 1913, repeated a statement which he
had made in 1906, to the effect that the total new investment of
the French people in securities, *both* at home and abroad
amounted to only about 1.5 to 2 billions a year (*Bulletin de l'Institut International Statistique*, Vol. XX, Part II, p. 1405).

This method of computing the growth of foreign investments can not, of course, pretend to a high degree of accuracy, since it involves mere estimates of certain of the service items. It does, however, mark out the general trend of increase over a long period of years with a fair degree of reliability. The error involved is considerably less than might at first be supposed, because of the fact that the particular items about which there is the most doubt are items which bulk relatively small in the totals.

The two large items in these accounts are the commodity and specie balance and the net interest income. The commodity and specie balance is an official figure that may be accepted as reasonably reliable for the years included in this statement. The estimates with regard to interest are computed on the basis of (1) Say's foreign investment figure for 1870—a figure generally accepted by students of French finance; (2) interest at a constant rate of 5 per cent on the net amount of French foreign investments—a liberal assumption; and (3) the year to year changes in net French holdings of foreign investments—the service items of minor importance in the international accounts of France thus becoming factors which enter into the computation of the interest item.

A question, therefore, may be raised concerning the extent to which the interest item is affected by errors in other items in the account. There is no reason to believe that errors in these items will all be in the same direction—under-estimates in some cases being matched by over-estimates in others, and possible omissions of negligible items of outgo being offset by similar gaps in the income figures. The net error in these estimates is, therefore, probably small when compared with the large items in the account. Now since it requires about 14 years for a sum at 5 per cent compound interest to double in amount, it will be seen that although errors in the minor accounts are carried over into the interest item, they will not greatly affect either that item or the net balance of accounts.

The figure at which we arrive is slightly above but very close to that of Neymarck, the outstanding French authority on investments, who for many years has made studies of this problem for the International Institute of Statistics. Neymarck's estimates, both gross and net figures, are shown in footnote 2, page 323. By the end of 1913 his net figure would probably have reached about 35 to 37 billions. Our analysis of the trade and specie items leads us to believe that Neymarck's estimates are a bit conservative. We have therefore taken 38 billions net, based on the table page 329, as the best approximation obtainable.

The method which we have used, it should be emphasized, leads to an estimate of net, not gross, holdings. New investments made by foreigners in French industry and French securities, automatically cancel in the international accounts against new French investments made abroad. To calculate the aggregate of French investments abroad, therefore, the net figure shown in the table on page 329 must be increased by the amount of this offset, which Neymarck estimated would be about 7 billion francs in 1912. Thus the estimated total for 1913, based on a study of the international income of France, becomes 44.5 billions to 46.5 billions, or roughly 45 billion francs.

B. GEOGRAPHIC DISTRIBUTION OF PRE-WAR INVESTMENTS

In the text, page 20, a table was presented which showed the geographic distribution of French foreign investments in 1914. The estimates there given were derived from two French studies for earlier years, supplemented by later data brought together from various sources.

In 1902 the French Minister of Foreign Affairs published a study of the character and distribution of French investments abroad, which was based on information furnished by consular and diplomatic agents abroad. At the time it was issued, Paul Leroy-Beaulieu severely criticized the study, characterizing it as "only an incomplete statistical beginning." Nevertheless, he concluded that "however faulty it might be, it gives some idea of the importance and diversity of French foreign investments." [8] In 1910, the United States Monetary Commission published a study, by Alfred Neymarck, which shows the amount and distribution of French foreign investments for the year 1907 or 1908—not stating definitely to which year the figures apply.

The figures from the official inquiry of 1902, and those from Neymarck's study of 1908, are presented on pages 333-4 in parallel columns.

---

[8] *L'économiste français*, Oct. 18, 1902, p. 513. It is also interesting to compare this study with an earlier one made by Raphaël-Georges Lévy (*Revue des deux mondes*, March 15, 1897, pp. 415-45) and to notice that in the main the geographical distribution given in the one corresponds fairly closely with that given in the other.

GEOGRAPHIC DISTRIBUTION OF FRENCH INVESTMENTS ABROAD, 1902
AND 1908
(In billions of francs)

1902 [a]		1908 [b]	
Total Europe..........	21.01	Total Europe	20.5-23
Russia	6.97	Russia	9 -10
United Kingdom	1.	England	5
Belgium	.6	Belgium, The Neth-	
Holland	.2	erlands	5
Serbia	.2	Germany, Turkey,	
Turkey in Europe......	1.82	Serbia, Bulgaria..	5
Roumania	.44	Roumania, Greece .	3 - 4
Greece	.28		
Italy	1.43	Italy	1 - 1.5
Austria-Hungary	2.85	Austria-Hungary ...	2
Switzerland	.46	Switzerland	.5
Spain	2.97	Spain, Portugal	3.5
Portugal	.9		
Norway	.29		
Monaco	.16		
Denmark	.13		
Sweden	.12		
Other countries	.19		
Total Africa..........	3.69	Total Africa	5 - 7
Egypt	1.44	Egypt, Suez	3 - 4
South Africa	1.56		
Tunis	.51	Tunis, French col-	
		onies	2 - 3
Other countries	.18		

[a] *Bulletin de statistique et de législation comparée*, October, 1902, p. 450.

[b] Neymarck, Alfred, *French Savings and Their Influence* (published by the United States National Monetary Commission, 1910), p. 176.

FRENCH INVESTMENTS ABROAD, 1902 AND 1908 (Continued)

(In billions of francs)

1902		1908	
Total America	3.97	Total America	3 - 4
United States	.6	United States, Canada	.5- 1
Canada	.14		
Argentina	.92	Argentina, Brazil, Mex-	
Brazil	.7	ico	2.5- 3
Mexico	.3		
Colombia	.24		
Chile	.22		
Uruguay	.22		
Venezuela	.13		
Cuba	.13		
Peru	.11		
Other countries........	.26		
Total Asia	1.12	Total Asia	1.
China	.65	China, Japan	1.
Turkey in Asia.........	.35		
Other countries	.12		
Total Oceania	.06		
Philippines	.03		
Other countries	.03		
Grand Total, 1902......	29.85	Grand Total, 1908....	
		Not less than 30 [c]	

[c] Neymarck sets the minimum total at 30 billions.

In 1914, the geographic distribution of French investments was approximately that shown in the table on page
20 of the text. The estimates in that table are based
partly upon the estimates for 1902 and 1908, and partly
upon fragmentary data concerning new investments since
that time. For convenience of reference the table is reproduced here, with an explanation of each of the estimates given.

Geographic Distribution of French Investments Abroad, 1914

(Figures in billions of gold francs)

Europe	30.4	Asia, Africa and America	14.6
Russia	11.3	Egypt, Suez and South	
Great Britain	.5	Africa	4.5
Belgium and the Nether-		Tunis and other French	
lands	.5	colonies	4.0
Turkey	3.5	United States and Canada	1.0
Bulgaria and Serbia.....	.6	Argentina, Brazil and	
Roumania	3.0	Mexico	3.0
Greece	.7	Other South American	
Austria-Hungary	3.5	countries	.6
Italy	1.3	Asia	1.5
Switzerland	.5		
Spain and Portugal......	4.0		
Scandinavia	.5	Total, All Countries....	45.0
Other European countries	.5		

Russia: The figure of 11.3 billions—which was published in the *Federal Reserve Bulletin,* August, 1922, p. 938—was supported by the study on *Russian Debts and Russian Reconstruction,* by the Institute of Economics, and recently has found added confirmation in a study published in the London *Economist;* December 27, 1924, p. 1048.

A higher figure is, however, sometimes given. In negotiations over French recognition of the Soviet government, France is demanding payment of 18.3 billion gold francs, of which 11.3 billions is claimed for pre-war debts and 7 billions for indemnifying French nationals for losses sustained because of the sequestration and nationalization of their property in Russia. (*L'Économiste Français;* October 18, 1924, p. 484.) This figure probably includes interest on securities for the later years of the war and for the post-war period, and undoubtedly exaggerates the importance of French enterprises operating in Russia. M. Germain Martin has set the figure at 15 to

17 or 18 billions (*La Situation Financière de la France;* 1914-1924, pp. 32 and 106).

Great Britain: The total of foreign funds invested in British enterprises is small, and, at the outbreak of the war, Great Britain had no foreign debt. French investments in Great Britain in 1902, according to Leroy Beaulieu, represented the savings of "timid investors" afraid to keep their savings at home. Altogether, it is not likely that the figure has changed greatly since 1908.

Belgium and the Netherlands: No new estimates are available, but there probably had been little change since 1908.

Turkey: The estimate of 3.55 billions is from the *Manchester Guardian Commercial,* March 8, 1923, p. 342, and the *Statist,* July 21, 1923, p. 85. According to the *Statist,* of the total of 3.5 billions, 2.5 billions represented the French share in the Ottoman public debt; and 1 billion, French investments in private enterprises.

Bulgaria and Serbia: The official inquiry of 1902 showed only 48 millions of French capital invested in Bulgaria—a figure so small that it was not included in the tabulated statement of investments. Some new loans were floated by Bulgaria in 1904 and 1907, but the French market took only a part of these, the rest going to London and Vienna. Capital invested in Serbia and Montenegro was estimated in 1902 at 201 millions, while a new loan to Serbia in 1914 amounted to 250 millions (*Annals of the American Academy;* November, 1916, p. 52). Very little foreign capital was invested in private enterprises in Bulgaria and Serbia.

Roumania: According to the Association Nationale des Porteurs Français de Valeurs Mobilières (*Annuaire;* 1915-1920, p. 119) the French share of the outstanding

Roumanian debt on January 1, 1917, amounted to about 1.24 billion francs. In addition to this, a large amount of French capital was invested in Roumanian industry.

Greece: The French consul at Piraeus estimated French investments in Greece in 1912 at about 600 million francs *(Bulletin de l'Institut International de Statistique;* Vol. XX, Part II, p. 1433), and this amount was increased somewhat by a new loan to the State in 1914 (Association Nationale des Porteurs Français, *Annuaire;* 1915-1920, p. 545).

Austria-Hungary: Leroy-Beaulieu estimated that the figure of 2.85 billions shown in the official estimate of 1902 should have been reduced to about 2 billion francs, a figure which Neymarck used in his study of 1908. It is known that between 1908 and 1914—and even on the very eve of the war—France made considerable investments in Austria-Hungary. Dr. Franz Bartsch, in his *Statistische Daten über die Zahlungsbilanz Oesterreich Ungarns vor Ausbruch des Krieges,* Vienna, 1917, pp. 20-21—which was published by the Austrian Ministry of Finance—gives the total of Austro-Hungarian indebtedness to France at the end of 1913, as 3.33 billion francs. This figure includes all known securities of every description, but probably does not include French enterprises operating in Austria-Hungary, French ownership of real estate in Austria-Hungary, and so on. An allowance for such property and for new loans early in 1914 would bring the total to not less than 3.5 billions.

Italy: From a study by Director General Stringher of the Bank of Italy *(Bulletin de l'Institut International de Statistique;* Vol. XIX, Part II, pp. 93-123) it appears that in 1909-10 France had invested in Italian government securities, more than 500 million lire; in private securities, about 300 millions; and in Italian companies, or Italian branches of foreign companies, about 425 millions, a total of about 1,225 million lire. A study by Alfred Neymarck (ibid., Vol. XX, Part II, pp. 1434-46) indicates that the amount in 1912 was about 1 to 1.5 billions. On the basis of these estimates, the figure of 1.3 billions has been used on page 335.

Switzerland and Scandinavia: There is no evidence of change with regard to these countries.

Spain and Portugal: According to Leroy-Beaulieu, the figure of 2.97 billions for Spain was probably not too large for 1902, though Neymarck scaled it down in 1908. Between 1908 and 1914, however, French investors were putting some capital into Spanish industries. M. René Masse has estimated pre-war investments in Spain alone at 4 billion francs (*La production des richesses;* 1925, p. 632).

Égypt, Suez and the Transvaal: Leroy-Beaulieu in his comments (*L'économiste français;* Oct. 25, 1902, p. 551) on the official inquiry of 1902 set the total of French investments in these three divisions of Africa at about 4.3 billions instead of 3.0 billions. In 1908 Neymarck, however, put the figure at 3 to 4 billions, omitting all mention of the Transvaal. Germain Martin says that Egypt alone had obtained from France at least 4 billion francs. Apparently, however, he has made no allowance in this estimate for depreciation or losses on such investments (*La situation financière de la France;* 1914-24, pp. 105-6).

Tunis and other French colonies: This estimate is based upon the well-known fact that before the war a considerable amount of French savings was being invested in the colonies. Germain Martin set the figure at about 4 billions (*ibid.*, pp. 30 and 106). This allows for a steady growth between 1908 and 1914.

United States and Canada: The *Federal Reserve Bulletin* (October, 1922, p. 1181) quotes a figure of 2.5 billion francs as an estimate of pre-war French investments in the United States alone, though attaching no great importance to the figure. According to Germain Martin, French holders were selling their American securities between 1908 and 1913 (*La situation financière de la France*, 1914-1924, pp. 101-2). In view of this fact and the pre-war policy of the government with regard to directing foreign investments in accordance with political purposes, a figure of 1.5 billions seems a reasonably high estimate.

Argentina, Brazil and Mexico: A study made for the Association Nationale des Porteurs Français de Valeurs Mobilières (*Annuaire*, 1915-1920, p. 107) fixes French investments in Mexico in April, 1914, at 1.2 billion francs. Probably 1 billion or more were placed in Brazil (*ibid.*, pp. 40-74). About 3.4 billions of Argentine securities were held abroad in 1913 (Corporation of Foreign Bondholders, annual report for 1913, p. 41). It is not known how much of this was held in France, but the amount was probably around 1 billion.

Other South American Countries: It is known that some French capital was being invested in other South American countries, for example, in Bolivia (*Bulletin de l'Institute International de Statistique*, Vol. XX, Part II, p. 1482), and in Chile (Association Nationale des Porteurs Français de Valeurs Mobilières, *Annuaire*, 1915-20, p. 246), but the total was relatively unimportant.

Asia: The Association Nationale des Porteurs Français de Valeurs Mobilières (*Annuaire*, 1915-20, pp. 75-

78), speaks of seven Chinese Loans floated since 1908,
and suggests that there were still others, in all of which
some French capital was invested. On this basis the
total French investment in China was probably more
than 1 billion francs in 1914. New Japanese loans were
also floated on the French market (ibid., p. 545), so that
the total amount invested in Asia in 1914 was around
1.5 billion francs.

III. CALCULATION OF PRE-WAR INTERNATIONAL INCOME

On page 16 of the text and 326 of this Appendix, a
statement of French international income is given for the
years 1871-1913. These averages were derived from a
year by year calculation or estimate of each of the several items entering into the account.

*The largest item of pre-war international income was
interest and dividends on foreign investments.* As a
basis for estimating this item, it was assumed that in
1870 France had a net sum of 10 to 12 billion francs
invested abroad—after allowance had been made for the
investments of foreigners in French undertakings—on
which she was receiving an annual income of 5 per cent.[9]
An estimate of the several service items, including interest, was then made to find the French income from
non-trading operations in 1871. This favorable balance,
offset by the adverse commodity and specie balance,
showed roughly the increase in foreign investments resulting from the year's operations. The interest income
for 1872 was then calculated on this new investment figure; and when combined with the other items in the
balance of payments, showed the net increase or decrease

[9] See pages 325 and 330-1.

in investments during the year 1872. As explained on pages 327-8 deductions from net investments were also made for the sacrifice of foreign securities, and the sale of French securities to foreigners, the proceeds of which, for the most part, went to meet the indemnity of 1871. The net amount of French investments abroad was thus estimated for each of the 43 years of the period 1871-1913, the figure for each year being used in calculating the interest for the following year.

Income from the tourist trade is the item of second importance in pre-war income. M. Léon Say estimated that this amounted to about 200 to 300 million francs just prior to the war of 1870. During the disturbed period of the seventies the figure was probably somewhat lower. M. René Masse [10] estimated the tourist income of France in 1900 at only 300 million francs, and Dr. F. S. Schmidt [11] set the figure at 600 million francs for the years immediately preceding the Great War. No one, however, has attempted to estimate the annual tourist income of the country over a long period of years. The estimates given in the table on p. 326 have been derived as follows.

In 1908 Sir George Paish estimated that American tourists abroad in 1908 spent, exclusive of passage money, 1,036 million francs. Probably one-fourth of this amount, possibly more (say 260 to 275 million francs), was spent in France. Some French writers have assumed that as much as one-half of American tourists' money went to France. That such a fraction is much too high is apparent from the observation that Americans travelled

[10] Masse, René, *La Production des Richesses*, 1925, pp. 667 and 674.
[11] Schmidt, F. S., *Internationaler Zahlungsverkehr und Wechselkurse*, p. 23.

very extensively in Great Britain; in Holland, Belgium and Germany; and in Switzerland, Austria. and Italy. The expenditures in each of these areas must have approximated the outlays in France, and a very considerable total was expended in other European countries and in other parts of the world.

Tourists from other countries, particularly from Great Britain, also came to France in large numbers. Assuming that all other tourists spent slightly more in France than was spent by Americans, the tourist income for France in 1908 amounted to probably 550 to 600 million francs.

The estimates for other years were worked out on practically the same basis. In estimating the tourist item for the later years of the pre-war period, account was also taken of the fact that foreign migratory laborers in France during part of the year, sent home or carried back with them considerable sums of money. M. Pupin estimates the amount at 100 million francs a year just prior to the war.[12] This item was treated as a reduction from tourist income rather than as a separate item in the accounts.

An estimate of shipping receipts should also be included in French international income. It is sometimes argued that since France pays for shipping as much, or possibly more, than she receives, the interest item should be entered as a deficit, if at all. This way of handling the matter, however, overlooks the fact that French *expenditures* for shipping are included in the valuation of French imports and have thus already been accounted for in the trade figures.

[12] Pupin, René, *Richesse privée et finances françaises*, 1919, pp. 25-26.

French imports are valued c.i.f. (cost, insurance, freight) at the French border. This means that all freight charges on imports—even those paid to French ships—are included as a part of the value of imports. Exports are valued f.o.b. (free on board) at the French border, so that the cost of carrying goods after they leave France is not included in the value of the exports.

From the fact that French imports are valued c.i.f.,' it is apparent (1) that the shipping charges on French imports carried by *foreign* vessels have already been included in the value of the imports and should not, therefore, be included a second time as an "outgo" shipping item; and (2) that the shipping charges on French imports carried in French vessels have also been included in the value of the imports, notwithstanding the fact that these merely represent payments from one group of Frenchmen to another, and should hence not be included in the international accounts. In other words, French imports have not cost the French nation as much (by the amount of the import shipping charges paid to French shipowners) as appears to be the case on the face of the import figures. For this reason, it is necessary to make an adjustment in the service accounts by considering the earnings of French shipowners in carrying French imports as a part of the international *income* of France.

It is also obviously necessary to include as French shipping income, the earnings of French ships on account of carrying French exports to foreigners, as well as any freight receipts earned by French ships in carrying goods from one foreign country to another. In brief, the shipping item must show the *total* earnings of French ships (no deduction being made on account of shipping charges paid to foreign ships, because such charges have already been taken account of in the import figures).[13] We may now turn to the problem of determining the amount of the income from shipping.

One method of determining the shipping figure would be to study the register of French shipping year by year for the years in question—1871-1913—in order to learn the total tonnage on the register and its probable effi- 'ciency. It would also be necessary to have a schedule, or an index number, of freight rates for these years. A study of this sort with regard to English shipping was made by C. K. Hobson in 1914.[14] Information about French shipping is much less adequate than that con- cerning British shipping, and hence the use of this method is not an easy matter.

A second and simpler method is to calculate French shipping earnings on the basis of (a) a percentage com- parison of French and British tonnage year by year, and (b) Hobson's estimates of British earnings. This is the method which we have followed in computing the ship- ping earnings given in the table on page 326.[15]

Lloyd's register and also the official merchant marine figures of the two countries were used in making the tonnage comparison. To make allowance for the rela- tively greater importance of sailing vessels on the French register, it was assumed that three sailing tons were

[13] For a fuller discussion of the problem of computing shipping earnings, including port charges, wages paid to foreign seamen, etc., Hobson, C. K., *Export of Capital*, pp. 171-187. See also Moulton and McGuire, *Germany's Capacity to Pay*, pp. 261-65.

[14] Hobson, *Export of Capital*, pp. 171-187.

[15] For the years 1911 and 1912 Hobson's estimate appeared un- duly large and has been scaled down. As a basis for the 1913 figure an estimate by Hobson appearing in *Economica*, May, 1921, p. 144, was used.

equivalent to one steam ton. It is probable that French shipping is not as efficient, ton for ton, as British shipping, and some account has been taken of this fact, particularly in the seventies when French shipping was struggling against especially keen competition. French earnings in the five years 1871-75 have been estimated at about 14 per cent of British earnings, and in the five years 1909-13, at about 9 per cent.

Insurance and commissions make up the only other important item of invisible income for France. In the British balance of payments this item is estimated at 2.5 per cent of the value of British foreign trade.[16] Judging from the fact that French ships carry only about 30 per cent of the French sea-borne imports and exports, and from the less active participation of France in international financial affairs, it seems probable that France earns from this source something like 1 per cent of the combined value of her imports and exports.

IV. INTERNATIONAL ACCOUNTS: August 1, 1914— JUNE 30, 1919

A condensed statement of the trade and financial operations of France for the war period was given on page 25 of the text. These accounts are presented in more detailed form in the table which follows. The sources of the data and the methods used in making the estimates are indicated in the discussion of the succeeding pages.

Since the computation of the interest item must take into account the foreign investment position of France in the war years, items shown under the heading "credit

---

[16] Hobson, *Export of Capital*, pp. 188-189.

operations" in the table above will be discussed before the explanation of the trade and service items. In this analysis, all operations having to do with the political debt are clearly distinguished from other credit operations, and from the trade and service items.

TRADE AND SERVICE OPERATIONS, AUGUST 1, 1914-JUNE 30, 1919

			Billions of Paper Francs
Deficit from trade and specie operations:			
Commodity imports	99.0 [a]		
Commodity exports	25.6 [a]		
	73.4		
Less net exports of bullion and specie	1.0		72.4
Net income from services:			
Interest:			
Income on foreign investments	4.5		
Outgo on accumulating foreign debt	2.4	2.1	
Commissions		.7	
Shipping		3.3	
Tourist items:			
Income from personal expenditures of foreign soldiers in France	8.0		
Income from expenditures of non-military foreigners (including commissions, relief agencies, etc.)	8.0	16.0	
Less outgo for expenditures of French diplomatic and commercial representatives and agencies abroad		.5	15.5
British and American government outlays in France		9.8	31.4
Net deficit from trade and service operations			41.0

[a] Special trade figures have been adjusted to include the reexport trade.

CREDIT OPERATIONS, AUGUST 1, 1914–JUNE 30, 1919

Commercial (i.e. exclusive of political borrowing and lending):
  Foreign borrowings (increasing foreign claims against France):
   Government commercial borrowings
    (6.8 at par) 7.5
   Less commissions 7
                                           —— 6.8
   Sale of domestic securities 10.0
   Sale of real estate......................... .5
   Commercial credits (open accounts), and
    sale of francs 2.0
                                                  —— 19.3
  Sale of foreign securities (decreasing French claims
   against foreigners; 3.5 at par)................ 3.9
                                                         —— 23.2

Political borrowing and lending:
  Receipts from government political borrowings
   (24.6 at part) 27.0
   Less capitalized interest included in
    the debt to Great Britain.......... 1.5
   Interest paid to the United States..... .7   2.2
                                                  —— 24.8
  Offsetting loans to the Allies................. 10.0
   Less interest paid from the Russian loan to
    French citizens, and bank discounts on
    various loans 3.0   7.0 17.8

Net receipts from new borrowings, required to meet the
   trade and service deficit........................... 41.0

A. CREDIT OPERATIONS

Government commercial borrowing abroad: Official
figures with regard to the foreign debt of France were
published by the Minister of Finance for the end of
1918 and 1919,[17] but not for June 30, 1919. Estimated
at par, the debt. figure for that date was about 31.4
billion gold francs—equivalent to about 34.5 billion paper
francs when allowance is made for an average 10 per cent

[17] *Exposé des motifs du projet du budget, 1919*, pp. 125-26, and
1920, pp. 171-72.

depreciation in the franc.[18]   This total is made up of 27.0
billion paper francs (24.6 at par) of political borrowings
and 7.5 billions (6.8 at par) of commercial borrowings
of the French government.   The net receipts from commercial borrowings, however, amounted to only about 6.8
billion paper francs, commission charges on the operations (for the most part at a 2 per cent rate) having
amounted to about 700 million francs.

Sale of domestic securities to foreigners: During the
war period, the total value of French stocks and bonds
floated in the French market (exclusive of bonus shares
and conversions) amounted to 87.5 billion francs.   In
addition, approximately 40 billions of Treasury and National Defense bills were also issued.   If Neymarck's
estimate—that about 10 per cent of the stocks and bonds
floated in the French market were purchased by foreigners—may be taken as applying to the war as well
as to the pre-war period, approximately 9 billions of
these securities were purchased abroad.   Assuming that
a very small proportion of the "bills" were also purchased abroad, we arrive at a figure of approximately
10 billions.   The data with regard to the flotation of
securities and bills have been compiled as follows:

(1) The "Association Nationale des Porteurs Français
de Valeurs Mobilières" sets the flotations on the French
market from the middle of 1914 to the end of 1918 at
9.25 billions; including in this securities of the Crédit
National, and excluding the issues of the government
and the large railway companies.[19]   This figure is for

[18] M. René Pupin uses the figure of 33.6 billions in his study of
the accounts for the war years: *l'Information financière,* Sept. 8, 1923.

[19] *League of Nations Monthly Bulletin of Statistics.* These figures show only the offerings; they do not show the total of actual
sales.

domestic securities alone, since foreign issues were practically excluded from the French market early in the war. The corresponding figure for the year 1919 is 8.5 billions, half of which may be taken as applying to the first part of the year. For the five-year period, therefore, this gives a total of about 13.5 billions.

(2) Published figures with regard to the internal debt of the French government show that the term debt of the country, represented by *rentes* and bonds, increased from August 1, 1914 to June 30, 1919, by about 64 billion francs.[20] This figure includes securities of the large railway companies, whose finances are closely bound up with those of the State.

As shown by the official debt figures, outstanding Treasury bills and National Defense bills increased between August 1, 1914, and December 31, 1918, by approximately 35 billions. The published figures for the end of 1919 show a further increase of 12 billions, about half of which we assume were issued in the first half of the year, making the total roughly 40 billions.

Sale of real estate: An estimate by M. René Pupin.[21]

Commercial credits, and sale of francs: No definite information as to the amount of these items is available. It is known, however, that some speculation in French francs and some commercial credit operations took place

[20] For the year 1919 the increase in the internal bonded debt was 31 billion francs, of which 30 billions represented the 4 per cent rentes of 1918. These rentes were authorized in September, 1918, and placed on the market a month later, although not included in the public debt figure until the close of 1919. The great bulk of this indebtedness, therefore, was actually incurred before the middle of 1919, the increase for the second half of the year being probably not more than 1 or 2 billion francs.

[21] *L'Information financière,* Sept. 8, 1923.

even during the war period, and that early in 1919 many
industries opened credits, under a semi-official arrange-
ment, for the purchase of foreign goods. We have set a
figure of 2.0 billions for these items, in order to balance
the accounts.

Sale of foreign securities: Sales by the government, as
well as by private citizens, reduced French holdings of
foreign securities. The need for foreign purchasing power
was so great that in May, 1916, the government worked
out a plan whereby it hoped to get control of a large
part of the best foreign securities belonging to the French
people. According to this plan, the government borrowed
the securities from the holders, with the understanding
that it might sell them in case of necessity, and that in
any case it was to compensate the owner for the use of
them. By this means the government was able to secure
more than 1.5 billions, which it eventually sold abroad.[22]

The plan did not prove a complete success, however,
because French capitalists found it more profitable to
sell the securities direct to foreign buyers than to loan
them to the government on terms laid down. How many
were disposed of by direct sale abroad we do not know.
M. André Théry states that "we know simply that the
sales were more important than the loans made to the
Minister of Finance in response to his appeal." From
this it would appear that all told at least 3.5 billions of
France's best foreign securities were parted with during
the war period.

---

[22] For details concerning the plan see Théry, André, *Les grands
établissements de crédit français*, pp. 218-20; Décamps, Jules, *Les
changes étrangers*, 2d edition, pp. 304-05; M. Pupin, like M.
Décamps, sets the sale of foreign securities by the government at
1.5 billions.

Political borrowings of the government: At the end of June, 1919, the political debt of the French government stood at approximately 27.0 billion paper francs (24.6 at par).[23] The actual net receipts of the government from these operations, however, were only about 24.8 billion paper francs.[24] The difference, 2.2 billions, represents interest and discount charges as follows:

1. Interest and discounts on the political debt of France to Great Britain amounted to approximately 1.5 billion paper francs at the middle of 1919. Interest was not actually paid to Great Britain as it fell due, but was capitalized and added to the amount of the debt to be paid at some future time, so that the total borrowings (27.0 billions) included interest as well as capital. The process was as follows: when the original loans were granted by Great Britain, the French government turned over to the British government French Treasury bonds. These bonds were discounted for a year by the Bank of England and renewable at each maturity date up to the end of the third year after the bringing into effect of the Treaty of Peace. Interest on these bonds is payable in advance, but as a matter of fact it has been met at each maturity date by the transfer of additional French Treasury bonds.[25] Until 1921, interest on a loan of 26.2 million yen by the Royal Bank of Japan was handled in the same manner. This item, however, amounted to only 10 million francs, and therefore no separate entry for it has been made in the account on page 347.[26]

[23] See p. 348 of this appendix.
[24] De Lasteyrie, *Exposé des motifs du projet du budget, 1923*, p. 65, and 1920, pp. 171-2.
[25] *Ibid.,* p. 65.
[26] *Ibid.,* p. 68, footnote 1.

2. Interest amounting to 128 million dollars or approximately .7 billion paper francs had been paid during this period on the political debt to the United States.[27] This payment was made partly in cash, partly by the cancellation of credits. No interest payments were made to the United States after May 15, 1919. The amount due and unpaid on June 30, amounted to approximately 10.9 million dollars or .1 billion paper francs. This amount, unlike the unpaid interest to Great Britain, was not added to the capital of the debt—that is, interest on the debt to the United States is calculated as simple interest, not as compound interest. Therefore no account is taken of the .1 billion francs of unpaid interest in the statement on page 346, although it is included in the statement of the investment and debt position of France on page 27 of the text.

Loans to Allied countries: According to the official statement published in the *Journal Officiel* for 1924,[28] French loans to Allied countries during this period totalled 9,991,795,000 francs—about half of which represents loans to Russia. The net sum which the Allies realized from these loans, however, amounted to not more than 7 billions; the difference between these figures representing interest, commissions, etc., which may be explained under three heads:

1. Bank discount on the loans to Russia amounted to 1,128 million francs.[29] This charge was included as a

[27] *Annual Report of the Secretary of the (U. S.) Treasury*, 1919, p. 67.

[28] *Documents parlémentaires—Chambre Annexe*, No. 6824, p. 756.

[29] League of Nations document—*Brussels Financial Conference, 1920, Recommendations and their Application*, July, 1923, Vol. IV, p. 5.

part of the Russian debt to France, the financial transactions involved being as follows: The French government issued treasury certificates of indebtedness which it offered for sale to the Bank of France. The Bank of France, however, would take them only at a discount amounting to 1,128 million francs, the balance being credited to the account of the Russian government. The Russian government was then able to use the proceeds to buy military supplies and other goods in France and to meet other external obligations, such as the interest on the previously contracted government debts in France, the maintenance of Russian troops in France, etc.[30]

2. Another offsetting item in connection with the Russian loans is a figure of 1,530 million francs which were specifically loaned for the purpose of enabling Russia to meet interest due to French holders of pre-war Russian securities.[31] This sum, which was paid by France to her own citizens, of course represented no transfer of goods or foreign bills across the French border.

3. There were doubtless small commissions on the other French loans, but with regard to these there are no available data. We have set these at a figure of about .3 billion francs, bringing the total offset against foreign loans to roughly 3.0 billions.

B. TRADE AND SERVICE OPERATIONS

Trade deficit: This figure is from the official data compiled by the government. A discussion of the re-

[30] For a discussion of the operation see Raffalovich, Arthur, *La dette publique de la Russie*, pp. 42-47.

[31] (London) *Economist*, Dec. 27, 1924, p. 1048. It is interesting to note here that even before the war France was loaning Russia funds with which to pay interest on earlier French loans to Russia. See Lysis, *Contre l'oligarchie financière en France*, 11th ed., p. 96.

liability of French trade statistics has already been given on pages 309-21.

Net exports of bullion and specie: The figure of 1 billion for the net export of bullion and specie is an estimate which is explained in the footnote on page 24 of the text.

Interest income on foreign investments: Of the total of foreign investments in 1914, amounting to about 45 billions, according to the itemized statement on page 20, about 23 billions were in Eastern and Southeastern Europe,—Russia, Turkey, Greece, Austria-Hungary, and the Balkans. The interest on these ceased at the outbreak of the war. Certain South American countries also shortly suspended payments on their obligations to France.[32] This would reduce the total of interest-bearing securities by perhaps another 3 billions. In addition, at least 3.5 billions of high-class foreign securities were sold during the war. This would leave a total of interest bearing securities amounting to around 16 billions. Interest on this sum at 5 per cent—allowance being made for the fact that the depreciation of the franc during this period averaged about 10 per cent—would amount to about 900 million francs a year, or 4.5 billion francs for the war period.

Interest on the accumulating foreign debt: Interest was actually being paid only on the so-called commercial borrowings of the French government, and on domestic securities held abroad. Interest on the political debt of the country—the debt of the French Treasury to the Treasuries of Great Britain and the United States—was handled in a different manner. The figure of 2.4 billions,

[32] Décamps, Jules, *Les changes étrangers*, (2d edition), 1923, p. 291.

shown in the table, for interest charges against France was estimated as follows:

(1) Of the total foreign debt of 34.5 billion (paper) francs contracted by the government during the war period, about 7.5 billions, as we have seen, were classified as commercial debt. On June 30, 1919, this debt had run on the average for more than two years with interest at an average rate of about 6 per cent. Interest for the period therefore amounted to approximately 900 million paper francs.

(2) Interest charges on the 10 billions of French (domestic) securities and bills sold abroad during the war would approximate one billion francs.

(3) At the beginning of the war, foreigners owned about 7 billions of French securities and French property. Some of this was doubtless of the non-interest paying variety, while a considerable part of it belonged to enemy countries and was confiscated. If as much as 2.5 billions remained in the interest-paying class, interest outgo for the five year period (at 4 per cent) totalled 500 million francs.

Commissions: Estimated by the method used for pre-war years (namely, at 1 per cent of the total foreign trade), the income from commissions for the war period would amount to about 1.4 billion francs. In view of the French position during the war, however, it seems probable that earnings from this source would not continue at the old rate. An estimate of half this amount, or 700 million paper francs has, therefore, been included in the statement on page 346.

Income from shipping: In estimating the pre-war shipping earnings for France we took the estimates of British shipping earnings as a starting point. Since no

estimates of British earnings have been published
years 1914 to 1918, an independent estimate must
made of French shipping income for this period. Such an
estimate must take into account changes in the total
tonnage belonging to France, changes in the activity of
French shipping, and changes in freight rates during
these years.

Tonnage figures for the war years are given in gross
tons in Professor Charles Gide's *Effects of the War upon
French Economic Life*,[33] and in net tons in the *Annuaire
Statistique*.[34]

FRENCH MERCHANT TONNAGE, 1914-1919
(Figures are in thousands of tons, for January 1, of each year)

Year	Net tons (Annuaire Statistique)	Gross Tons (Gide)
1914 [a]	1,582	2,498
1915	1,629	2,494
1916	1,628	2,471
1917	1,548	2,322
1918	1,303	1,966
1919	1,259	1,863

[a] August 1, 1914.

The decrease in activity of the fleet was even greater
than the decrease in total tonnage. This is indicated
by the following figures, in thousands of net tons, showing
total entrances and clearances of French steamships in
French harbors: 1913—15,350; 1914—12,288; 1915—
10,121; 1916—8,607; 1917—7,469; 1918—6,467.[35]

Data with regard to freight rates are particularly unsatisfactory. The evidence available indicates that, with

[33] Pp. 15-16.

[34] 1919-20, p. 72. *Lloyd's Register* is not used because it does not
give French tonnage figures for 1917 and 1918.

[35] *Annuaire statistique*, 1919-20, p. 73.

the average rates for 1913 taken as 100, rates for war years stood roughly as follows: 1914, about 100; 1915, about 250; 1916, about 500; 1917, about 600; 1918, about 700.[36]

On the basis of the estimated earnings of French shipping in 1913 (250 million francs) and the freight rate index given above, and using the entrance and clearance figures as a rough index of activity, earnings for the war period appear to have been about as follows: Last half of 1914—100 million francs; 1915—425 millions; 1916—700 millions; 1917—760 millions; 1918—775 millions.

For the year 1919 estimates of British shipping have been published, and accordingly we may derive an estimate of French earnings for the first half of the year by the method of comparison.[37] French tonnage in 1919 was a little less than 10 per cent of British tonnage for the same year.[38] Taking the French shipping earnings as about 9 per cent of the British earnings would give a figure for the first half of 1919 of approximately 500 million francs.

[36] Based on an analysis of data from the following sources: Johnson, Emory R., *Ocean Rates and Terminal Charges*, 1919, particularly the table on p. 13; Gide, Charles, *Effects of the War upon French Economic Life*, table, pp. 20-25, particularly a comparison of freight rates given here for "Transatlantic trade," and a statement at the bottom of page 19 with regard to French rates in general; Salter, J. A., *Allied Shipping Control*, particularly the table on p. 351.

[37] British shipping income for 1919 was estimated by Sir Frederick Lewis of Furness, Withy & Company, Ltd., at 350 to 400 million pounds sterling (*The Economist*, Oct. 11, 1919, p. 750).

[38] Based on official shipping figures of France and the United Kingdom and on *Lloyd's Annual Register*.

This rough computation gives an aggregate figure for the five-year period August 1, 1914—June 30, 1919, of 3,260 million francs.

Tourist items: Two items of income and one of outgo are included in this account, which shows a net total of 15.5 billion francs. The income items are: (1) The personal expenditures of the military forces, set at from 8 to 10 billions in a study by M. René Pupin.[39] We have made an independent estimate, based upon the average number of American, British, and other foreign troops in France which indicates that 8 billions is a generous estimate. (2) Expenditures of non-military foreigners, which include the outlays of tourists, war residents of France, various special commissions, relief agencies—the Red Cross, the Y. M. C. A., and other similar organizations. Such published data as are available indicate that an estimate of 8 to 10 billions made by M. Pupin is not seriously in error. We have taken the lower figure.

The outgo item represents expenditures of French diplomatic and commercial representatives and agencies abroad. M. Jules Décamps has estimated the amount of these items for the year 1923 at from 150 to 200 million francs.[40] During the war years the total outlay on this account was doubtless somewhat larger. We have also made some allowance here for remittances by a reduced number of migratory workers in France. In view of the relatively higher value of the franc, however, we place the total at about 100 million francs a year or 500 millions for the war period.

British and American government outlays in France: These outlays on military account refer not to British and American loans, but to dollar and pound reimburse-

---

[39] *L'Information financière*, Sept. 8, 1923.

[40] *Revue de Paris*, March 1, 1924.

ments for materials, supplies, etc., furnished by the French Government to British and American military forces in France. The figure of 9.8 billions is taken from M. Jules Décamps.[41] The Minister of Finance, set the amount of such expenditures by the American government alone, at 5,686,989,648 francs.[42]

V. INTERNATIONAL ACCOUNTS, JULY 1, 1919— DECEMBER 31, 1923

The condensed statement of post-war trade and credit operations shown on page 30, is simplified below.

TRADE AND SERVICE OPERATIONS, JULY 1, 1919-DECEMBER 31, 1923

Deficit for—			Billions of Francs
Trade and specie:			
Commodity imports .... 148.6 [a]			
Commodity exports .... 106.4 [a]			
	42.2		
Less net exports of bullion and specie......	.5	41.7	
Interest:			
Outgo on accumulating foreign debts.......	8.8		
Income from foreign investments...........	6.5	2.3	44.0
Net income from—			
Insurance and commissions.......................		1.0	
Shipping		5.0	
Tourist items:			
Income from expenditures of tourists in France		12.0	
Outgo for remittances of migratory workers, and expenditures of French diplomatic and commercial representatives and tourists abroad		2.5	10.5
Reparation receipts and costs:			
Receipts in cash and kind, including the Saar mines		4.8	
Less costs of army of occupation, advances under Spa Protocol, etc.		4.2	.6	17.1
Net deficit from trade and service operations..............			26.9

[a] Special trade figures have been adjusted to include the re-export trade.

[41] *Les changes étrangers*, 2nd edition, pp. 303 and 322.

[42] *Débats, Chambre*, April 29, 1925, p. 2345.

CREDIT OPERATIONS, JULY 1, 1919-DECEMBER 31, 1923

Commercial (i.e., exclusive of political borrowing and lending):
Receipts:
Foreign borrowings (increasing foreign claims against France):

Municipal and industrial borrowings, less discounts (.32 at par)........	.7		
Sale of domestic securities	10.5		
Sale of francs	14.5		
Commercial credits (open accounts)	.5		
		26.2	
Sale of foreign securities (decreasing French claims against foreigners).............		1.8	28.0

Outgo:

Repayment of government commercial debt (1.5 at par)		3.3	
New investments absorbing part of reparation receipts, the Saar mines (375 million gold francs)......................		.8	4.1	23.9

Political borrowing and lending:

Receipts from government political borrowings (5.9 at par)		13.0	
Less interest on the debt to Great Britain (2.8 at par)		6.2	6.8
Offsetting loans to allies and neighbors of France...		3.8	3.0

Net receipts from new borrowings, required to meet the trade and service deficit 26.9

The table is followed by a discussion of the sources of the data and of the methods used in estimating certain of the items.

Credit operations are again discussed first, because some of these operations throw light upon items appearing in the trade and specie accounts.

A. CREDIT OPERATIONS

Municipal and industrial borrowings abroad: Certain municipal and industrial corporations floated small loans in foreign markets during the year 1922, the face value of which totaled about 360 million gold francs. When allowance is made for a considerable discount in the selling price, and for commissions, the sum realized from these operations may be set at around 320 million gold francs, or roughly 700 millions paper.

Sale of domestic securities: During the four and a half years under consideration the total value of French stocks and bonds floated in the domestic market—exclusive of bonus shares and conversions—amounted to about 118 billion francs. Of this total about 62 billions represent government *rentes* and bonds, including issues of the large railway companies; and about 56 billions are for all other securities floated in the French market, including the securities of the Crédit National and the *"groupements sinistrés."* About 16 billions of Ordinary Treasury bills and National Defense bills were also absorbed by the market. Estimated by the method used for war years, sales to foreigners would total about 12.0 billions. Assuming that the purchases of foreigners were reduced somewhat because of French borrowings in foreign markets, this estimate may be put at 10.5 billions.

Sale of francs and new commercial credits: The sale of francs to foreigners assumed large proportions during this period. Some estimates run as high as 20 billions. M. Décamps, however, places the total outstanding at the end of 1923 at not more than 15 billion francs.[43] The amount of commercial credits extended to France during this period is estimated by M. Décamps as being relatively small, the total outstanding in 1923 being per-

[43] Both of these estimates were given us direct by M. Décamps. So far as we know they have not been published heretofore.

haps 2 to 3 billion francs. Together these items total about 17.0 billion francs at the end of 1923, as compared with 2.0 billions at the middle of 1919. The increase during the period thus amounted to about 15.0 billions, of which perhaps 14.5 billions represent the sale of francs; and 500 millions, new commercial credits.

Sale of foreign securities: No official statement of the amount of French foreign securities liquidated since the war has been made, and so far as we are aware, no individual has ventured an estimate. It is known, however, that considerable quantities of foreign securities pledged as collateral for loans in Spain, Switzerland, Holland, and the Scandinavian countries, were sold after the war. The Spanish Urquijo loan of 149 million pesetas (149 million francs, at par), secured by French-owned Spanish railway securities has practically been liquidated by the sale of the collateral. Two similar collateral loans from Switzerland aggregating 165 million Swiss francs (165 million French gold francs), have been repaid, largely from the sale of the collateral. Loans contracted in the Scandinavian countries amounting to 116 million crowns (163 million gold francs) were entirely paid off in 1920-21 through the sale of collateral which consisted of French-owned Scandinavian securities.[44] Similar loans that were contracted in Holland and Japan have not as yet been liquidated.

These sacrifices of securities aggregate roughly 450 million gold francs, or approximately 900 million paper francs. Private holdings of foreign securities have also doubtless been sacrificed to some extent during the same

[44] These facts are taken from *Exposé des motifs du projet du budget, 1923*, pp. 66-68.

period. In fact, it is known that some have been used in connection with arbitrage transactions made profitable by the fall of the franc after the control was removed at the end of the war. It is not improbable that the total of such sales were equivalent to another 900 million paper francs.

Repayment of government commercial debt: The government commercial debt, according to official figures, was 5,255,337,000 francs at par,[45] at the end of 1923. As compared with June 30, 1919, this represents a decrease of 1.5 billion francs at par. Reduced to paper francs, this repayment figure becomes 3.3 billions.

New Investments—The Sarre Mines: According to the terms of the Peace Treaty, the Sarre mines were ceded to France as part of her share of German reparation. These mines were valued at 300 million gold marks,[46] or about 800 million paper francs in terms of the paper francs of this period. Since these mines are not located in territory belonging to France, it is clear that they are the equivalent of a new foreign investment for France.

Government political borrowings: On December 31, 1923, the political debt of the French government amounted to 30.5 billion francs at par.[47] This represented an increase of 5.9 billion francs at par, or about 12.9 billions in terms of paper. Interest on the political debt due Great Britain, however, amounted to approximately 2.8 billion francs at par,[48] or roughly 6.2 billion paper

[45] Lachapelle, Georges, *Les finances publiques àpres la guerre* (1919-1924).
[46] Clémentel, *Inventaire de la situation financière,* p. 151.
[47] Lachapelle, *ibid.*
[48] Based on debt figures published in the *Exposé des motifs du projet du budget,* 1920, 1922 and 1923, the figure published by

francs, so that the net receipts from new borrowings during this period amounted to about 6.8 billions.

Loans to foreign countries: According to the official figures set forth in the *Journal Officiel* for 1924,[49] loans to foreign countries in November, 1923, totaled 13,767,-011,047 francs, as compared with 9,991,795,000 at the middle of 1919. New loans extended during the post-war period, therefore, amounted to 3.8 billion francs.

B. INCOME AND EXPENDITURES FOR TRADE AND SERVICES

Trade and specie deficit: The trade and specie figures are from the official reports of the government.

Interest income on foreign investments: The interest-yielding foreign securities belonging to France totaled about 15.5 billion francs [50] at the beginning of this period. Since then securities amounting to a value of about 1 billion gold francs have been sold. On the other hand, new investments (the Sarre mines), valued at about .4 billion gold francs, have been added. On the average, we may take the productive investments as aggregating 15 billions, which, at 5 per cent, would give an annual interest yield of 750 million francs (at par of exchange), or a total for the four and a half years of about 3.4 billions. Attention should, however, be called to the fact that the interest receivable on these investments was payable in part in French francs and in part in the cur-

M. Georges Lachapelle, *ibid.*, and figures given by M. Clémentel, *ibid.*, pp. 69-70.

[49] *Documents parlémentaires—Chambre Annexe* No. 6824, p. 756.
[50] See pp. 27-8, and 354.

rencies of other countries. The income can not, therefore, be taken as strictly a return on 15 billion gold francs. Accordingly, in converting this interest income to paper francs, we must take account of the general depreciation in the currencies in which payment was received. Taking the exchange rates of 16 important countries as a basis of conversion, we find that 1 franc at par was equivalent during this period to about 2 paper francs. In paper francs, therefore, the interest income for the period amounts to roughly 6.5 billions.

Interest outgo on accumulating foreign debt: The total outgo on this account amounted to about 8.8 billion francs. It is convenient to discuss this item under three separate heads.

(1) The government commercial debt at the middle of 1919 was about 6.8 billion francs at par, and at the end of.1923 it was 5.3 billions. Interest on the par value of the debt at 6 per cent—the average of rates applying to the several parts of the debt—totaled about 1.6 billion gold francs for the period. As payments had to be made in the currencies of the lending countries—about 60 per cent in dollars, 32 per cent in pounds sterling, 4 per cent in yen, and the rest in various other currencies—the ratio for converting from gold to paper francs must be based on exchange rates for these countries. The weighted average works out at about 1 gold franc to 2 paper francs. Interest outgo on the government commercial debt may therefore be set at about 3.3 billion paper francs.

(2) At the close of the war about 10 billions of domestic securities and bills had been sold abroad, and by December 31, 1923, this had increased to about 20.5 billions. Interest rates on new borrowings during the

latter part of this period were as high as 8 to 9 per cent, while the average rate for loans floated during and immediately after the war averaged close to 6 per cent. In computing the amount of interest paid to foreigners on domestic securities, no allowance need be made for franc depreciation, since the debt was contracted in terms of paper francs. Assuming an average interest rate of 7 per cent on domestic securities, (and including with this about .1 billion for interest due on municipal and industrial securities floated in foreign markets) the total paid to foreigners on this class of debt approximated 5.0 billion paper francs.

(3) About 2.5 billions of pre-war French securities belonging to foreigners (see p. 355) may still have remained in the interest-paying class. Interest on these at 4 per cent would equal about 500 million francs.

Insurance and commissions: Estimated at 1 per cent of the total trade of France (the pre-war estimate), the insurance and commissions figure would stand at roughly 2.5 billion francs. This estimate, however, appears unduly high in view of the difficult financial position of France in post-war years. When account is taken of the large increase in the French foreign debt and the losses sustained by French banking and insurance concerns during this period, it appears doubtful whether net income from this source amounted to more than 1 billion paper francs.

Shipping: The shipping income of Great Britain was reckoned at 350 to 400 million pounds sterling for 1919 (half of which may be taken as the earnings of the latter six months of the year); at 350 millions for 1920; at 85 millions for 1921; at 90 millions for 1922; and at 100 millions for 1923. If French shipping income is estimated at about 12 per cent of British (basing this percentage on tonnage comparisons), the total income for the period amounted to about 5 billion paper francs.

Tourist items: Against the income which France received from foreign tourists may be placed the outgo on account of the remittances of migratory workers in France, and the expenditures of French diplomatic and commercial representatives and tourists abroad. Taking into account both the income and outgo items, the net tourist income of France for the post-war period ending December 31, 1923, was probably about 10.5 billion francs. This estimate is arrived at as follows:

(1) The income received from foreign tourists has been the subject of considerable discussion since the war. For the year 1923 various estimates have been made, some of them running as high as 8 [51] billion francs. M. Décamps, however, puts the total as low as 3 billion francs for that year. The United States Department of Commerce has estimated the expenditures of all American tourists in Europe in 1923 at about 400 million dollars,[52] equivalent to approximately 6.5 billion paper francs. Assuming that a third of this total was spent in France and that tourists from other countries spent half as much in France as American tourists, the total for

[51] *Rapport du Directeur de l'Office National du Tourisme,* 1923 (published as an Annex to the *Journal officiel,* November 19, 1924), p. 816. This report describes the work of the National Tourist Office, but attempts no independent estimate of French income from the tourist trade, although it does comment on the wide range of current estimates and brings together certain British and American figures bearing on the tourist trade.

[52] *Trade Information Bulletin,* No. 215, April 7, 1924, p. 10.

the year 1923 would amount to about 3.3 billions. A similar computation for the year 1922, when Americans spent 350 million dollars [53] abroad, would give a total tourist income of about 2 billion paper francs. The figure for 1921 may be taken as approximately the same as for 1922. In 1920 and the last half of 1919 the totals were probably swelled somewhat by the continuing expenditures of foreign sojourners and of relief and other war organizations. A total of from 11 to 13 billions would seem an ample figure for the four and a half years. We have used 12 billions in the statement on page 360.

(2) M. Décamps estimates that in 1923 there were about 150,000 foreign migratory workers in France who sent home or took away with them a total of about 500 million francs.[54] The large migration of foreign laborers to France did not begin immediately after the close of the war. We have therefore estimated the total for this item at 1.7 billion francs.

(3) Expenditures of French diplomatic and commercial representatives and agents abroad were estimated by M. Décamps at from 150 to 200 million francs for 1923.[55] In view of the somewhat lower rates of exchange in earlier years we take a figure of 800 millions for the whole period.

Reparation receipts, costs of armies of occupation, etc.: In the table reparation receipts are placed at 4.8 billion

[53] *Trade Information Bulletin,* No. 144, September 14, 1923, p. 15. Also No. 235, June 2, 1924, p. 16.

[54] Through a typographical error this was set at 1 billion in the *Revue de Paris,* March 1, 1924, p. 207, but the error was corrected by M. Décamps in a letter published in the *Journal des Débats,* March 17, 1924, p. 3.

[55] M. Décamps, *Revue de Paris,* March 1, 1924.

paper francs; costs of the army of occupation, advances under the Spa protocol, etc., at 4.2 billion paper francs; leaving a net gain of only .6 billion paper francs. This figure, it should be pointed out at this place, does not include German property surrendered in Alsace-Lorraine, or elsewhere in France. These figures are from a study published in the *Journal Officiel* for March, 1924.[56]

In this study two sets of figures were quoted, both of which brought the data down to June 30, 1923: one from Reparation Commission data, the other from figures published by M. Poincaré, then Premier. The one important difference between these figures was a sum of 348.5 billion gold marks that had been realized from the requisition of paper marks. No account of this was taken by the Reparation Commission, while M. Poincaré included it among the receipts from Germany and also among the costs of the armies of occupation. We have used Poincaré's figures in the table on page 359, converting from gold marks to gold francs at par, and estimating 2.2 paper francs as the equivalent of 1 gold franc.

Included in the 4.8 billion paper francs of reparation receipts is a figure of .8 billion paper francs (300 million gold marks or 375 million gold francs) for the value of the Sarre mines which were turned over to France by the Peace Treaty. Since this part of the reparation receipts represents an addition to French investments abroad, it is also included under the head of "Credit Operations."

VI. INTERNATIONAL ACCOUNTS FOR THE YEAR 1924

The income and expenditures accounts for the year 1924 are presented in the following table.

[56] *Documents parlémentaires, Chambre Annexe*, No. 6600, March 9, 1924, pp. 286-87.

TRADE AND SERVICE OPERATIONS, 1924

		Billions of Francs

Deficit for interest:
Outgo on accumulating foreign debts.............. 2.6
Income from foreign investments 2.0
                                                         ——— .6

Net income from—
Trade and specie:
  Commodity exports .... 41.4 [a]
  Commodity imports .... 40.1 [a]
                                          ——— 1.3
  Of bullion and specie................... .1
                                                  ——— 1.4
Insurance and commissions....................... .4
Shipping 1.2
Tourist items:
  Income from expenditures of tourists in
    France 5.0
  Outgo for remittances of migratory workers,
    and expenditures of French diplomatic
    and commercial representatives and
    tourists abroad 8
                                                  ——— 4.2
Reparation receipts balanced by administrative costs
    and costs of occupation ....
                                                         ——— 7.2

Net surplus from trade and service operations............. 6.6

[a] Figures for the re-export trade are not yet available, but would make only a slight change in the special trade figures.

The data incorporated in the table have been obtained from various sources, as enumerated below. Before discussing the various items, however, it is necessary to point out that the table shows the international accounts of France proper, with the colonies treated as though they were foreign countries. A word of explanation is necessary in this connection.

All of the colonies, except Indo-China, use the French franc; and for this reason transactions between France and the colonies involve problems of domestic rather than foreign exchange. It will be apparent therefore that a

CREDIT OPERATIONS, 1924

Commercial (i.e., exclusive of political borrowing and lending):
  Receipts:
    Foreign borrowings (increasing foreign claims against France):

Government commercial borrowings in excess of repayments	.2	
Borrowings of railways and corporations (260 millions at par)	.9	
Sale of domestic securities	1.0	
		2.1

Outgo:
  Repurchases of French francs from foreigners (decreasing foreign claims against France)......   5.0
  Loans to foreigners (increasing French claims against foreigners):

Bankers' loans	1.0	
New private investments ("flight of capital")	2.5	
	3.5	
		8.5

Net outgo	6.4

Political loans:
  Outgo on account of new government loans..............   .2

Net reduction of foreign claims as a result of the trade and service surplus 6.6

favorable balance between France and her colonies does not create bills of exchange which could be used in making foreign investments or in paying foreign debts. Since we are interested in the debt-paying capacity of France as revealed by her international trade and service accounts, it is necessary to make an adjustment of the net figures arrived at in the above table.

If one were to make a complete statement of the paying capacity of France, with the colonies considered as an integral part of the nation, it would be necessary to estimate the amount of both the trade and service operations. There are no reliable estimates for the service operations and the trade data for the various colonies leave much to be desired. They are uniform neither in the method used in compiling them, nor in the time at which they are issued. During the war years, however, the export trade of the colonies was stimulated and their balance with France was favorable. Since the war the reverse has been true. The trade of the colonies with the outside world has also fluctuated considerably. During the years 1916 to 1920 the colonies were importing more from foreign countries than they were exporting to them, but in 1921 the tide again turned. On the whole the statistics show that if the colonial trade and service accounts are consolidated with those of France, the net adverse balance of payments for the ten-year period 1914-1923 is not materially changed. Because of the difficulty in getting anything like adequate data for all of the items, we have omitted the colonial accounts from consideration and treated the international income accounts of France independently of the colonies.

In the interest of uniformity we have also omitted the colonial data from the table for the year 1924, although it is probable that an adjustment for the trade with the colonies should be made for this year. During 1924 French exports to the colonies exceeded imports from the colonies by 1.2 billion francs. On the other hand the international income of the colonies from service operations may be estimated at perhaps 200 millions francs. Therefore, if France and the colonies are thought of as one nation, the foreign-debt-paying capacity of the nation may be set at about 1.0 billion less than the figure shown in the table on p. 370. One more item is needed, however, if the account is to be presented in full—namely, the amount of the deficit or surplus in the trade of the colonies with other countries. But data on this point are lacking, since the published trade statistics of the colonies are not yet available.[57] It is therefore impossible to arrive at a net figure showing the extent to which the net income of the "French Republic" was reduced or increased by the international trade and financial operations of her colonies, although some adjustment for these items obviously should be made.

A. CREDIT OPERATIONS

Government commercial borrowings: The *commercial* debt of the government was increased during 1924 by a net amount of 122 million francs at par of exchange. The government repaid 396 million gold francs,[58] but incurred new obligations amounting to 518 millions. The net receipts of the government from these operations was less, however, than the net increase in the debt because of the fact that the 100 million dollar 7 per cent loan floated in the United States was issued below par—at 94—while a 5 per cent banking commission reduced the amount which France received to 89.[59] The government, therefore, received from this loan only 461 million gold francs or 1.6 billions paper. Allowing for the 396 million gold francs paid on the commercial debt during 1924, the

[57] A French economist, M. Pierre Meynial, has recently estimated that the trade of the colonies with other countries in 1924 resulted in a deficit of 600 million francs. We have decided, however, not to attempt an estimate for this item. (For a discussion of M. Meynial's article see pp. 381-93 of this appendix.)

[58] M. Clémentel, *Inventaire de la situation financière de la France au début de la treizième legislature*, p. 81. This statement shows a reduction in the debt between December 31, 1923, and July 31,. 1924, of 250 millions, and states that a further reduction of 146 millions was to be made before the end of the year.

[59] *Journal officiel, Débats, Sénat*, Dec. 30, 1924, p. 1688.

net receipts from government commercial transactions amounted to 65 million gold francs or about 240 million paper francs.

Railway and corporation borrowings abroad: French railway and shipping companies floated loans in the United States, with an aggregate nominal value of 55 million dollars, issued to yield about 50 million dollars,[60] or about 900 million paper francs.

Sale of domestic securities: During the year 1924 about 7.3 billions of domestic securities,[61] exclusive of government *rentes* and bonds and railway securities, were issued in the French market. An item by item comparison of the government debt statements of June 30, 1924, and December 31, 1923,[62] leads to the conclusion that not more than 600 millions of new *rentes* and bonds (exclusive of conversions and of securities issued to the *sinistrés*) and about 1.8 billions of ordinary Treasury bills and National Defense bills, had been floated on the market in the first part of the year. The new ten-year Treasury bonds floated in the latter part of the year were subscribed to the amount of 4.9 billion francs, but of this 3.9 billions represented conversion operations—the return of previous issues of Treasury bills, National Defense bills, etc.—while only 1 billion represented real income of the Treasury.[63] Summarizing these data, it seems prob-

[60] Monthly bulletin of the Banque Suisse, September, 1924, No. 9, p. 203. *New York Times,* Financial Section, Oct. 7, and Dec. 3, 1924. *Commerce Reports,* Jan. 26, 1925, pp. 185-6.

[61] *Statist,* Jan. 24, 1925, p. 124. This includes the *Crédit National* issue of January, 1924. Details with regard to corporation and company loans floated in 1924 are given in the *Journal officiel* (*documents parlémentaires*), *Sénat,* 1925, p. 12.

[62] M. Clémentel, *Inventaire de la situation financière,* p. 81.

[63] *Journal officiel, Débats, Sénat,* Dec. 31, 1924, p. 1697.

able that the total of new *rentes*, bonds and shares issued on the domestic market during the year was around 9 billions, exclusive of National Defense and Treasury bills. Assuming that foreigners took 10 per cent of the *rentes*, bonds and shares, and some of the bills, the amount taken by foreigners during 1924 may be set at about 1 billion paper francs.

While no data is available concerning the total of commercial credits outstanding at the close of 1924, it is probable that this figure had changed but little during the year.

Repurchase of francs: The total amount of paper francs in the hands of foreigners was reduced during the year, according to M. Décamps,[64] from about 15 to 10 billions. This represents an outgo in 1924 for the redemption of foreign obligations incurred through the sale of francs in previous years. The explanation of this development is as follows: In the early months of the year the franc fell rapidly in value, due to internal economic and political instability, accentuated by extensive short sales of francs by foreign—particularly Austrian—speculators. These speculators, expecting the franc to go the way of the mark, thought they would shortly be able to purchase francs for delivery in fulfillment of the short-sale contracts at prices much lower than those at which the sales were consummated. When the proceeds of the Morgan Loan were made available for the stabilization of the franc, however, the game of these short speculators was spoiled. Meanwhile, the French were able to repurchase francs held abroad at prices much below those at which they had previously sold them to foreigners.

[64] This estimate was given us direct by M. Décamps.

This operation may be regarded as a profitable one for France, however, only on the assumption that, except for this "temporary" decline in exchange rates, these francs held abroad would ultimately have been redeemed at say 6 or 7 cents instead of at 3 or 4. If the franc is ultimately stabilized at a figure below 3 cents, or if the franc should go the way of the mark and become virtually worthless, these repurchases of francs at 3 cents will in the long run have proved a bad bargain. In any event, their repurchase in 1924 represented an outgo to foreigners amounting to about 5 billion francs.

Bankers' loans to foreign countries: French bankers took 5 per cent of the 800 million gold mark German loan floated in September, 1924, amounting to 40 million gold marks or about 180 million paper francs.

It is also reported that the Czechoslovak Minister of Finance placed a loan of 1.5 billion Czech crowns with French bankers during the latter part of 1924. Converted to paper francs, this loan amounts to about 800 millions.[65]

New private investments: By the law of May 1, 1916, the French market was practically closed to foreign securities; by the law of August 1, 1917, anyone who delivered, bought or sold foreign securities, foreign exchange, or foreign money of any sort was required to make an accounting to the president or one of the *juges de Tribunal de Commerce;* and by the law of April 3, 1918, the export of French capital to other countries was forbidden.[66] Since then there have been rumors that the Fi-

[65] *Commercial and Financial Chronicle,* Oct. 11, 1924, p. 1695.

[66] Théry, André, *Les grands établissements de crédit Français* (1921), pp. 215-16. A paragraph in the London *Economist,* March 1, 1924, p. 474, shows one reason why evasion of the law was fairly easy for several years.

nance Minister would introduce a bill allowing the free
export of capital, but so far these have been only rumors.
It is well known, however, that ways are found of evading these laws and that some of the proceeds of French
export trade are being deposited in foreign banks, or used
for foreign investments. The Minister of Finance called
attention to this fact in October, 1924, and again in February, 1925, the explanation for this evasion of the law
being that "the depreciation of the franc causes uneasiness to investors, who, notwithstanding legal restrictions,
manage to send their capital abroad." [67]

From our analysis of the various trade and service
items for 1924 it appears that some 2.5 billion paper
francs, at the lowest, must have been invested abroad
by private investors in 1924. The exchange crisis in
February, 1925, indicated that the flight of capital was
becoming increasingly serious. In view of the favorable
balance of international income it is difficult to account
for a new exchange crisis except by the flight of capital,
superinduced by growing uneasiness over the internal
budgetary, currency, and cost of living difficulties.

 Government loans to foreign countries: The total
amount due the French government from foreign countries on June 30, 1924, was set at 15,133,074,000 francs,[68]
as compared with 13,767,011,047 francs on November 15,
1925,[69] an increase of 1,366 million francs. This increase
is to be accounted for in several ways: (1) by the difference in the rate of exchange at which conversion was
made from foreign currencies to francs. (2) By the in-

[67] New York Times, Oct. 13, 1924, and Feb. 9, 1925.
 [68] Minister of Finance, M. Clémentel, Inventaire de la situation
financière, p. 175.
 [69] Documents parlémentaires, Chambre Annexe, No. 6824, Dec.
18, 1923, p. 756.

clusion of interest charges and (in the case of the Russian debt) the inclusion of bank discount for the renewal of bonds. (3) By the inclusion of certain items that were left out of previous statements—for example, the French share of the guarantee of the Austrian loan. (4) By actual new loans made by France during the year 1924. The published data do not distinguish between the increases due to these several causes. From an item by item comparison of the two statements, however, it appears that new loans during 1924 must have approximated 250 million francs.

B. TRADE AND SERVICE OPERATIONS

Interest outgo: The total outgo on interest account amounted to 2.6 billions in 1924.

(1) Interest on the government commercial debt amounted to about 263 million francs at par. Converted at 3.5 paper francs to 1 franc at par—a weighted average based on exchange rates in countries where the debt was contracted—this sum becomes .9 billion paper francs.

(2) At the close of 1923 municipal and industrial borrowings abroad—apart from those included as part of the commercial debt of the French government—totaled a nominal value of about 360 million gold francs. Interest on this amount calculated at an average rate of 7 per cent, amounts to about 25 million gold francs, equivalent to about 90 million paper francs when converted on the basis of dollar exchange—3.7 paper francs to 1 gold franc.

(3) At the close of 1923 foreigners held about 21.5 billions of French securities. Calculated at an average rate of 7 per cent, interest on this sum amounts to 1.5 billions.

(4) Assuming that foreigners still hold as much as 2.5 billions of pre-war investments in France, and that they have been unable to convert these into investments bearing a higher rate than the 4 per cent average of pre-war days, interest on this class of debt amounted to about 100 million paper francs.

Interest income: At the close of 1923 French productive foreign investments equalled about 18 billions, interest payments having been resumed on about 3 billions of South American securities which were not productive during the preceding years. Interest on this amount at 5 per cent equals 900 million francs. Making allowance, as in the preceding period,[70] for the depreciation of the franc and other currencies in which interest was paid, this interest income of 900 millions equals about 2 billions paper.

Trade and specie surplus: These figures are from the official reports of the government.

Commissions: Estimated on the same basis as for the preceding period, the income from commissions in 1924 would amount to about .4 billion francs.

Shipping: British income from shipping has been estimated at 130 million pounds sterling for 1924.[71] If French earnings are estimated at 12 per cent of this amount (basing this percentage on a comparison of French and British tonnage figures) and conversion from pounds sterling to paper francs is made at the average rate for the year, the French income from shipping may be set down at 1.2 billion paper francs.

Tourist income: Estimated on the basis used for previous years, and taking account of the fact that

[70] See p. 365.
[71] *Board of Trade Journal*, Jan. 29, 1925, p. 145.

American tourists in 1924 spent in Europe about 500 million dollars,[72] the tourist income of France for 1924 may be set at about 5 billion paper francs.

The number of migratory workers in France increased considerably in 1924; but since wages did not rise as rapidly as the cost of living, the amount that could be remitted home was not proportionately increased.[73] Accordingly, we estimate about 600 million francs for remittances of migratory workers; while the expenditures of French diplomatic and commercial representatives abroad may be set at about the same total as in 1923, roughly 200 million francs. The net income from the tourist trade, therefore, approximates 4.2 billions.[74]

Reparation receipts and Ruhr occupation costs: Official reports concerning French reparation receipts from Germany and the net costs or receipts from the occupation and exploitation of the Ruhr are so contradictory and unsatisfactory, that it is impossible to give a definite figure. Careful study of the material has led to the conclusion that the costs practically balanced the receipts.

VII. NEW FRENCH ESTIMATES

Just as this book goes to press, two French studies bearing upon the French balance of accounts make their

[72] Estimate of the United States Department of Commerce.

[73] French exchange on the countries concerned remained practically stationary. It is interesting to note that because of the continuation of the migration of foreigners to France since the war; a measure has been brought before the French Parliament by which undesirable foreigners will be refused admittance and all foreign residents will be required to register with the police. (*Documents parlémentaires, Chambre Annexe*, No. 430, pp. 1372-8, Dec. 11, 1924.)

[74] The London *Economist*, Jan. 31, 1925, p. 195, quotes an estimate of 4 billion francs for the French tourist income in 1924.

appearance. In one of these, published in the Revue d'Économie Politique for January-February, 1925, a French economist, M. Pierre Meynial, gives a comprehensive analysis of the balance of payments of France during the war and post-war period to the close of 1924. The primary purpose of this investigation was to refute the contention of M. Décamps of the Bank of France that foreign holdings of French francs, securities, and floating credits were so large as to present a serious obstacle to the maintenance of exchange stability. In the other, published by l'Information, a study of the French security markets is used as a basis for estimating the market value in December, 1924, of French holdings of foreign securities and of foreign holdings of French securities. This study strengthens the contention that a considerable volume of French securities were in the possession of foreigners at the close of 1924.

A.   M. MEYNIAL'S ESTIMATE COMPARED WITH OURS

M. Meynial concludes that France was able to liquidate her war and post-war trade and service deficits with practically no sale of francs or of domestic securities, and that at the close of 1924 there were practically no outstanding credits against her on open account. Our estimates, on the other hand, indicate that the net total of foreign securities, French francs, and commercial credits that had been required to meet the trade and service deficits for the 11 years, 1914-24, amounted to about 34 billion francs. The differences are to be explained largely by the fact that M. Meynial has recalculated the foreign trade figures, and thereby greatly reduced the figure for the trade deficit that had to be met. It is in lesser degree due to his omission of certain items of income and expenditure which we have included. Other differences are of relatively minor importance.

It is impossible to set forth a detailed comparison between the two sets of estimates since M. Meynial has presented his data to show the five calendar years 1914-1918 together, and the five calendar years 1919-23 separately; while we have grouped the data for the war period, August 1, 1914—June 30, 1919, and for the four and a half post-war years July 1, 1919—December 31, 1923. The year 1924 alone is strictly comparable.

For the years 1914-23, M. Meynial presents his data in tabular form, but not for 1924. We have brought together his 1924 data, and present it in tabular form along with the data for the 10 years 1914-23.

Detailed differences between M. Meynial's estimates and those which we have presented in the course of this study are indicated by the table below. This summarizes the eleven-year period 1914-24 so that comparisons may be made between the net totals for each of the several items.

The trade deficit: In the trade and service accounts the item for which the discrepancy between the two estimates is greatest is the one showing net exports of commodities. The difference here amounts to a 24.4 billion franc reduction in the trade deficit. The explanation of this difference is two-fold.

1. M. Meynial has recalculated the value of French imports for the years 1914-1920, refusing to accept the figures given in the official trade statistics. His main argument for doing so is that during the war, goods imported on government account (chemicals, food, arms and munitions, and in fact all kinds of merchandise) were valued in the trade figures at current prices, in spite of the

M. PIERRE MEYNIAL'S ESTIMATES OF THE FRENCH BALANCE OF ACCOUNTS, 1914-1924*

(In millions of francs)

Items	1914-1918	1919	1920	1921	1922	1923	1924	Net Total 1914-1924
Merchandise import or export surplus	-47,284	-20,290	-20,020	-2,295	-2,552	-2,177	1,300	-93,318
Colonial trade with France	2,319	1,889	-500	621	-764	-915	-1,200	1,450
Colonial trade with other countries	...	...	140	1,450	950	...	-600	1,940
Precious metal import or export surplus	2,438	-139	473	212	-48	18	...	2,954
Income from the tourist trade	1,000	600	2,200	2,800	3,000	4,000	4,800	18,400
Migratory workers	...	...	-330	-336	-388	-720	-1,000	-2,774
Expenditures of foreign armies	8,650	5,100	...	...	...	...	...	13,750
Shipping	5,200	1,600	3,200	1,200	1,120	1,500	1,500	15,320
Insurance	300	80	75	60	70	78	...	663
Transit	125	60	95	82	85	91	...	538
Interest:								
Paid to France	10,100	2,300	2,000	2,500	2,500	2,500	2,500	24,400
Paid by France	-1,000	-300	-300	-300	-300	-300	-200	-2,700
Paid by French government	-782	-816	-2,153	-832	-788	-807	-800	-6,978
Interest on short-term credits	...	...	-100	-300	-240	-200	...	-840
Reparation receipts in excess of occupation costs, etc.	...	...	1,705	456	656	...	2,500	5,317
Imports of capital:								
Sale of foreign securities	2,200	800	3,000	...	...	...	...	6,000
Receipts from foreign loans	4,223	436	1,974	1,600	1,487	150	1,650	11,520
Credits obtained abroad	23,938	6,820	2,614	...	...	...	...	33,372
Exports of capital:								
Repayments of credits	...	-1,129	-1,913	-2,064	-575	-1,081	...	-6,762
Repayments of loans	...	...	-3,878	-141	...	-250	-906	-5,175
Loans to Allies and repayments received	-9,906	-1,368	-1,015	-632	61	-971	...	-13,831
Foreign securities sold on the French market	...	...	-202	-215	-256	-1,122	...	-1,795
Unexplained surplus(+) or deficit (—)	1,521	-4,357	-12,935	3,866	4,018	-206	9,544	1,451

*The minus sign is used to indicate debit balances in M. Meynial's estimate; all other accounts show credit balances.

COMPARATIVE SUMMARY OF TRADE AND SERVICE OPERATIONS

(Figures in billions of francs)

Items	Net figures, 1914-24 [a]		Amount by which M. Meynial's Estimate	
	Estimate of M. Meynial	Our Estimate	Decreases the Deficit	Increases the Deficit
Trade and service operations:				
Imports of commodities	− 89.9	− 114.3	24.4	...
Exports of bullion and specie	+ 3.0	+ 1.6	1.4	...
Income from foreign tourists (less outgo for migratory workers, etc.)	+ 15.6	+ 14.2	1.4	...
Income from expenditures of foreign armies	+ 13.8	+ 9.8	4.0	...
Personal expenditures of foreign soldiers and relief organizations	...	+ 16.0	...	16.0
Shipping	+ 15.3	+ 9.5	5.8	...
Insurance and commissions	+ .7	+ 2.1	...	1.4
Transit trade	+ .5	...	.5	...
Interest:				
Income	*+ 24.4*	*+ 13.0*		
Outgo	*− 10.5*	*− 13.8*		
Net	+ 13.9	− .8	14.7	...
Reparation receipts in excess of costs on reparation account	+ 5.3	+ .6	4.7	...
Net	− 21.8	− 61.3	56.9	17.4
			Net decrease of	39.5

COMPARATIVE SUMMARY, Continued

(Figures in billions of francs)

	Net figures, 1914-24 [a]		Amount by which M. Meynial's Estimate	
	Estimate of M. Meynial	Our Estimate	Decreases the Surplus	Increases the Surplus
Credit operations:				
Receipts from borrowing abroad, in excess of re-payments	+33.0	+36.9	3.9	
Sale of foreign securities	+6.0	+5.7		.3
Commercial, credits	...	+2.0	2.0	
Sale of domestic securities	...	+21.5	21.5	
Sale of francs	...	+10.0	10.0	
Sale of real estate	...	+.5	.5	
Net outgo for loans to Allied governments	−13.8	−11.0	2.8	
New investments abroad	−1.8	−4.3		2.5
Net	+23.4	+61.3	40.7	2.8
			Net decrease of	37.9

[a] The plus sign represents a surplus; the minus sign, a deficit.

fact that government purchases were made on more advantageous terms. As proof of his contention that imports were over-valued, he compared the French valuation of imports from Great Britain with the British figure of exports to France. He also compares the value of French imports from the United States with that of American exports to France. The results obtained—adjustments being made in the British and American figures for the shipping item [75]—are tabulated below.

FIGURES USED TO TEST FRENCH IMPORT STATISTICS
(In millions of francs)

French Imports	1914-18	1919	1920
From Great Britain:			
Based on French import figures...	23,050	8,800	10,312
Based on British export figures....	12,650	5,670	8,072
Difference	10,400	3,130	2,240
From the United States:			
Based on French import figures...	26,894	9,217	10,846
Based on American export figures.	22,394	8,717	10,096
Difference	4,500	500	750

The discrepancies between the French and British figures average about 2.25 billions a year; between the American and French figures, about 800 millions.

A comparison of the French figures of *exports* to Great Britain and the United States, with British and American figures of imports from France, discloses considerably smaller discrepancies.

On the basis of these comparisons M. Meynial cuts the French import total for 1914-18 from 87,938 million

[75] French imports are valued c.i.f., while British and American exports are valued f.o.b.

francs to 73,037 millions, a cut of about 17 per cent. For 1919 he makes a 10 per cent cut in imports, reducing them from 35,799 million francs to 32,169 millions; and for 1920, a 6 per cent cut, reducing imports from 49,905 million francs to 46,914 millions. He makes no change in export figures given by the customs administration for the whole period 1914-24, nor in the import figures for 1921-24. The total cut in the trade deficit which is achieved by this recalculation of imports for the years 1914-20 amounts to 21.6 billion francs.

2. For the purpose of the trade balance, M. Meynial has regarded the French colonies as an integral part of France. The one exception to this rule is Indo-China, which is treated as a foreign country for the reason that it does not use the franc but has a currency of its own.

By this method of handling the trade he has offset the total trade deficit of 93.3 billion francs (according to his figures), for the eleven-year period, by net imports from the colonies amounting to 1.5 billions, and net exports from the colonies to other countries other than France amounting to 1.9 billions, making a total offset of 3.4 billions. It must be noticed, however, that through a clerical error the 1921 figure of 621 millions of net exports to the colonies [76] is set down as a plus or credit item, instead of a minus or debit item.

It must also be noticed that M. Meynial has assumed that all of the foreign trade of the colonies is carried in French ships, and that on this assumption he has adjusted the trade value figures for the three years 1920-22 in such a way that the net import surplus of 368 million francs reported by the customs officials of the colonies,

[76] See M. Meynial's article, p. 15.

becomes a net export surplus of 2,450 millions. Such an adjustment is open to question—particularly in view of the fact that it, in effect, adds considerably to the shipping estimate, which is already quite high. Without this adjustment, the colonial import and export figures practically cancel, so that the French trade balance is unchanged by the inclusion of the colonial trade figures. average of 250 million francs a year.

The interest item: Another item which serves to cut the trade and service deficit shown by M. Meynial's figures, considerably below that given in our estimate is the interest item. The net figures for interest, according to M. Meynial's estimate, show income considerably larger than outgo, whereas our estimate shows outgo slightly greater than income. The result is that the deficit in the trade and service items shown by M. Meynial's estimate is cut 14.7 billion francs below that shown by our figures. Here again the explanation of the difference is two-fold.

1. M. Meynial assumes that during the war period the foreign securities remaining in the French portfolio were yielding interest at a higher rate than in pre-war years. For the post-war period, also, he estimates that the remaining securities (19 billions, according to his estimate) were not only bearing interest at a higher rate than before the war, but that the depreciation of the franc automatically and proportionately increased the paper franc value of the interest income. No account is taken of the fact that a large share of the foreign securities still belonging to the French people at the close of the war were in the form of bonds on which interest was payable in French francs and that the number of francs required to meet the interest charge remained fixed unless the

agreement specifically stipulated that payment should be made in gold.[77]

2. M. Meynial assumes that practically no French securities have been sold to foreigners and that a great part of the war and post-war trade deficit was met by short-time credits on open account. He estimates that practically all of these have now been paid off, and that the total interest charge on this account amounted to only 840 million francs. This low figure is explained by the fact that (1) his recalculation of imports cut down the figure for the deficit that had to be met; and (2) he has assumed that this deficit was met by short-term credits at low rates of interest. Our analysis indicates that a large volume of French securities was bought by foreigners during and since the war, and that interest payable by France on account of these securities totaled about 7.5 billion francs for the eleven-year period. The difference between the two estimates amounts to about 6.7 billion francs.

Soldiers' expenditures: A large offsetting difference between the two estimates is found in M. Meynial's failure to include an estimate of French income during the war from personal expenditures of foreign soldiers and relief organizations. Our estimate for this item is 16 billions.

[77] In case an agreement specifically requires payments to be made in gold, French law requires the debtor—if he be a foreigner —to pay his obligations in gold. This is true even at a time when irredeemable paper currency is legal tender in France. In case nothing is said in the agreement with regard to the money of payment, paper currency may be used. Jèze, Gaston, "La Monnaie de paiement," *Revue de science et de legislation financièr,* January-March, 1924, pp. 72-95. This question of the money of payment has been the cause of considerable litigation since the outbreak of the war.

Other items: Differences between other items in the two estimates are considerably smaller in amount. We have included no separate estimate for the transit trade, an item which M. Meynial estimates at a total of 500 million francs for the eleven-year period.

M. Meynial adjusts, as do we, the figures for gold and silver imports and exports during the war, refusing to accept the official trade statistics with regard to this item. His estimate places net exports of gold and silver at 1.4 billions greater than our estimate. His apparent failure to take account of the Russian gold imported by France under terms fixed in the treaty with Germany may account for part of this difference.

The shipping item accounts for a reduction of 5.8 billions in the trade and service deficits shown by his figures as compared with our estimate. In view of published data with regard to British income from shipping, his estimate for this item appears somewhat high, but it must be remembered that the difficulties in the way of arriving at a figure for the shipping item for any country are sufficient to account for considerable differences between two independent estimates.

The lack of complete and satisfactory evidence with regard to French reparation receipts and costs is likewise sufficient to account for considerable differences between figures given for net reparation receipts.

Credit operations: In the estimates with regard to credit operations, practically the whole difference between the two sets of figures is accounted for by two items, sale of domestic securities and sale of francs. Whereas our estimates showed that deficits in the trade and service accounts to the extent of approximately 22 billions had been met by the sale of domestic securities and

real estate, and 10 billions by the sale of francs, M.
Meynial's theory is that practically no French francs and
only a relatively small volume of French securities are
held by foreigners—a theory which he has sought to
establish by his recalculation of import values.

B. VALIDITY OF M. MEYNIAL'S ASSUMPTIONS AND CONCLUSIONS

According to M. Meynial's estimate, the deficit on trade
and service account for the eleven-year period 1914-
1924 was 39.5 billions francs below that which our figures
show. The difference, as we have seen, is largely due
to the fact that M. Meynial's recalculation of import
values has served to cut down the figure for the trade
deficit and for interest outgo. Other differences between
the two estimates with regard to trade and service operations, largely offset each other.

It is common knowledge that official trade figures are
not entirely satisfactory. The question is whether the
errors are such as to exaggerate or to understate the
trade deficit. M. Meynial has attempted to prove that
during the war period the net result of the errors was to
overstate the value of imports and thereby to increase
the deficit enormously. He assumes that the export figures are correct. He asserts that at the present time
this tendency to over-value imports still holds, though he
makes no correction in the figures for 1921 or later. The
proof which he offers, however—a comparison of French
trade figures with those of Great Britain and the United
States—is hardly conclusive.

Trade statistics are a by-product of commercial activity, and are not matters of primary importance to

those engaged in foreign trade. This fact alone is a sufficient explanation of many of the differences that may occur between the figures which country A publishes for her exports to country B, and the figures which country B publishes with regard to her imports from country A.

The exporter, for example, is not particularly interested in recording the exact destination of his goods. He is interested in getting his goods aboard ship and on their way. Likewise, the primary interest of the importer is in getting possession of his goods, not in declaring their precise country of origin. If the goods are put aboard a tramp which has instructions to put in at certain ports where it will receive further sailing orders, the exporter will probably make his declaration to show the country to which he thinks the goods will go. The ultimate destination of the goods, however, may prove to be altogether different. If a shipment is to be broken, part going to one country, part to others, there are further possibilities for confusion. The exporter may include only one of the several countries in his declaration—and that country may not prove to be the one to which the bulk of the goods finally goes. The importer, on the other hand, may not distinguish between the country from which the goods actually came and the country where the boat stopped to unload part of its cargo.

Anyone who is in doubt concerning the wisdom of using import-export comparisons for a limited number of countries, as a basis for revising the total trade of a country should explore this question further. A comparison of American exports to the United Kingdom with United Kingdom imports from the United States in 1913, furnishes a good example of the discrepancies that may be expected. The American export figures show that 31.8 million bushels of wheat and 3 million barrels of flour were sent to the United Kingdom in 1913; but the United Kingdom import figures show that 69.7 million bushels of wheat and 4.2 million barrels of flour were received from the United States. Exports of 12 head of cattle to the United Kingdom are recorded in the American statistics, against the British figure of 11,417 head received from the United States. Examples such as these are not hard to find.

War-time necessity for maintaining secrecy concerning goods shipped to the belligerents served to increase the probability of inaccuracies in the exporter's declarations. It would not necessarily have the same effect on import declarations. Once a shipment had arrived safely at its destination and the war need for preserving secrecy no longer held, goods which had started out under camouflaged sailing orders, might have had their country of origin correctly declared by the importer. This would in some measure explain discrepancies between the statistics of two countries.

C. STUDY PUBLISHED BY *L'INFORMATION*

The study of the security markets recently published by *l'Information*,[78] is based on a survey of transactions in the principal security markets of France, with additional information used to supplement and correct the results of the survey. It arrives at the conclusion that foreigners hold French securities with a present value of about 34 billion paper francs. No attempt is made to

[78] This article is summarized in *Wirtschaftsdienst*, May 15, 1925, p. 776; and in the monthly bulletin of the *Banque Suisse*, July, 1925, p. 180.

estimate the amount of French currency held by foreigners.[79]

The check between this estimate and the conclusions which we reach on the basis of our study of the balance of accounts is reasonably close and may be taken as a rough confirmation of our work. Our figures show that on December 31, 1924,[80] foreigners hold French domestic securities for which they had paid about 28 billion paper francs,[81] and that French indebtedness to foreigners in the form of commercial credit granted on open account amounted to about 2.0 billion francs.

In concluding this detailed analysis of the French balance of account it is, of course, scarcely necessary to say that we make no pretense of absolute accuracy in our estimates. We do believe, however, that we have come about as close to the truth as is possible in view of the

[79] An estimate is also made of the value of French investments in foreign securities. They are put at 68 billion paper francs held in France, plus 7.5 billions held abroad. This estimate probably includes investments made practically valueless by the war—and at present non-interest bearing, whereas our estimate of 43 billions includes only interest bearing obligations. This fact may not, however, account for the entire difference. The rest is presumably due to the fact that we used an average rate of only 2.2 in converting pre-war values to paper francs of 1924. We use this rate for the reason that many of the foreign holdings are payable in paper francs or in the depreciated paper of the borrowing countries. It is possible, however, that this ratio, and therefore our estimate of French foreign investments, may be somewhat low.

[80] See p. 35.

[81] Whether or not the quotation value of these securities in the French market would be higher or lower than 28 billions would, of course, depend on the policy that had been followed by the borrowing corporations and firms with regard to new issues.

unsatisfactory character of the data bearing on the problem. Moreover, we have a good deal of confidence in the substantial accuracy of our conclusions for the single year 1924.

APPENDIX B

THE FRENCH BUDGET SYSTEM

THE French budget has never been a simple, unified, inclusive statement of revenues and expenditures, which he who runs may read. It has usually consisted of an ordinary budget, a series of annexed budgets, an extraordinary budget, and numerous special treasury accounts. In the year 1920 France had still another budget—the so-called "recoverable" budget—in addition to all of these. The exact budget situation at any given time can therefore be ascertained only by bringing together all of these various budgets and accounts.

I. THE ORDINARY BUDGET

The ordinary budget, in strict theory, comprises all the current receipts from non-borrowing sources of revenue, and all regular government outlays. In practice it sometimes includes the proceeds of loans, and it commonly does not include *all* of the ordinary current expenditures. We shall see that many expenditures which properly belong in the regular budget have commonly been classed as *extraordinary*.

The budget bill as presented by the Finance Minister to the Chamber of Deputies is made up, on the one hand, of the *expenditure* estimates of the different ministers for their respective departments; and on the other hand, of the revenue estimates compiled by the Finance Minister

396

himself. As a rule, the departmental estimates with regard to expenditures are drawn up in October or November, about 14 or 15 months before the budget concerned is put into operation, and the completed bill is sent on to the Chamber of Deputies about three months later, or a full year before it is to be put into effect.

This practice—which is jealously insisted upon by the Chamber of Deputies—greatly impairs the value of the estimates, for, as M. René Stourm says, "commercial crises, good or bad crops, market prices of merchandise, etc., can within a year's time greatly modify the (budgetary) figures." [1] Budgetary deficits, requiring the granting of additional credits, may perhaps in part result from this practice. Curiously enough, however, it seldom gives rise to budgetary surpluses.

The budget in France is voted for a single fiscal year, the limits which coincide with the calendar year. At the end of the year, however, the government, like an individual, must wait before closing its books, until work started within the year and chargeable to it has been completed and paid for. The full time elapsing up to the date when the accounts are closed is known as the fiscal period or "exercice."

For many years the accounts were kept open indefinitely in France, there being no fixed closing date. At the present time the fiscal period is regulated by the law of February 25, 1899. This law "recognizes definitely five schedules of delay in closing the fiscal periods: January 31 of the second year, for the purpose of completing works under way; March 31, for the liquidating and passing of payment vouchers covering expenditures;

---

[1] Stourm, René, *The Budget* (1913 edition, translated by the Institute of Government Research, 1917), p. 99.

April 30, for collections and payments; June 30, for the authorization and regularization of certain expenditures, by means of supplementary appropriations; July 31, for rectification of the records." [2]

Claims outstanding at the end of the fiscal period are listed and inserted in the "law of regularization of the accounts," and any such claims not included in this list are payable only if they are included in supplementary appropriations voted by the Chamber. The accounts for the fiscal period are finally audited and published by the *Cour des Comptes.* At the present time, the work of auditing the accounts is very much delayed, 1916 being the last year for which an audited statement has been published.

II. THE ANNEXED BUDGETS

The annexed budgets which are attached to the general budget include a series of small special budgets—which deal specifically with the revenues and expenditures of various enterprises administered by the State. These budgets are for the following services: Issuing money and minting medals; National Savings Banks; National Printing Office; Legion of Honor; Fund for Invalid Sailors; Central School of Arts and Crafts; Railroads and Port of Réunion; State Railways, etc. Not all industrial enterprises are, however, budgeted separately; again illustrating the lack of uniformity in French practice. For example, the manufacture of tobacco, gunpowder, matches, playing cards, and maps, are carried in the general budget, while the posts, telegraphs, and telephones have sometimes been included in the ordinary budget, and at other times carried in one of the annexed budgets.

[2] Stourm, René, *The Budget* (1913 edition, translated by the Institute of Government Research, 1917), p. 523.

The annexed budgets are submitted to Parliament along with the ordinary budget, and indeed the net figures are incorporated in the final returns of the general budget. That is to say, the surplus or deficit in the accounts of each of the several services covered by the annexed budgets is carried into the general budget at the close of the accounting period or *exercice*. In case of a surplus, the general budget gets the income; in case of a deficit the general budget makes good the deficiency. While the annexed budgets are sound in principle, they have led to some confusion, and there has been considerable discussion of the desirability of their elimination.

III. THE EXTRAORDINARY BUDGET [3]

The extraordinary budget may include three different categories of expenditures: first, inescapable emergency expenditures, such as those incident to a great war; second, optional expenditures—such as appropriations for public works, which are deemed desirable, but are not usually imperative; third, unjustifiable expenditures—meaning by unjustifiable, all expenditures appearing in the extraordinary budget which properly belong in the ordinary budget.

The extraordinary budget opened the doors to fiscal practices of a vicious character. While the abuses are to be found primarily in the second and third classes, even the first type of extraordinary budget has nothing to commend it. The extraordinary budgets for public works have led to great extravagance in public expenditure, and the launching of many enterprises of doubtful char-

[3] The discussion under this heading is based on Stourm, *The Budget*, Chapter X.

acter. Anyone who is familiar with the American "pork barrel" will readily appreciate the opportunities for waste afforded by the French extraordinary budget.

The third type of extraordinary budget is wholly bad. In practice this type of extraordinary budget tends to consist of the excess of estimated expenditures over estimated revenues from taxation, government monopolies, etc. The classification of expenditures between ordinary and extraordinary is wholly arbitrary. In the words of Léon Say, "The expenditures are ordinary when the Budgetary Commission declares them to be ordinary. They become extraordinary when the Commission defines them as such." According to Stourm, the extraordinary budget could be extended at will. "The mass of projects which clamor for inclusion in the extraordinary budget nearly always succeed in being so incorporated." [4]

The French extraordinary budget is a device of venerable age. Under the old régime in France, it dominated the fiscal system, and the French Revolution was conducted almost exclusively on extraordinary resources. While Napoleon's official budgets were apparently unified, it appears that under the name of "extraordinary domain," the little Corsican maintained a huge secret extraordinary budget. It received the proceeds of enforced contributions from vanquished and occupied countries, revenues from state property abroad, etc. Napoleon thus established a war fund in the cellars of the Tuilleries, from which he endowed his generals and soldiers, met his war expenditures, and made loans for the encouragement of industry.

The extraordinary budgets were in more or less common use throughout the period from the Napoleonic era

[4] Stourm, *The Budget*, p. 250.

until 1870. A law of 1840 abolished the extraordinary budget established in 1837 for public works, and consolidated it with the general budget. The extraordinary budgets were revived, however, in the forties, and played an important rôle during the next three decades. They were again abolished by Finance Minister Thiers in 1871. During the period from 1872-1878, the only thing resembling an extraordinary budget was a liquidation account, the expenditures from which were devoted to repairing war loss, and reconstructing the military organization. The funds were derived almost entirely from loans.

The extraordinary budget reappeared in 1878, and the succeeding 12 years constituted perhaps its period of greatest abuse. In 1882, seven different ministers succeeded in participating in the allotments of the extraordinary budget, acquiring the right under one plausible pretext or another. Expenditures were constantly shifted from one budget to another, and notoriously regular expenditures were charged against the loans of the extraordinary budget. As a result of the vigorous agitation for fiscal unification, the extraordinary budgets were abolished in 1890. It was not until the period of the Great War that they again reappeared, continuing in use until they were once more suppressed in 1922.

IV. THE RECOVERABLE BUDGET

The recoverable budget, which was in a sense an extraordinary budget, was revised as a means of recording, on the one side, expenditures which were considered as chargeable to Germany, and, on the other side, the amounts received from Germany. This budget was suppressed at the close of 1924, so that the general or ordinary budget of 1925 now includes the items which in 1920 and 1921 were distributed among ordinary, extraordinary, and recoverable budgets.[5]

V. SPECIAL TREASURY ACCOUNTS [6]

The Special Treasury Services or Accounts are to some extent analogous to the extraordinary budgets. Since these accounts originally fell altogether outside the budgetary regulations, it was not necessary to submit them to Parliament for ratification, nor were they submitted to audit. The original purpose of the Special Treasury Accounts appears to have been quite legitimate; namely, to facilitate the recording of transactions that properly belonged outside the regular budget.

Expenditures handled in this way were commonly of a temporary sort, shortly to be covered by specific receipts, so that there appeared to be no necessity of encumbering the budget with them. Some of these accounts, however, were, and still are, in the nature of funds: as for example, the accounts entitled Capital of surety bonds; Proceeds of legacies and gifts to the nation; Proceeds from the tax on horse-race betting, to be used in encouraging breeding; etc.

The Special Treasury Accounts made possible enormous unauthorized expenditures. Many of such outlays, moreover, were never recovered. For example, in 1832, the French treasury participated in a temporary loan to Greece. In 1857, an international commission stipulated

---

[5] For further discussion of the recoverable budget see pp. 73-84. of the text.

[6] Stourm, *The Budget*, pp. 270-7; *Exposé des motifs du projet du budget, 1923*, pp. 29-35 and 322-365.

that Greece should reimburse the advances in annual installments. In 1886 it was computed that at the existing rate of payments, the obligation would be discharged in 135 more years. In 1887, the loan was cancelled from the accounts of the treasury. Again "temporary loans" were made to industries in 1860. But of 36,840,166 million francs thus loaned, 9,716,878 francs were carried to the "loss" account in 1888.[7]

After 1870 the Special Treasury Accounts, like the extraordinary budgets, were largely devoted to the promotion of public works and the improvement of the military establishment. The special accounts survived the budgetary reform of 1893, and they continued to be utilized throughout the pre-war period.

During the war a great many of the government's activities were recorded in the Special Treasury Accounts rather than in the budget. For example, a special account was opened in which a record was kept of the loans which the French government made to foreign countries. In another account, a record was kept of loans made to Chambers of Commerce, in order to facilitate the mobilization of troops, the feeding of the civil population, etc. A separate account was opened for each Chamber of Commerce receiving such a loan, the debits in the account showing the loans made by the State, the credits showing the amounts that were repaid.

The aid which the government gave to industrial establishments in order to encourage the adaptation of industry to war needs was made the subject of another one of these accounts. Still other accounts were opened to record the operations in connection with the feeding

[7] Cernesson, André, *Le principe d'unite budgetaire en France,* 1911, pp. 48-61.

of the civil population during the war. In one of these a record was kept of the purchase and resale of wheat and flour. A second had to do with other commodities—sugar, coffee, petrol, fertilizers, butter, cheese, oil seeds, rice, pastry, meats, etc., handled by the government. War materials purchased from the United States were handled in another account. The debits represented the cost of storage, transportation, and expenses in connection with the sale of the goods, as well as the principal and interest of the amounts due the United States for the goods; while the credits represented receipts from the sale of such goods.

The net sums paid out by the government and charged to these accounts have reached enormous figures in the years during and since the war, the large deficits being mainly due to loans to foreign governments, to the provisioning of the civil population, and to railway grants. The Finance law of April 30, 1921, therefore, provided that all operations covered by these accounts—except for a certain list specifically enumerated in the law—should be subject to the same rules concerning authorization, execution, and control as the receipts and expenditures included in the general budget of the State. As a matter of fact, a large number of these accounts were no longer required and were closed out during 1922-1924.

The nature of these services is shown by the tabular statement given below, which shows the Special Treasury Accounts outstanding on June 30, 1924. The first 28 of these accounts, it will be observed, had been created prior to August 1, 1914.

STATE OF THE SPECIAL TREASURY ACCOUNTS, JUNE 30, 1924 *

(In millions of francs)

Name of Account	Net Balance of Account	
	Re-ceipts	Ex-pendi-tures
I. Accounts Created Before August 1, 1914		
Capital of surety bonds, in cash.................—.........	100.5	...
Funds for expenditures of public interest..........	237.8	...
Legacies or gifts to the nation or to various public "administrations"	5.4	...
Transfer of military lands (laws of Jan. 2 and 14, 1890)	.6	...
Transfer of land at one time fortified.............	.2	...
Tax on race-track betting, to be used for encouraging stock breeding............................	33.5	...
Annual payments by the Bank of France (law of Nov. 17, 1897)............................	38.3	...
Advance of 40 millions to the Treasury by the Bank of France	13.2	...
Proceeds from short-term bond issues (law of Feb. 17, 1898)................................	125.6	...
Proceeds from the short-term bond issues for repayment of surety bonds (law of Dec. 26, 1908)....	35.0	...
Subventions for construction or rebuilding of school houses, and subsidies for building sites (law of July 7, 1904).............................	.5	...
Funds set aside for repayment of Bank of France loans to *sinistrés* (law of March 8, 1910)........	1.8	...
Tax on the manufacture of alcohol, to be used for indemnifying denaturers of alcohol (laws of Feb. 25, 1901, and Mar. 30, 1902).................	.8	...
advance of 20 millions to the Treasury by the Bank of France...........................	...	...
Deposit with the Treasury of the value of blue bank notes (*la valeur des billets à impression bleue*) of the Bank of France...........................	5.0	...
Advance to the local budget of Guadeloupe for repairing damages due to the earthquake of April 29, 1897	...	.7
Advance to the local budget of Mayotte for repairing the damages caused by the cyclone of Feb. 27-28, 1898	...	...
Loans to industry (law of Aug. 1, 1860)..........	...	.7
Liquidation of old accounts of village roads and academic buildings	...	24.6
Advances to French railroad companies for guaranty of interest.......................	...	103.4
Perfecting of armaments and re-installation of military services (law of Feb. 17, 1898)...........	...	173.6
Advances to the government of Crete (law of Apr. 6, 1902)................................	...	1.0
Advances to the departmental or regional treasuries (law of Apr. 5, 1910).......................	...	.1
Advances by the Treasury under the law of March 30, 1902................................	...	59.3

* *Exposé des motifs du projet du budget*, 1925, pp. 358-363.

STATE OF THE SPECIAL TREASURY ACCOUNTS, JUNE 30, 1924—(*Cont'd*)
(In millions of francs)

Name of Account	Net Balance of Account	
	Re-ceipts	Ex-pendi-tures
Proceeds from the issue of short-term bonds (law of July 30, 1913)............................	44.8	...
Advance to Albania............................	...	.01
Proceeds from the issue of 3½ per cent amortissable *rentes* (law of June 20, 1914).................	453.5	...
Military occupation of Morocco..................	.7	...
	1,097.2	363.4
II. Accounts Created Since August 1, 1914		
Advances to Allied governments or foreign estab-lishments (divers laws).....................	...	13,710.0
Cessions of materials to foreign governments (law of Sept. 29, 1917)............................	...	377.0
Advances to Chambers of Commerce because of the war of 1914 (divers laws)[a].....................	...	12.2
Loans to divers manufacturers to forward activities necessary for national defense (decrees of Mar. 27 and July 15, 1915; laws of Sept. 28, 1915, and Jan. 27, 1917)............................	...	52.0
Wheat and flour supply for the civil population (laws of Oct. 16, 1915, Apr. 20, 1916, Oct. 30, 1916, Apr. 7 and 8, 1917, and Apr. 4, 1918)[b]....	...	3,621.7
Bread supply (law of Aug. 9, 1920)[b]............	...	238.8
Advances to the European Commission of the Dan-ube (laws of Nov. 9, 1915, and Jan. 22, 1917)...	...	.8
Advances to workers' productive and credit co-operative societies (law of Dec. 18, 1915).......	2.7	...
Advances to the peoples' credit banks and to small commercial and industrial concerns (law of Mar. 13, 1917)................................	13.9	...
Advances to consumers' co-operative societies (law of May 7, 1917)............................	4.3	...
Grants to Agriculture (laws of Apr. 7, 1917, and May 4, 1918)[a]............................	6.5	...
Outlays for the reconstruction of railway roadbeds of general interest, destroyed or damaged by war (law of June 29, 1917)[c].....................	...	1,745.9
Outlays for reconstruction of railway roadbeds dam-aged by war (laws of Dec. 30, 1917, and Jan. 10, 1919)[c]	...	1,906.8
Agricultural reconstruction of invaded departments (law of Aug. 3, 1917)[d].....................	191.8	...
Industrial reconstruction of invaded departments (law of Aug. 6, 1917)[e].....................	141.8	...
Maritime insurance against war risk (law of Sept. 29, 1917)	105.0	...

[a] Account closed Dec. 31, 1923 (law of Dec. 28, 1923).
[b] Account closed Nov. 1, 1922 (law of Dec. 1, 1922).
[c] Account closed June 30, 1922 (law of Dec. 31, 1921).
[d] Account closed June 30, 1924 (law of Dec. 28, 1923).
[e] Account closed Mar. 31, 1924 (law of Dec. 28, 1923).

(In millions of francs)

Name of Account	Net Balance of Account	
	Re-ceipts	Ex-pendi-tures
Advances to shipowners for the purchase and con-struction of ships (law of Apr. 13, 1917) [f]	...	41.3
Maritime transports—purchase and construction of ships (laws of Mar. 25, 1918, and June 30, 1919)	818.1	...
Fleet in operation (law of Dec. 29, 1919)	8.1	...
Increase in pay of demobilized soldiers	...	11.7
Supplying chemical fertilizers (law of June 20, 1918) [b]	112.8	...
Operations concerned with extraordinary taxes on war profits (law of June 28, 1918)	5,758.6	...
Supplementary payment by the Bank of France (law of Dec. 20, 1918)	...	...
Balance of supplementary payments by the Bank of France to be assigned to different services	78.5	...
Civil requisitions and cessions (law of Nov. 23, 1918) [a]	...	...
Supplying shoes (law of Nov. 23, 1918) [a]	13.8	...
Advances to the general budget of French Equatorial Africa for urgent work noted in the law of July 13, 1914, which authorized the colony to contract a loan of 171 million francs (law of Dec. 17, 1918)	...	...
Maintenance of troops of occupation in foreign countries (law of Dec. 31, 1918)	...	2,044.4
Replacement of emergency war currency issued in the invaded areas (law of Feb. 11, 1919)	...	323.6
Exchange of German money belonging to Alsace and Lorraine, French prisoners of war and in-habitants of the liberated regions (law of Apr. 23, 1919)	...	1,986.3
Liquidation of materials ceded by the U. S. (law of Oct. 21, 1919) [g]	2,227.7	...
Liquidation of railway rolling stock, roadbeds, etc., ceded by Great Britain (law of July 31, 1920) [a]	38.0	...
Loans to small commercial and industrial concerns demobilized (law of October 24, 1919)	16.9	...
Proceeds of tax on betting to be used for agricul-tural education (law of Aug. 5, 1920)	8.5	...
Liquidation of consortiums and buying concerns cre-ated during the war (law of July 31, 1920)	29.3	...
Service of benzols and petrols (law of July 31, 1920) [a]	349.0	...
Payments effected in execution of the Allied protocol of July 16, 1920 (law of Aug. 6, 1920)	...	772.3
Common funds of the large railway system (law of Oct. 20, 1921)	41.2	...
Alcohol accounts	25.5	...
Supply of fuel [h]	...	37.3

[f] Account closed June 30, 1924 (law of Aug. 8, 1924).
[g] Closing of this account on December 31, 1924, proposed in the draft of the Finance law of 1925.
[h] Account closed May 31, 1924 (law of May 14, 1924).

STATE OF THE SPECIAL TREASURY ACCOUNTS, JUNE 30, 1924—(*Cont'd*)

(In millions of francs)

Name of Account	Net Balance of Account	
	Re-ceipts	Ex-pendi-tures
Advances of the Treasury for the construction of customs stations at the German-Sarre boundary (law of July 17, 1923)....................	...	...
Advances of the Treasury to facilitate the distribution of electric power in the rural districts....	...	
Audit of Special Treasury Accounts (Law of December 1, 1922) ⎰ Old food supply account No. 1..	...	103.5
Old food supply account No. 2..	206.2	
Old agricultural chemicals account	3.0	
Old account of benzols and petrols	16.2	
Old account of stocks of British railway materials	57.2	
Old husbandry work account—Section A	.1	
Old account of the Industrial Reconstruction Service	38.2	...
Old account of the Agricultural Reconstruction Service......	...	...
Old shoe supply account.......	.7	...
Old fuel supply account.......	.001	...
	10,813.6	26,985.6

VI. THE CHARACTER OF FRENCH BUDGET REVENUES

As shown in the classification of receipts on page 88, the French government derives its revenues from (1) direct taxes, (2) indirect taxes, (3) monopolies, and (4) miscellaneous sources. A brief discussion of each class of receipts follows:

Direct taxes: The direct taxes comprise three classes, one of which is temporary in nature. They are the income tax; the so-called assimilated taxes; and the war-profits tax. The old theory of taxation in France has been that taxes should be levied on the basis of "exterior signs." The individual Frenchman preferred to be taxed on the basis of the front he presented to the world—the rental value of his residence, the number of doors and windows in his house, etc.—rather than to expose to any prying eyes the actual state of his private affairs. This, of course, is in direct disagreement with the spirit of the modern income tax.

The present income taxes of France were incorporated into the French taxation system by a series of laws which date back no further than March 29, 1914. Their history, however, covers a great many years of persistent effort towards fiscal reform. In 1907, after many similar bills had been rejected, a draft law was presented to the Chamber of Deputies by Caillaux which was accepted in part by that body in 1909 (with other sections adopted at later dates). It was finally forced through the Senate piecemeal in 1914 and later years, the provision with regard to the general income tax being attached as a rider to the Finance Law of 1914.[8]

The present system of income taxes is intended to reach all classes of income. It includes a general tax on incomes and a group of "schedule taxes" which classify taxable income into six groups, providing a set of rules and rates for each category.[9] The six classes of income

[8] In this connection it is interesting to recall that Ruskin, writing in 1871, speaks of an income tax bill that had recently been up for discussion and voted down by the French Senate. (*Fors Clavigera*, vol. II, p. 111.)

[9] The history and significance of the income tax system of France is thoroughly discussed by Allix, M. Edgar, *Traité élémentaire de science des finances*, 1921, pp. 481-578. The French income tax laws, including the matter of rates, exemptions, etc., have been summarized in English in an excellent study prepared by Bernard, A., *Taxation of Incomes, Corporations, and Inheritances in Canada, Great Britain, France, Italy, Belgium, and Spain* (published as Senate Document No. 186, 68th Congress, 2nd Session), pp. 65-102.

covered by the schedule taxes are derived from the following sources: (1) real estate, both urban and rural, with and without buildings (an old tax); (2) securities (also replacing an old tax) and mortgages, notes, deposits, and surety bonds (a new tax); (3) industrial and commercial profits (the old *patents* tax revised and changed); (4) agricultural profits, as distinguished from a tax on land (a new tax); (5) salaries, wages, pensions, annuities, etc. (a new tax); and (6) professional incomes (in part a new tax, in part a revision of an old tax).

The rates in force up to the middle of 1925 on these various classes of income are as follows:

	Rate Per Cent
Real estate	12
Securities, mortgages, notes, etc.	12
(14.4 per cent in case of income from foreign securities.)	
Industrial and commercial profits	9.6
Agricultural profits	7.2
Salaries, wages, pensions, etc.	7.2
Professional income	7.2

The net income of each taxpayer, after deductions have been made for the amount paid under each of the schedule taxes, is then subject to the general income tax. This tax, which roughly corresponds to the British super-tax, is assessed at a proportionally increasing rate, rising from zero on net incomes below 6,000 francs to 60 per cent on incomes in excess of 500,000 francs. The amount to be paid under the general income tax is increased by 25 per cent in the case of unmarried persons above the age of 30 who have no dependents, and by 10 per cent in the case of all married taxpayers without dependents.[10]

[10] Data with regard to tax rates is from the (London) *Economist*, May 23, 1925, p. 1008.

The general income tax and schedule taxes have now superseded the four old direct taxes—mentioned on page 53 in the State taxation system. The old taxes are still of importance, however, because they furnish the basis for assessing the principal revenues of the departments and communes. Under the old régime, the direct taxes levied by the State were increased by certain percentages—known as the *centimes additionnels*. The proceeds from these added rates were collected by the State and turned over to the departments and communes. When the national system of direct taxes was changed, no provision was made for changing the local taxation system. The result is that the *centimes additionnels*, which still continue in existence, are now levied on a fictitious basis.

The so-called "assimilated" taxes include a number of important contributions. The only characteristic which these *taxes assimilées aux contributions direct* have in common is the method by which they are administered. Otherwise they are quite different, one from another. For example, they include the mortmain tax—a tax levied on lands and buildings owned by corporations or similar institutions [11]—the tax on mine royalties, the horse and vehicle tax, billiard tax, club tax, fees for boiler inspection, and verification of weights and measures, oleo manufacture inspection, and license fees for pharmacists, sellers of mineral waters, etc.[12]

[11] Bernard, *Taxation of Incomes, Corporations and Inheritances*, p. 110.

[12] For the itemized returns from the assimilated taxes for the years 1910-1921, see *Bulletin de statistique et de législation comparée*, April, 1923, p. 634.

The war profits tax was imposed by the law of July 1, 1916. It is levied on excess profits made by persons or corporations who carried on business transactions with the government during the war, on persons or corporations subject to the business license tax, and on mine owners whose profits exceed their average rate of profits for the three trade years preceding August 1, 1914. This tax which was made retroactive, affected excess profits made between August 1, 1914, and the end of the twelfth month following the cessation of hostilities.

While this tax has ceased to be assessed on profits made after June 30, 1920, a considerable part of the proceeds due the State from this source are still outstanding and collectible.[18] For example, the Finance Minister, M. Clémentel, estimated that in 1925 the State would collect about 750 million francs from the operation of this tax. The amounts to be collected in subsequent years will, of course, become progressively smaller.

Indirect taxes. The line between direct and indirect taxes is not hard and fast, some receipts which are classed as indirect being closely akin to others which are included under the head of direct taxes. Those which we have classified as indirect taxes are the following: the registration, stamp, bourse, stocks and bonds, customs, excise, and consumption taxes; a *special payments* tax; and the luxury and turnover taxes. Strictly speaking, the net proceeds from the fiscal monopolies—tobacco, matches, and gunpowder—should also be included with this group. They are separated only because of their method of administration.

The registration tax is levied on transfers of property, mortgages, written contracts, etc., at the time such trans-

[18] Bernard, *Taxation of Incomes, Corporations and Inheritances,* pp.102-4.

actions and documents become matters of official record.
Most of these receipts may properly be classified with
other indirect taxes. For historical reasons, however,
they include the inheritance taxes, which belong under
the head of direct taxes.

In the beginning, the inheritance tax in France was
very moderate, corresponding closely to the tax on ordinary property transfers for value—both in the rate of
the tax and in the way it was collected. Little by little,
however, the character of this tax was changed, and the
rate increased, until at the present time it yields a very
considerable revenue to the government.[14] In 1923 it
yielded 990 million francs out of a total of 3,391 millions
received from the registration tax; and for 1925 the estimated yield is 1,774 million francs out of a total registration tax of 5,430 millions.

The tax on inherited wealth is of two kinds. The estate
of a deceased person who leaves less than four children
is subject to the *taxe successorale*, a graduated tax which
rises from 0.3 per cent on the first 2,000 francs in case
three children or their descendants are living, to 46.8 per
cent on any excess over 500 million francs where there
are no children. There is also the *droits de mutation par
décès* which is levied upon the net amount received by
a legatee, and varies according to the amount of the
legacy and to the degree of kinship to the deceased. On
that part of an inheritance in excess of 50 million francs,
received from relatives beyond the fourth degree or from
non-relatives, the rate rises to 70 per cent.

[14] The historical development of this tax is discussed by Allix,
Traité élémentaire de science des finances, pp. 597-610. For a dis-
cussion and tabulation of the inheritance tax rates, see Bernard,
Taxation of Incomes, Corporations and Inheritances, pp. 111-8.

The stamp tax, which is of very ancient origin, of course takes its name from its method of collection, a stamp being required to legalize practically all public documents and a great variety of private papers. With regard to the bourse tax, tax on stocks and bonds, and customs duties, nothing need be said in this survey, the nature of these taxes being clearly enough indicated by their names.

The excise and consumption taxes (*Produit des contributions indirectes, sucres et saccharine*) cover a wide variety of commodities: wines, beer, alcohol, mineral waters, charged water, lemonade, vinegar, salt, sugar, coffee, cocoa, tea, vanilla, animal and vegetable oils, candles, railways, public vehicles for land and water travel, bicycles and motorcycles, and manufacture of gold and silver, playing cards, etc.

Taxes of this sort had an important place in the fiscal system of the old régime, but were suppressed altogether at the time of the revolution on the theory that they were contrary to the principle of freedom of commerce. Budgetary deficits, however, gradually necessitated their revival. This revival was exceedingly unpopular, and constituted one of the serious grievances which the people held against Napoleon in 1814.[15]

The special tax on payments was instituted by the law of December 31, 1917, and in 1920 was replaced by the "business turnover tax." This tax was intended as a tax on consumption. It is levied on certain non-commercial transactions, such as payments for licenses, payments of farm rents, payments of house rents, etc., and on the retailing of goods valued at more than 15 francs.[16]

[15] Allix, *Traité élémentaire de science des finances*, pp. 639-81.
[16] *Ibid.*, 630.

The luxury tax was also imposed by the law of December 31, 1917. It was levied on the sale of photographic supplies, brandies, liqueurs, antiques, etc., and on certain other classes of goods the value of which exceeded certain stipulated amounts, as well as on hotels, restaurants, etc., that were classed as *établissements de luxe*.

The luxury tax and the tax on payments, particularly on retail sales, were exceedingly difficult to put in operation, merchants being required to keep a special set of books in which they entered all transactions subject to these taxes. In the law of June 25, 1920, they were, therefore, both incorporated in the business turnover tax.

The business turnover tax differs from the payments tax in one essential respect. It replaced the tax on particular retail transactions by a tax on the general turnover of a business. It is levied on: (1) all persons who buy goods for resale and those engaged in occupations which are subject to the tax on commercial and industrial profits, the rate in these cases being 1.3 per cent of the turnover; (2) the value of food or drink consumed in restaurants, inns, etc., the rate being 12 per cent for "first class" establishments and 3.6 per cent for "second class"; (3) the sale of certain luxury goods, also at a rate of 12 per cent. It does not apply to those engaged in the "liberal professions," to agriculturists selling their own products, nor to co-operative organizations which are not operating for commercial profits, and there are certain other exemptions particularly enumerated in the law.[17]

Monopolies: The gross receipts of the government from two classes of monopolies—the fiscal monopolies, and the posts, telegraphs, and telephones—are included in

[17] *Ibid.,* pp. 629-39.

the table of receipts on pp. 61 and 88. The fiscal monopolies of the state include the manufacture and sale of
tobacco, powder, and matches. The wholesaling of
powder and tobacco, regardless of who manufactures
them, is carried on by government agents who sell only
to licensed retailers on cash terms. In the case of the
match monopoly, the State does not take a direct hand
in the wholesaling of the goods, but does supervise the
wholesalers and retailers, and tries to prevent smuggling
from abroad. Orders for matches are filed with the col-
lectors of indirect taxes and are forwarded by them
directly to the factories.[18]

A certain part of the government's receipts from these
monopolies are, of course, required to cover manufacturing and selling costs. Receipts over and above such costs,
however, are equivalent to a tax on the consumption of
these monopoly products. In 1913, for example, the gross
receipts of the tobacco monopoly amounted to 545.1 million francs, expenditures to 108.7 millions, and the net
proceeds of the State—equivalent to a tobacco tax—
amounted to 436.4 million francs. For the same year the
figures for the match monopoly were: gross receipts, 44.6
millions; expenditures 12.6 millions; net receipts 32 millions. In 1923 the figures for the tobacco monopoly were
gross receipts 1,806.7 millions; expenditures, 524.2 millions; net receipts 1,282.5 millions. Comparable figures
for the match monopoly were gross receipts 127.3 millions; expenditures, 55.6 millions; and net receipts 71.7
million francs.[19] Figures given in the table of receipts,
pp. 61 and 88, represent the gross receipts from these
monopolies.

[18] Stourm, *The Budget*, pp. 410-22.
[19] M. Clémentel, *Inventaire de la situation financière*, pp. 135-6.

The item posts, telegraphs and telephones represents the gross receipts of the government from this group of monopolies. French budgetary practice with regard to these services has not been uniform. At various times they have been covered by one of the annexed budgets and at other times by the general budget. Prior to 1923, for example, they were entered in the general budget, but since that time they have been included among the annexed budgets.[20]

The other items shown among the budgetary receipts listed on page 88 are State properties, receipts by order and sundry receipts, and sale of war materials. Two of these are self-explanatory: receipts from State properties, the larger part of which come from the national forests; and the sale of war materials, for the most part the sale of war materials bought from the United States and Great Britain at the end of the war. The other item, receipts by order and sundry, is a general group which includes several classes separately itemized in the ordinary budget, (receipts by order, sundry receipts of the budget, proceeds recoverable in Alsace, Lorraine and Algeria), and two classes from the recoverable budget, also headed receipts by order and sundry receipts.

In the general budget the item "receipts by order" includes a group of "routine revenues" which either in part or *in toto* represent offsets to particular expenditures. This includes, for example, deductions (stoppages) for pensions of civil employees, maintenance fees of pupils in government schools, proceeds from the universities, etc., which in part offset corresponding expenditures. It also includes total repayments made by the City of Paris for government expenditures on the "Guard of

[20] Stourm, *The Budget,* pp. 216-22.

Paris," repayment by the government of the Bey for expenditures in connection with the gendarmerie, repayment by mine owners for government advances in connection with accident insurance, etc.

Under the heading of "sundry receipts" are grouped a variety of unrelated revenues, such as the proceeds of the tax on patents, profits made by the *Caisse des Dépots et Consignations*, the income from convict labor, reimbursement of expenditures for control and supervision over railroads, etc.

Proceeds recoverable in Alsace, Lorraine, and Algeria represent the revenues which the State receives by way of the departmental or colonial budgets of these regions.

Under the recoverable budget the receipts by order and sundry receipts are, in theory, comparable to similar classifications in the general budget. As a matter of fact, however, the heading "receipts by order" includes certain items which do not represent actual receipts, but only indicate that government obligations of one sort have been transformed into government obligations of another sort—that government bonds have been turned over to the *sinistrés* in lieu of payments in cash or kind in connection with reconstruction work.[21]

VII. FINANCES OF THE DEPARTMENTS AND COMMUNES [22]

To obtain a complete picture of the governmental receipts and expenditures of a country it is necessary to take account of the financial operations of the local as

[21] See p. 79.
[22] This summary statement is based on Allix, *Traité élémentaire de science des finances*, pp. 791-838.

well as of the national government. In France there are
only two local divisions which have separate fiscal organizations: the departments and the communes. In
France, unlike the condition that exists in many other
countries, there is a very close relationship between the
financial operations of the State and those of the local
governments.

From the time that the departments were created by
the Constituent Assembly of Revolutionary days until
1892, the financial operations of the departments were
covered by the national budget. At first the department
was only a geographic division, but by the law of May
10, 1838, it became practically a separate corporation,
and in 1866 certain funds were definitely assigned to the
departments. The budgetary figures of the departments
were still included in the ordinary budget of the State,
however, until 1862, when they were first set forth in
one of the special budgets of the State. Finally in 1892
this special budget was done away with and a complete
division was made between the budget of the State and
those of the departments. The history of the communal
budgets closely parallels that of the departments, communal receipts and expenditures also having been transferred from the ordinary budget to a special budget of
the State in 1862 and having been separated from the
State budget in 1892.

The finance year of the departments and communes,
like that of the State, extends from January 1 to December 31. The fiscal period for the local divisions, however,
is much shorter than that of the State. In the case of
the departments it extends to January 31 of the following
year for the liquidation of expenditures and until the end
of February for the payment of receipts; and in the case

of the communes it extends to March 15 of the following year for expenditures and to March 31 for receipts.

The principal revenues of the departments, as indicated above, are provided by the *centimes additionnels* to the direct and assimilated taxes of the State rather than by special local taxes. These taxes are collected by the State, and are turned over to the local organizations in 12 monthly installments. Additional revenue is provided from departmental property, grants from the State, receipts from local railways, street railways, etc. The communes likewise receive an important part of their revenues from the *centimes additionnels*.

Another important source of revenues, yielding on the average about one-third of the total income of the departments is a set of taxes representing a price paid for services:—tax on weights, tax on markets, grants for the use of public property, etc. The communes, on the other hand, have a special set of taxes, known as the *octrois*, from which they derive a considerable part of their revenue. These taxes are consumption taxes, collected on commodities consumed within the communes, being collected not only on goods brought into the commune but also on goods produced there. The *octrois* are only established on request of the municipal council, and only in case the commune has insufficient revenues. The maximum rates which may be assessed are set forth in a decree of October, 1919; as are also the following six classes of goods to which the operation of the tax is restricted:—drinks and liquids; food; fuel; fodder; building material; and a miscellaneous group of specified commodities.

The communes, like the departments, also receive some revenue from property belonging to them; from sundry grants by the State, and from certain other optional taxes which they may levy, if they have obtained legislative sanction to do so. Taxes on theatres and cinemas belong to this class. There is only one tax which all communes must levy—the dog tax—the rate of which may vary between certain limits set by the law of July 31, 1920.

The question of local tax reform is one that is under serious consideration in France at the present time; the *centimes additionnels* and the *octrois* being the outstanding subjects for discussion.

In favor of the *centimes additionnels* it is argued that they aid the local groups by putting at their disposal taxes "already levied, and collected by the State officials at the time State taxes are collected." It is argued against them that because they are connected with the taxes of the State they make the State taxes inelastic and difficult to reform; that they exaggerate any inequalities that exist in the State taxes; and that they increase the apparent burden of the State taxes so that the resentment of the taxpayer over tax increases is likely to be turned against the State. Furthermore, the substitution of the income taxes for the four old direct taxes has done away with the basic state taxes to which the local *centimes* were attached. Reforms in the national tax system thus necessitate reforms in the local tax systems.

The *octrois* have long been unpopular, the charge being made that they bear heavily on the poor people. On the other hand, it is argued in their favor that by means thereof a part of the expenditures of the communes are borne by tourists and travelers who are well able to pay. Both of these contentions, it may be remarked, apply to a large number of the indirect taxes of the State. At the

present time, when the need for revenue is so great, it is
unlikely that local fiscal reforms can do much toward
doing away with the *octrois* for, as Professor Allix remarks, "it is much easier to suppress the *octrois* than it is
to replace them."

VIII. COLONIAL FINANCES [28]

The finances of the French colonies are very closely
tied up with those of the mother country. The lack of a
clean-cut separation between the colonial budgets and
that of the mother country is an added source of difficulty
in presenting a precise statement on the French budget
situation proper.

In the main the colonies provide the revenues to meet
all of the expenditures which apply to them directly
except expenditures for military services, and they may
be called upon to bear a part of those costs. Colonial
expenditures which are included in the budget of the
mother country include "expenditures for the common
interest," that is, the costs of the central administration,
of government inspection of the colonies, etc.; military
expenditures, due to the maintenance of troops stationed
in the colonies; the cost of penitentiaries; pensions to
colonial functionaries; and certain budgetary expenditures on posts and telegraphs.

The receipts which the State takes from the colonies
are not very large and for the most part offset particular
expenditures. Most important are the receipts required
to meet military expenditures in the colonies. This cost,
as a matter of fact, is borne almost entirely by Indo-
China and Algeria, the financial condition of the other
colonies not permitting them to make such contributions.

[28] Allix, *Traité elementaire de science des finances*, pp. 840-73.

The taxes imposed in the colonies are quite similar to those of the mother country. Customs duties, in fact, are levied at the same rates that apply to the mother country. Since January 11, 1892, the principal colonies have been considered, from the point of view of customs, as provinces of the mother country. The effect of this is that, with certain exceptions, French goods imported into the colonies may enter free of duty; and vice-versa, colonial exports to France are tax free.

APPENDIX C

THE WEALTH AND INCOME OF FRANCE

THE estimates of national wealth and national income used at various places in the text have been derived from sources and by methods explained in the following paragraphs. The figures, as will be seen, leave much to be desired in the way of precision.

I. PRE-WAR ESTIMATES

Various writers are in substantial accord in estimating the national income of France in 1913 at around 36 billion francs. M. François-Marsal, former Finance Minister, in a letter to the London *Times*, (Feb. 20, 1925, p. 10) set the figure at 35.9 billions. The London *Economist* put the figure at 35 billions (March 15, 1924, p. 576). M. Edmond Théry estimated the national wealth of France in 1914 at 304 billions (*Conséquences Economiques de la Guerre*, 1922, p. 337) which represents a national income of from 36 to 38 billions. After surveying various estimates, Professor Edwin R. A. Seligman set the figure at 36 billions. (*Political Science Quarterly*, March, 1924, p. 142.)

For the period of the nineties few estimates apparently have been made, the only one we have been able to discover being that of M. Edmond Théry for the year 1892.

424

M. Théry estimated the national wealth for that year at 243 billion francs, which would be equal to 29 or 30 billions of gross income (*Fortune Publique de la France,* 1911, p. 247.) That this figure is much too high is evident in the light of estimates for 10 and 15 years later. Professor Seligman sets the figure for 1900-01 at about 26 billions; and for the period 1906-08 various writers put the total wealth at about 220 billions, equivalent to about 27 billions of income. (See Stamp, Sir Josiah, *Journal of the Royal Statistical Society,* July, 1919, p. 470.) M. Théry himself put the wealth figure for 1908 at 287 billions, an increase of only 44 billion francs in 16 years. Failing to find much light or agreement from these writers, we have estimated the national income for 1893 by the rough method indicated in the following paragraph.

In 1893 French wholesale prices averaged about 81 per cent of the 1913 prices. The 36 billions of national income in 1913 are therefore roughly equivalent to only 29 billions in terms of 1893 prices. If M. Théry's figure of 29 to 30 billions of income for 1892 were correct, it would follow that the real income of the nation in 1892 and 1913 was the same: that there had been no increase in national wealth during the 20 years just prior to the war—merely a rise in price level. This is a conclusion contrary to all the evidence. Therefore, the national income in 1893, in terms of 1893 values, must have been considerably below 29 billions. In Appendix A it was noted that the rate of increase of French savings was estimated at about 2 billion francs a year, which would amount to roughly 40 billion francs for the twenty-year period 1893-1913. Since the national income is usually estimated at about 12½ per cent of national wealth, the

increase in national income during the period would be
roughly 5 billions. Subtracting 5 billions from 29 billions gives a national income for 1893 of approximately
24 billion francs.

II. ESTIMATES FOR 1924

Several rough estimates of the national income of
France have been made for the years 1923 and 1924.
The first to which reference should be made is given in
the London *Economist*, March 15, 1924, p. 576. Two
bases were used in making this estimate: (1) the annual
savings as shown by investments, and (2) the import
trade data.

(1) The annual savings, as shown by subscriptions to
bond issues, were estimated at about 25 billions a year
in 1922 and 1923. Before the war annual savings were
reckoned at about one-seventh of the national income.
Assuming savings now to represent only one-sixth of the
national income, the total income would be 150 billion
francs.

(2) Before the war French imports equalled in value
about one-fifth of the national incomes. Assuming that
the same proportion has obtained since as before the war,
the total income in the years 1921-23 would have been
about 130 billion francs.

From these two sets of data the conclusion of the
Economist is that the national income of France ranges
somewhere between 130 and 150 billions, with a middle
figure of 140 billions a safe estimate. In money values
the income is thus roughly four times that of 1913; and
the *Economist* notes in this connection that the currency

circulation in 1924 was almost exactly four times that of 1913, a rough corroboration of the figure of 140 billions.

The high figure of 150 billion francs for 1922-23 based on the statistics of bond subscriptions is open to a vital criticism. It has been shown in Chapter VII that these bonds were to a large extent purchased with bank credit and hence they are a poor gauge of actual savings. Judged by bond subscriptions the income of France would have appeared very much smaller in 1924 than in the relatively depressed years of 1922 and 1923.

M. François-Marsal, (London *Times*, Feb. 20, 1925, p. 10) makes a rough computation of the income for 1924 simply by multiplying the income for 1913 (35.9 billions) by four in order to make allowance for the depreciation of the franc. This, of course, assumes that the general productivity of the country has remained unchanged by the events of the last 10 years. He thus arrives at a figure of 143 billion francs.

A third estimate of 125 billion francs is given by M. Marcel Héraud in the Chamber of Deputies (*Journal Officiel, Débats, Chambre*, Feb. 15, 1925, p. 850). The basis for the reckoning was, however, not given.

The estimates summarized above may be roughly checked by the following method. From the data presented in Chapter VIII we conclude that in 1924 the quantity production of France, including Alsace-Lorraine, was about 105 per cent of that of 1913, with Alsace-Lorraine excluded. In terms of 1913 values the income of 1924 would equal 105 per cent of 36 billion francs (the national income of 1913) or 37.8 billion francs.

The Federal Reserve Board's index numbers for France averaged in 1924 as follows:

Goods produced..................   430
Goods imported.................   529
Goods exported.................   465
Raw materials..................   459
Producers goods................   455
Consumers goods...............   428
All commodities...............   446

Multiplying 37.8 billion francs (national income of 1924 stated in 1913 values) by 4.46 (the index of all commodities) would give a total paper franc value in 1924 of 169 billion francs. This total, however, is undoubtedly too high, for the index numbers are for wholesale prices, and in 1924 wholesale prices rose faster than other prices, and incomes generally. It should be observed also that imported goods, which do not represent French income, are included in the index of all commodities and that they tend to raise the average considerably. A 10 per cent reduction for these considerations would give an income of 152 billion francs.

A further deduction must be made for the loss of income on foreign investments and the incurring of external interest obligations in connection with new private obligations abroad [1]—an important item which the estimates discussed above do not take into account. France derived in 1914 about 1.9 billion gold francs of net income from foreign investments, while in 1924 her income from this source was only about 300 million paper francs. Converted to paper francs at the average rates of ex-

[1] In this computation, interest on the external government commercial debt, amounting in 1924 to 900 million paper francs, is excluded, for the reason that we are interested in the income of the people before taxes are levied and hence income that is taken from them by taxes for the purpose of meeting foreign debts should not be deducted.

change for the year 1924, the 1.9 billion gold francs (interest in 1914) is equivalent to approximately 7 billion paper francs. Subtracting the income of 300 million paper francs in 1924, makes a net loss of income on this account of about 6.7 billion paper francs. This reduces the total national income to about 145 billion francs.

APPENDIX D

GOVERNMENT BORROWINGS AND THE PUBLIC DEBT

THE summarized data on the character of French war borrowings and the growth of the public debt since 1914 were presented in Chapters IV and V of the text. Detailed figures showing the growth of the debt and the types of borrowing operations are given below.

The first table shows the total amount which the government realized each year from borrowing operations between 1914 and 1921, and the sources from which these amounts were secured. The figures after 1921 are not available.

PROCEEDS OF FRENCH WAR BORROWINGS, 1914-21 *

(In millions of francs)

Description	1914	1915	1916	1917	1918	1919	1920	1921
INTERNAL LOANS	2,323	16,752	18,433	18,588	24,293	27,653	34,499	23,103
Perpetual and long-term loans [a]	465	6,265	5,425	5,174	7,246	655	18,313	...
Short-term bills	1,858	10,487	12,955	13,054	16,611	25,454	15,569	22,724
Deposits	...	...	53	360	436	1,544	617	379
FOREIGN LOANS [b]								
The United States	51	2,806	8,800	11,885	8,695	11,348	3,578	1,452
England	51	1,845	1,624	7,532	5,388	9,267	3,295	1,449
Spain	...	814	6,968	3,997	1,594	1,759	205	...
Switzerland	...	...	131	67	570	...	78	...
Scandinavian countries	...	147	47	46	164	73	...	...
Other countries	...	...	30	232	979	249	...	3
ADVANCES OF THE BANKS OF ISSUE [c]	3,925	1,150	2,350	5,160	4,680	8,370	865	...
OPERATIONS TO FACILITATE PAYMENT OF WAR								
DAMAGES [d]						3,960	3,880	6,565
Loan of the Crédit National						3,960	3,880	1,871
Payment in annuity securities and bonds						...	...	4,694
Total	6,299	20,708	29,583	35,633	37,668	51,331	42,822	31,120
LESS REPAYMENT OF LOANS	42	402	347	512	442	2,676	5,136	3,816
Treasury bonds and bills (pre-war type)	...	149	...	...	...	...	...	...
Deposits	42	68	...	...	...	...	...	...
Foreign loans [e]	...	185	347	512	442	2,676	4,901	2,966
Advances by the banks	...	...	...	...	...	...	235	850 [f]
NET RECEIPTS FROM LOANS	6,257	20,306	29,236	35,121	37,226	48,655	37,686	27,304

* *Exposé des motifs du projet du budget, 1923*, pp. 70-1.

a Net proceeds, not including consolidations and conversions.

b Conversions at average rates for the respective years.

c Chiefly the Bank of France, with the Bank of Algeria advancing small sums.

d Not including the 1,070 millions of National Defense bills accepted in the subscriptions of November, 1921.

e Conversion at the average rate for the year.

f Deduction made from the credit balance for amortization (1,250 millions).

The second table presents the classified debt statement
of France at the beginning and at the end of the war.

NATIONAL DEBT OF FRANCE, 1914-18
(In millions of Francs)

Classification	July 31, 1914 [a]	December 31, 1918 [b]
I. INTERNAL DEBT		
Perpetual and long-term debt............	32,235.3	67,248.0
3% rentes.............................	21,922.2	19,745.4
Amortissable 3% rentes..............	3,288.7	3,089.4
" 3½% rentes..............	884.6	34.0
5% rentes (1915 and 1916).............	....	25,480.1
4% rentes (1917)......................	....	13,182.6
4% rentes (1918)......................	....	....
Capitalized value of annuities paid by the State............................	5,546.5	5,139.3
State railway bonds...................	593.3	577.2
Short-term debt:	342.0	531.1
Short-term Treasury bills (5 to 10 years)	342.0	....
National Defense bonds (5 to 10 years).	....	531.1
Floating debt:	1,608.7	56,015.2
Ordinary Treasury bills...............	427.5	579.9
National Defense bills................	....	35,385.0
Advances of the Bank of France........	....	18,000.0
Advances of the Bank of Algeria.......	....	300.0
Special funds from the general Treasury	27.7	286.5
Sundry special current accounts........	....	218.3
Other deposit accounts in the Treasury..	1,153.5	1,245.5
Total Internal Debt [c]..............	34,186.0	123,794.3
II. FOREIGN DEBT		
Political debt............................	....	23,130.9
Commercial debt........................	....	6,188.1
Total Foreign Debt................	....	29,319.0
GRAND TOTAL............................	34,186.0	153,113.3

[a] *Exposé des motifs du projet du budget, 1918*, pp. 144-9, and
153.

[b] Figures for the internal debt are from the *Exposé des motifs
du projet du budget, 1920*, pp. 164-70, and 173. The foreign debt
figures are at par of exchange calculated from figures given in
Exposé de motifs du projet du budget, 1919, pp. 125-6. At average

The effects of post-war borrowing operations are revealed in the third table which gives the debt figures for December 31, 1923, and November 30, 1924, the latest date for which a statement had been published at the time this book went to press.

PUBLIC DEBT OF FRANCE, DECEMBER 31, 1923, AND
NOVEMBER 30, 1924 *

(In millions of francs)

Classification	December 31, 1923	November 30, 1924
I. INTERNAL DEBT		
Perpetual and long-term debt:	148,136.2	153,716.9
3% *rentes*......	19,740.4	19,740.4
Amortissable 3% *rentes*......	2,840.2	2,790.4
Amortissable 3½% *rentes*......	12.9	12.4
5% *rentes* (1915 and 1916)......	19,063.6	18,855.3
4% *rentes* (1917)......	9,064.7	9,003.2
4% *rentes* (1918)......	20,804.0	20,609.6
Amortissable 5% *rentes* (1920).. {Capital value......	11,452.1	11,284.3
Premium for amortization	4,422.2	4,496.4
6% *rentes* (1920)......	26,655.8	26,447.2
6% *rentes* (given for war damages).....	747.5	948.3
3% perpetual *rentes* of Alsace-Lorraine..	73.5	73.5
Crédit National bonds (loans authorized by law of October 10, 1919).........	12,978.0	17,262.6
Capitalized value of annuities given to *sinistrés*	8,119.3	8,605.1

current rates of exchange, the foreign debt as calculated by the Minister of Finance amounted to a total of 30,598.2 million paper francs, of which 23,832.4 millions represent the political debt, and 6,765.8 millions represent the commercial debt.

ᶜ Unlike the "Annuities paid by the State," the *Viagère* or pension debt is not capitalized in the statements of the Minister of Finance, and therefore is not included in the figures given above.

* Compiled from debt statement given by Bérenger, M. Henry, *Sénat Rapport* 19 (*annexe au procés verbal de la séance du 27 Janvier, 1925*), pp. 519-27.

PUBLIC DEBT, Continued.

Classification	December 31, 1923	November 30, 1924
Capitalized value of government annuities to the railways, the *Caisse de dépots*, etc.	10,884.5	12,360.7
State railway bonds...................	1,277.5	1,227.5
Short-term debt:	40,110.8	39,845.0
Short-term Treasury bills (2 to 10 years)	24,534.8	25,953.0
National Defense bonds (5 to 10 year)..	4,343.0	7,349.0
Crédit National bonds (*bons*)..........	11,000.0	6,309.0
Bonds issued to the banks of Alsace and Lorraine	233.0	234.0
Floating debt:	89,251.0	90,688.4
Ordinary Treasury bills................	2,997.0	2,855.0
National Defense bills.................	54,723.0	57,045.0
Advances of the Bank of France........	23,500.0	22,800.0
Special funds from the General Treasury	6,269.0	6,728.0
Deposit accounts in the Treasury.......	927.0	627.0
Balance of postal checks...............	835.0	633.4
Total Internal Debt................	277,498.1	284,250.3
II. FOREIGN DEBT [a]		
Political debt, including capitalized interest on debt to Great Britain.............	30,469.6	31,009.5
Accrued interest, at 5%, on the political debt to the United States [b]..........	3,369.2	4,193.0
Commercial debt........................	5,255.3	5,017.4
Total Foreign Debt................	39,094.1	40,219.9
GRAND TOTAL.....................	316,592.1	324,470.2

[a] Conversion from foreign money to francs is at par of exchange. At current rates of exchange the foreign debt (including accrued interest on the political debt to the United States) was as follows: Dec. 30, 1923; total debt, 137.7 billion francs; of which 119.7 billions represented the political debt; 18.0 billions, the commercial debt. November 30, 1924: total debt, 143.3 billion francs, of which 125.7 billions were for the political debt; 17.6 billions, the commercial debt.

[b] The figures for "accrued interest . . . to the United States" are those published by the United States Treasury for November 15 of the respective years.

The external debt of France at the end of 1918 and on November 30, 1924, was as follows:

FOREIGN DEBT OF FRANCE, DECEMBER 31, 1918, AND NOVEMBER 30,1924
(In millions of francs, at par of exchange)

Classification	December 31, 1918 [a]	November 30, 1924 [b]
I. POLITICAL DEBT		
Great Britain...........................	11,831.9	15,815.6
United States...........................	11,298.9	15,193.9
Accrued interest on the debt to the United States (at 5%).........................	.....	4,193.0
Total political debt................	23,130.8	35,202.5
II. COMMERCIAL DEBT		
Great Britain:		
Treasury bills turned over to the Bank of England	1,639.4	1,261.0
Treasury bills sold to the public by the Bank of England....................	252.2	.....
Sale of English war supplies............	.....	188.5
United States:		
Anglo-French loan....................	1,295.8	11.0
Loans by a consortium of banks........	518.3	.....
Loan of 1920..........................	.....	429.9
Loan of 1921..........................	.....	385.3
City of Paris loan.....................	259.2	.....
Three cities loan......................	186.6	210.2
Loan of April, 1917...................	518.3	.....
Sale of American war supplies..........	.....	2,110.0
Japan	129.2	64.5
Bank Loans:		
Spain	510.0	.....
Sweden	55.6	.....
Norway	69.4	.....
Argentina	488.0	97.1
Switzerland	140.3	.....
Holland	.....	114.6
Uruguay	.....	64.3
Canada	.....	29.7
Egypt	.....	51.2
Total commercial debt.............	6,062.3	5,017.3
GRAND TOTAL	29,193.1	40,219.8

[a] *Exposé des motifs du projet du budget*, 1919, pp. 125-6.
[b] Bérenger, *Sénat Rapport* 19 (*Annexe au procés-verbal de la séance du 27 Janvier, 1925*), pp. 526-7.

APPENDIX E

FINANCIAL DATA

THE banking data to which reference was made in Chapter VII are presented in the tables below. The data were furnished us by M. Décamps, Director of Economic Research of the Bank of France.

I. QUARTERLY DATA FOR THE PRINCIPAL CREDIT BANKS, 1914-24

Crédit Lyonnais, Comptoir d'Escompte, Société Générale, Crédit Industriel et Commercial

(Figures in millions of francs)

Dates	Cash	Portfolio and Treasury Bills	Advances Against Securities	Current Accounts Debited	Deposits and Accounts Current	Capital and Surplus
1913—December 31..	488.3	3,621.7	1,157.9	1,803.2	5,681.0	1,078.8
1914—March 31.....	494.2	3,770.7	1,226.1	1,837.2	5,955.2	1,094.1
June 30.......	616.8	3,541.6	1,101.7	1,928.9	5,834.6	1,096.4
December 31..	1,268.0	1,357.8	998.3	1,477.6	4,058.1	1,097.1
1915—April 30.......	1,214.7	1,688.8	834.2	1,309.3	4,005.2	1,087.7
June 30.......	1,315.0	1,810.1	790.4	1,236.1	4,056.8	1,087.8
September 30..	1,322.5	1,923.3	748.4	1,212.3	4,148.5	1,087.8
December 31..	1,032.1	2,042.3	732.3	1,207.7	3,932.6	1,087.8
1916—March 31.....	1,098.7	2,211.1	668.0	1,175.2	4,150.1	1,021.3
June 30.......	1,114.8	2,415.7	654.1	1,130.8	4,361.9	1,021.8
September 30..	1,183.5	2,671.2	661.9	1,131.2	4,692.8	1,021.8
December 31..	1,063.8	2,655.0	667.6	1,184.9	4,587.9	1,021.9
1917—March 31.....	1,370.3	2,846.8	672.6	1,221.8	5,142.1	1,022.2
June 30.......	1,277.6	3,393.8	660.2	1,222.4	5,592.4	1,023.0
September 30.	1,467.3	3,612.6	665.1	1,218.4	6,001.9	1,023.3
December 31..	1,265.3	3,969.0	664.2	1,351.8	6,263.2	1,023.5
1918—March 31.....	1,381.7	3,888.6	671.0	1,311.9	6,161.8	1,023.6
June 30.......	1,735.5	4,036.0	634.6	1,357.0	6,808.7	1,024.6
September 30.	1,449.3	4,801.6	621.9	1,395.7	7,317.3	1,024.8
December 31..	878.4	4,817.4	613.4	1,688.9	7,047.3	1,024.8

Dates	Cash	Portfolio and Treasury Bills	Advances against Securities	Current Accounts Debited	Deposits and Accounts Current	Capital and Surplus
1919—March 31.....	1,062.5	5,288.3	597.1	1,749.6	7,698.7	1,025.1
June 30.......	1,458.0	6,153.5	642.7	2,051.1	9,267.6	1,051.3
September 30.	1,087.3	7,850.2	663.4	2,129.7	10,654.1	1,051.7
December 31..	1,098.6	8,746.4	777.2	2,847.9	12,293.0	1,052.2
1920—March 31.....	1,286.8	8,586.0	883.4	3,652.4	13,121.9	1,055.7
June 30.......	1,245.6	9,303.0	849.8	3,695.9	13,723.9	1,057.3
September 30.	1,252.0	9,328.6	811.8	3,921.4	13,925.3	1,111.4
December 31..	1,563.7	9,261.0	734.9	3,455.2	13,548.9	1,129.4
1921—March 31.....	1,234.8	9,687.2	646.3	3,004.9	13,268.6	1,132.1
June 30.......	1,221.3	9,691.7	585.0	2,695.9	12,948.8	1,133.6
September 30.	1,106.4	10,257.9	625.1	2,532.5	13,303.9	1,133.6
December 31..	1,298.3	10,307.5	615.4	2,664.4	13,620.6	1,133.6
1922—March 31.....	1,222.5	10,024.7	564.1	2,576.3	13,141.7	1,134.8
June 30.......	1,347.4	11,073.9	568.9	2,610.0	14,084.1	1,137.5
September 30.	1,322.0	10,913.0	598.9	2,392.7	13,862.3	1,137.6
December 31..	1,584.3	10,963.2	636.8	2,428.6	14,206.8	1,137.7
1923—March 31.....	1,589.1	10,607.5	673.0	2,652.5	14,131.6	1,140.4
June 30.......	1,454.3	11,065.6	680.2	2,779.4	14,473.8	1,142.1
September 30.	1,597.5	11,927.1	733.7	2,693.2	15,387.4	1,142.2
December 31..	1,643.7	10,899.7	834.4	3,196.4	15,171.9	1,150.4
1924—March 31.....	1,640.1	11,209.8	914.7	3,542.6	15,737.4	1,152.0

II. Condition of the Principal Commercial Banks of Paris, 1913-1923

(Figures, in millions of francs, are for the close of the fiscal year)

Year	Cash	Portfolio and Treasury Bills	Advances against Securities	Current Accounts Debited	Securities	Deposits and Accounts Credited	Capital and Surplus
1913........	214.5	592.3	384.9	862.3	384.2	1,206.2	757.7
1914........	266.9	313.3	314.1	702.4	429.9	956.5	727.0
1915........	249.7	497.2	230.2	516.2	393.1	996.4	701.8
1916........	296.4	780.8	223.2	538.4	382.1	1,315.4	720.6
1917........	340.5	1,358.0	220.4	737.5	367.7	2,141.7	751.0
1918........	406.2	1,615.4	390.9	732.5	402.0	2,622.5	755.1
1919........	712.3	3,472.6	559.9	1,344.6	462.1	5,812.0	967.2
1920........	1,404.2	4,130.5	744.9	1,933.2	610.2	7,176.5	1,350.9
1921........	1,132.7	3,619.9	716.3	1,837.5	613.4	6,113.0	1,521.1
1922........	1,037.8	3,874.4	637.3	1,864.5	536.5	6,203.9	1,464.1
1923........	1,235.1	4,113.4	893.8	2,112.8	539.4	7,184.8	1,401.8

III. National Defense Bills and Treasury Bills in Circulation,
1921-1924

(In millions of francs)

1921—December	31	....	67,362.8
1922—January	31	....	68,755.6
February	28	....	68,855.9
March	31	....	69,101.0
April	30 [a]	....	62,833.5
May	31	....	64,584.4
June	30	....	65,714.1
July	31	....	64,550.5
August	31.	....	64,962.2
September	30	....	65,973.1
October	31	....	63,024.0
November	30	....	59,845.3
December	31	....	61,051.9
1923—January	31	....	60,819.7
February	28	....	60,068.6
March	31	....	58,513.0
April	30	....	55,594.0
December	31	....	58,405.0
1924—June	30	....	60,218.0
November	30	....	59,900.0

[a] Figures corrected in April, 1922. The figures for preceding
months are too high by about 7 billion francs, the error arising
from the fact that some bills were included in the total twice at
the time of former consolidation loans.

APPENDIX F

HOW FRANCE MET THE INDEMNITY OF 1871.[1]

The rapid payment of the indemnity of 5 billion francs imposed upon France after the Franco-Prussian War of 1871 has excited almost universal admiration. The treaty of peace was signed at Frankfort on May 10, 1871; the first payment was made on June 1, 1871; and the last payment, not due until May 2, 1874, was made on September 5, 1873. A discussion of the economic processes by means of which this debt was liquidated throws some interesting light upon the international debt problems of the present. The data used in the following pages, except where otherwise specifically noted, are taken from an official French report made in 1874,[2] by Léon Say, who was at the time a member of the National Assembly.

The following means were employed in paying and adjusting the indemnity, which with some interest and incidental costs amounted to 5,315 million francs, or 4,250 million marks.

1. France surrendered to Germany the franchise right to that portion of the Railroad of the East which was located in the ceded territory of Alsace-Lorraine. This was valued at 325 million francs. Since the French gov-

[1] This analysis first appears in Moulton and McGuire's *Germany's Capacity to Pay.*

[2] *Rapport fait au nom de la commission du budget de 1875, sur le paiement de l'indemnité de guerre et sur les opérations de change qui en ont été la conséquence.*

ernment did not own this railroad, it was necessary that
it should obligate itself to pay the railroad corporation
in due time the amount specified.

2. There was a minor credit balance of 98,400 francs
due the City of Paris from the German government,
which was credited to the indemnity account.

3. France was by special agreement permitted to pay
in paper money (bills of the Bank of France) to the
extent of 125 million francs.

4. The sum of 105,039,145 francs of German coin and
bank notes, a large part of which had been brought into
France by the German army, was collected by the French
government and turned over to Germany.

5. French gold to the amount of 273,003,058 francs was
transferred to Germany. Of this amount, 150 million was
advanced to the government by the Bank of France.

6. Silver to the amount of 239,291,876 francs was paid,
of which 93 millions were procured from the Bank of
Hamburg.

The total of the above six items is 1,067,432,479 francs.

7. The remainder, amounting to 4,248,326,374 francs,
was adjusted by turning over to Germany foreign bills
of exchange.

The question now is, by what means did the French
government obtain the ownership of this large amount
of foreign bills of exchange,—that is to say, how did the
French government procure the ownership of the money
of other countries? First, the French government issued
two large loans which yielded a total of 5,792 million
francs.[3] Of this amount, approximately two-fifths, or

[3] Gaston, Jèze, *Cours de science des finances et de législation
financière française*, Paris, 1922, p. 391. According to Léon Say
the yield of the two loans amounted to 5,724 million francs.

2,316 million francs were sold in foreign countries for foreign money,[4] and, interestingly enough, a considerable part of the bonds that were floated abroad were sold in Germany. Second, approximately 2 billion francs of existing foreign investments of French citizens were utilized.

Since these foreign investments belonged to French private citizens, it will be seen that the French government had its own problem of getting possession of them. Instead of using money derived from taxation to buy these bonds, the French government, in effect, borrowed them. The process was as follows: the French government issued its own bonds and induced its citizens to take these, suggesting that in exchange they should turn over to the government foreign currency procured by selling foreign bonds which they held. The government also accepted foreign bonds from its citizens in direct payment for their purchases of the new government bonds. In this case the government could either deliver the foreign bonds directly to Germany—the evidence is not clear as to what extent this was done—or, could sell the foreign bonds for foreign money which it could use in paying Germany.

The French government borrowed in one way or an-

---

[4] Based on Victor Canon, *Précis d'histoire de la finance française 1870-1878*, p. 261, and on reports in the *London Times* of June 29, 1871, and of Aug. 2, 1872, and in the *London Economist* of Aug. 3, 1872. The face of the first loan was 2,799.5 million francs, of which 20 per cent, or 556 million francs were issued to foreigners. The face value of the second loan was 4,140.5 million francs, of which 58 per cent or 2,401 million francs were issued to foreigners. The total amount issued to foreigners (2,956 million francs) was thus 40 per cent of the total face value of the two loans (6,920 million francs).

other practically all of the funds used in paying Germany. It borrowed 325 million francs from the Railroad of the East; it borrowed 805 millions from the Bank of France, of which 150 millions in gold and 125 millions in paper were used in paying the indemnity; and it borrowed all of the funds necessary to procure the foreign bills of exchange. Indeed, a further analysis of the French government's loan operations indicates that the government went into debt during the years in question to a considerably greater extent than it got out of debt through the payment of the indemnity.

The French government floated two large bond issues. The face value of the first issue, floated in 1871, was 2,779.5 million francs; the rate of interest was 5 per cent; the bonds were sold at 82.5; and the yield of the loan was 2,293 million francs.[5] The second loan, put out for subscription July 28, 1872, had a face value of 4,140.5 millions and it also bore a rate of 5 per cent. It sold at 84.5, yielding a total of 3,499 million francs. The two loans combined thus yielded the government the sum of 5,792 million francs, and increased the funded debt by 6,920 million francs. Besides these loans, the debt of the government increased to the extent of 805 millions,[6] by virtue of its direct borrowings from the Bank of France and 325 millions on account of the debt to the Railway of the East. All told, therefore, the French government, while paying off the indemnity of 5,315 millions, incurred new obligations of 8,050 millions.

[5] Jèze, *ibid.*

[6] André Liesse, *Evolution of Credit and Banks in France* (Report of National Monetary Commission), p. 139. The total debt of the Government to the Bank at this time was 1,530 million francs. Jèze, *ibid.*

We must now inquire to what extent these new bond issues of the government were paid for out of French savings. The two large loans put out for public subscription together yielded 5,792 million francs. Of this amount, approximately two and a quarter billions were subscribed by foreigners, and another 2 billions were paid for through the sacrifice of foreign investments owned by French citizens. This leaves roughly 1.5 billions to be accounted for, a sum which possibly may have been paid out of current savings.

There is no means of ascertaining to what precise extent the payment of this 1.5 billions was made by the French public at the expense of ordinary consumption; that is to say, to what extent the French people tightened their belts in order to buy bonds. Data are not available to indicate whether a considerable part of it may not have been paid with funds borrowed from the banks just as during the Great War we "paid" for Liberty bonds by borrowing the funds from the banks. Nor does it appear to what extent the banking institutions themselves purchased government bonds. Some bonds, no doubt, were purchased with money drawn from hoards.

At the very outside then—assuming no inflation of the currency in connection with the flotation of these bonds—the French public bought 1.5 billions out of current savings or with accumulated hoards. Meanwhile, the interest burden had been increased by the following amounts: 346 million francs, the annual charge on the 6,920 million francs increase in the public funded debt; 20.5 million francs, the sum annually due, according to agreement, to the corporation of the Railway of the East; 8.1 million francs, representing interest at 1

per cent due the Bank of France on loans received from
that source after the war,—a total of 374.6 million
francs.   In addition to this, the treasury had agreed to
repay the loan to the Bank at the rate of 200 million
francs a year.[7]

*Taxes were not increased sufficiently to meet even the
increased interest charges.* The following table shows
the total French revenues from taxation for the years
1867-1878 inclusive, classifying these into direct and
indirect taxes—the latter being those derived from customs, registration, and stamp duties, and from excise
duties on alcoholic liquors, salt, sugar, tobacco, powder,
etc.

The total revenue from taxation during the year 1873
was 2,371 million francs, as compared with a total of
1,805 million francs for the year 1869, the year preceding the war year of 1870—an increase of 566 million
francs.   This leaves a margin of only 191.4 million francs
over the increased interest charges.   Meanwhile other
revenues of the government had increased only slightly,
while other expenditures had very greatly increased.

The fact that the government secured 5,792 millions
from the two bond issues, and 805 millions from the
Bank of France—the total indemnity payments being
5,315 million francs—indicates that the French government during the years in question was borrowing to
meet ordinary fiscal requirements as well as to procure the funds with which to pay the indemnity.   In fact,
only 70 per cent of the proceeds of the first bond issue,
and 87 per cent of the second, were actually intended for
indemnity purposes.

[7] Jèze, *ibid.*, p. 437.

FRENCH TAX RECEIPTS, 1867-1878.

(In millions of francs)*

Year	Direct Taxes	Indirect Taxes	Total
1867.............	545	1,177	1,722
1868.............	562	1,207	1,769
1869.............	576	1,229	1,805
1870.............	586	1,083	1,669
1871.............	581	1,239	1,820
1872.............	605	1,524	2,129
1873.............	673	1,698	2,371
1874.............	669	1,748	2,417
1875.............	684	1,933	2,617
1876.............	697	1,996	2,693
1877.............	698	1,970	2,668
1878.............	704	2,036	2,740

* Compiled from data contained in the British *Statistical Abstract for Principal and other Foreign Countries,* 1885, p. 206.

This increase in the French public debt has left a permanent fiscal burden. The face value of that portion of the two loans that was earmarked to provide funds with which to meet the indemnity, was 5,548 million francs. The annual interest charge on this sum at 5 per cent is 277 million francs. From the time the loans were floated until 1883 this sum had to be provided for annually in the French budget. Meanwhile, it appears that most of the bonds which had been sold abroad had been repurchased in France, and in 1883 a refunding operation [8]

[8] For data with regard to the refunding operations, see Edmond Thèry, *Conséquences economiques de la guerre pour la France,* 1922, pp. 311-4. Thèry gives the interest charge on the total war loans. Our figures represent the separate amount directly chargeable to the part of the loans which was used for the payment of the indemnity.

reduced the rate to 4½ per cent and slightly reduced the debt. From 1883 to 1894, the annual interest charge on account of the indemnity was, therefore, reduced to 245 millions. From 1894 to 1902 the rate was only 3½ per cent, the interest charge then amounting to 190 million francs. From 1902 on to the present time, the rate has been 3 per cent, and the annual interest chargeable to the indemnity has amounted to 165 million francs a year.

It thus appears that from the point of view of the internal budgetary problem, France has never got rid of the indemnity burden. The notoriously large French public debt, which for decades has seriously embarrassed the financial administration, is in no small degree directly attributable to the fact that the French people never did, through economy and heavy taxation, liquidate the indemnity.

From the point of view of international trade and finance, the payment of the French indemnity did not give rise to serious difficulties. The first six items enumerated on pages 439 and 440 which total 1,067,432,479 francs in specie payments and credits, did not involve the transfer of commodities across French borders. The borrowing transactions did, however, directly influence the international financial and trade situation. The sale of 2 billions of French-owned foreign investments built up in the years before the war, meant a direct loss of interest from foreign sources, while the flotation of 2.25 billions of French bonds in foreign markets amounted to the same thing, since it served to reduce the net amount of French foreign investments.

France's international balance of payments was distinctly favorable during the indemnity period. There was a slight adverse balance of trade, amounting to roughly 100 million francs in the three years; but the invisible credits—mainly the interest on foreign investments—yielded approximately 900 millions per year, giving a net favorable balance for the three years 1871-73 of 2,600 million francs. It was the existence of these large invisible credits that enabled France to repurchase rapidly the bonds that had been sold abroad when the indemnity loans were floated.

The total indemnity with interest, etc., was 5,315 million francs. Of this 1,067 millions were paid, as already noted, by specie transfers and credits. The normal international income (derived from interest on foreign investments and from foreign trade) during the years when the indemnity was being paid (2,600 million francs) was thus about five-eighths of the amount required to meet the 4,248 millions not settled by specie payments or credits.

The import and export figures (including re-exports) for the years 1867-1873 inclusive, are as follows:

FRENCH FOREIGN TRADE, 1867-1878.
(Special commerce and re-export trade, in millions of francs)

Year	Imports	Exports	Net
1867	3,202	3,085	− 117
1868	3,415	2,974	− 441
1869	3,269	3,257	− 12
1870	2,935	2,915	− 20
1871	3,599	2,925	− 674
1872	3,603	3.814	+ 211
1873	3,651	3,925	+ 274
1874	3,574	3,806	+ 232
1875	3,585	3,968	+ 383
1876	4,046	3,689	− 357
1877	3,737	3,552	− 185
1878	4,246	3,297	− 949

It will be noted that the unfavorable trade balance of 1871 and earlier years was converted into a favorable balance in 1872 which continued favorable until 1877. This resulted not from a reduction of imports, which in fact slightly increased, but from a considerable expansion of exports. Again, there is no evidence of rigid self-denial on the part of the French people. The favorable balance of trade in 1872-73 resulted merely from the thriving export business,—an export business which necessitated increased imports of raw materials, and which was possible only because France's credit and economic plant and equipment had not been gravely impaired.

It is interesting to observe that French sales in Germany increased markedly during the period of the indemnity payments. Exports to Germany in the two years before the war averaged 260 million francs; while in the two years 1872 and 1873 they averaged 436 million francs. It was the proceeds of the favorable trade .balance in the years 1872-75 and the returns from foreign investments throughout the period that enabled France to purchase the bonds which had been sold abroad and to replenish the gold reserves of the Bank of France.

APPENDIX G

A TENTATIVE APPRAISAL OF THE CAILLAUX ADMINISTRATION.

The foregoing analysis was completed before the advent of M. Caillaux as Finance Minister. Even now (July, 1925) the expected "comprehensive program of financial reconstruction" has not been disclosed; there has merely been presented a number of particular measures designed to tide the country over present emergencies. In these measures, however, the broad outlines of a policy have to some extent been foreshadowed, and accordingly an appraisal of the Caillaux program as thus far developed is permissible.

Almost immediately upon coming to power, M. Caillaux was faced with the necessity of paying, or refunding, a large volume of short-time bills:—3,290 millions maturing on July first; 8,236 millions on September twenty-fifth; and 10,090 millions on December eighth. In order to renew these loans at lower rates of interest, M. Caillaux proposed their conversion into perpetual bonds, with interest payable in francs bearing a fixed relation to the pound sterling. Specifically, a holder of 10,000 francs of maturing bonds, the interest on which has been payable in paper francs of whatever value obtained at the moment of payment, would exchange his bond for a new perpetual bond of 10,000 francs, the interest on which would be paid on the basis of a franc valued at a rate of not more than 95 francs to the pound sterling. This would give a franc value equivalent to about 5.06 cents in United States currency. This means that if the franc stood at a rate of exactly 95 to the pound, the holder would receive 400 francs paper, or 4 per cent per annum. But if the franc should fall, so that it took 120 to equal a pound, the holder would receive 500 francs, instead of only 400. On the other hand, if the franc should rise in value he would not be penalized, for the government would continue to pay 400 francs a year. At the present value of the franc, which is practically 100 to the pound, the cost of this borrowing to the government amounts to about 4¼ per cent. If the franc should fall to 110 to the pound, the cost would be 4.60 per cent; and if it should fall to 130, the cost would be 5.60 per cent.

Assuming that this conversion operation succeeds (and early indications are favorable) the government will have safely passed an emergency, and will at the same time apparently have effected some slight saving in interest. The amount of the reduction in interest charges will, however, depend on the future course of the franc, not only during the period when the conversion is being made, but in the long run as well.

Various observers see in this fixing of a ratio of 95 francs to the pound an indication of the rate at which M. Caillaux expects permanently to stabilize the franc. But the stabilization of the franc depends, as we have seen, upon the ability of the government to affect a genuinely balanced budget. This emergency device and first step in what appears to be a general policy can not therefore be finally appraised until the results of M. Caillaux's larger fiscal policy are apparent. The measures proposed in this connection will be discussed presently.

The second step in the Caillaux program—if program it can be called—consists in the raising of the note issue limit at the Bank of France from 45 to 51 billion francs, and increasing the limit of government borrowings from the Bank by a like amount. The purpose of this increase is both to enable the government to procure from inflation the funds required to meet operating expenses not covered by taxation receipts, and to lessen the commercial credit shortage from which business has been suffering. This measure can in no sense be regarded as constructive. It continues the policy of renewed borrowing from the Bank, which was begun with such reluctance and concern at the end of 1924, and it encourages a continuation of the commercial boom at a time when the whole economic situation would be benefited by a period of deflation. (See discussion on p. 185-8).

Accompanying this currency expansion, there has, moreover, been a reduction of the rate of interest at the Bank of France from 7 to 6 per cent. This reduction was calculated, on the one hand, to facilitate the flotation of the conversion loan at 4 per cent; and, on the other hand, to cheapen money for business purposes. In other words, the managers of the Bank are obviously not free to formulate banking and currency policies in the light of financial and commercial considerations; they are under the necessity of allowing Treasury considerations to take precedence over everything else. The result of this general policy has been to sustain the commercial boom, which earlier in the year had shown signs of recession, and to lead to a renewal of the upward trend of prices. A further decline of the franc is therefore inevitable—unless the exchange can be temporarily held up by means of foreign credits.

This consideration leads naturally to the third phase of the Caillaux policy, which is apparently that of procuring a large foreign loan. Thus far, however, no definite pronouncement on this score has been made, nor can definite commitments be made until some kind of an adjustment is reached on the matter of the political debts to Great Britain and the United States. Some months will doubtless have to elapse before this phase of the program will assume definite form.

The crucial test of the Caillaux program will come in connection with the 1926 budget. Although some small increases in taxes have been voted and some minor economies effected, it is admitted that there is no hope of a balanced budget in 1925. While there has been a good deal of talk about the improvement of the budget situation, there is no reason whatever to believe that the total excess of government expenditures over non-borrowed revenues, will be any smaller in 1925 than it was 1924. The favorable budget figures that are presented still omit from the reckoning the bulk of the reconstruction expenditures and war pensions and numerous other extra-budgetary outlays. At the same time, the system of granting supplementary credits as the necessities of the situation require, continues.[1]

A balanced budget is as usual promised for the ensuing year. Apparently it is to be achieved in part by minor economies in expenditures and small savings in interest charges, but mainly it is to result from an increase of taxes. It is estimated that higher taxes on

---

[1] See discussion, pp. 72 and 397.

agricultural, commercial, and industrial profits, on real estate and mining industries, and on French securities, and higher postage rates and telegraph and telephone tolls, will increase the revenue by about 3,275 million francs. If successful, this budget reform would lessen the budget deficit by possibly as much as four billion francs. But such a reduction will not bring the total of government revenues into balance with the total of government expenditures; for the real deficit, it must be repeated, is not three or four billion francs, as the published statements would lead one to believe, but several times that amount. The present government continues the policy of "balancing the budget" by throwing many billions of francs of outlay outside the official Budget proper.

While it would be premature to attempt any final appraisal of M. Caillaux's administration, it is clear that the program as thus far outlined does not by any means reach to the heart of the problem.

INDEX

For Product Safety Concerns and Information please contact our EU
representative GPSR@taylorandfrancis.com
Taylor & Francis Verlag GmbH, Kaufingerstraße 24, 80331 München, Germany